LEXINGTON
and
CONCORD

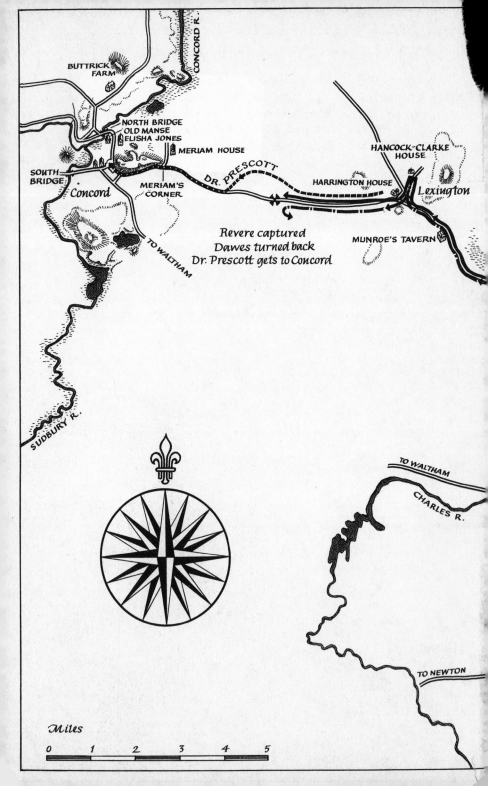

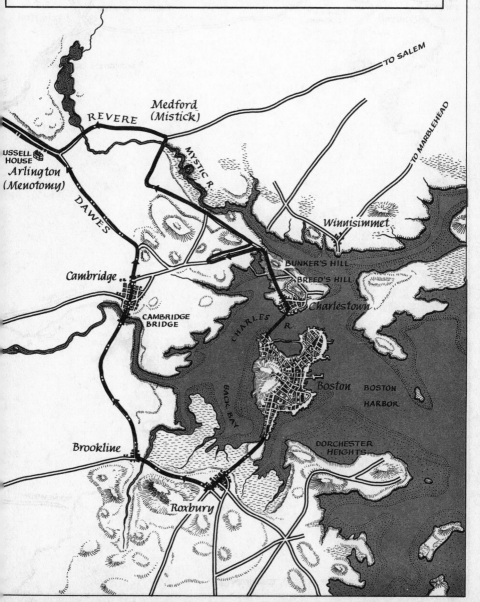

THE MIDNIGHT RIDERS

Dawes was the first to leave Boston with news of the
British expedition, but he took the long route over Boston Neck,
and got to the Hancock-Clarke house after Revere,
who was rowed across the Charles.
Dr. Prescott joined Revere and Dawes at Lexington
and was the only rider to get to Concord.

TO SALEM

Medford
(Mistick)

REVERE

USSELL
HOUSE
Arlington
(Menotomy)

DAWES

MYSTIC R.

TO MARBLEHEAD

Winnisimmet

Cambridge

BUNKER'S HILL
BREED'S HILL

CAMBRIDGE
BRIDGE

Charlestown

CHARLES R.

BACK BAY

Boston

BOSTON
HARBOR

Brookline

DORCHESTER
HEIGHTS

Roxbury

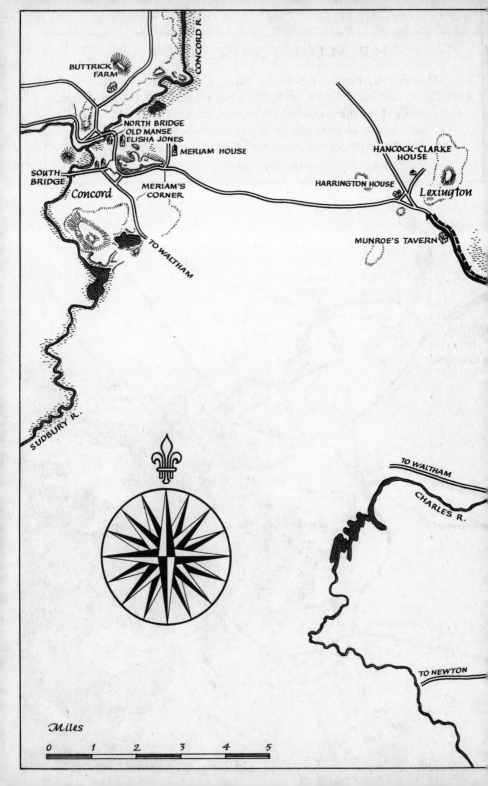

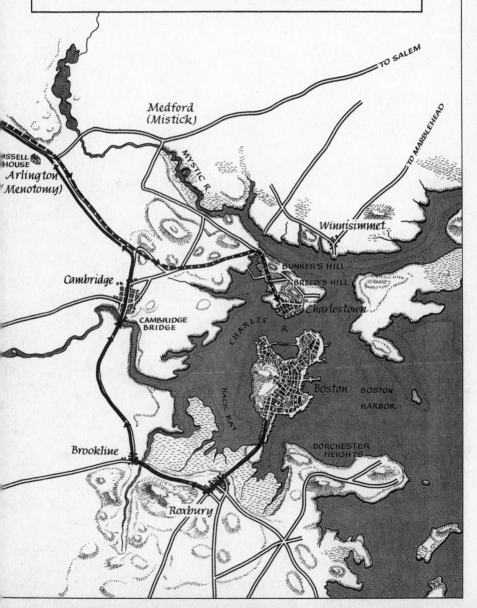

PERCY'S RETREAT

Because the provincial militia barricaded the Cambridge bridge over the Charles, Percy could not get back to Boston. But he managed to get his troops over the narrow neck into Charlestown, under the protection of the British men-of-war in the Charles basin.

TO SALEM

TO MARBLEHEAD

Medford (Mistick)

MYSTIC R.

RUSSELL HOUSE

Arlington (Menotomy)

Winnisimmet

BUNKER'S HILL

BREED'S HILL

Charlestown

Cambridge

CAMBRIDGE BRIDGE

CHARLES R.

Boston

BOSTON HARBOR

BACK BAY

DORCHESTER HEIGHTS

Brookline

Roxbury

LEXINGTON
and
CONCORD

*The Beginning of the War
of the American Revolution*

ARTHUR BERNON TOURTELLOT

W · W · NORTON & COMPANY

New York · London

First published as a Norton paperback 1963 by arrangement
with Doubleday & Company, Inc.; reissued 2000

Originally published under the title
William Diamond's Drum

Cartography by Rafael Palacios

ISBN 0-393-32056-1
ISBN 978-0-393-32056-5

Library of Congress card number 59-9144

W. W. Norton & Company, Inc.
500 Fifth Avenue, New York, NY 10110
www.wwnorton.com

W. W. Norton & Company Ltd.
10 Coptic Street, London WC1A 1PU

Printed in the United States of America

FOR

Jonathan Bernon

AND

Christopher Trayne

Contents

Illustrations

ILLUSTRATIONS

Maps

Maps follow page 270

Preface

Every student of the beginnings of hostilities in the War of the American Revolution must acknowledge the extraordinarily perceptive work of the late Allen French of Concord and the sharply speculative essays of the late Harold Murdock, read before the Massachusetts Historical Society and the Colonial Society. In the case of this book, I owe a more special debt to each.

Mr. French completed his invaluable inquiries into the events of April nineteenth, 1775, some thirty-three years ago, before all the documentary evidence was known, and concentrated thereafter on his major work, *The First Year of the American Revolution,* which does not treat of Lexington and Concord. However, he was later the first American scholar to make a careful examination of the papers of General Thomas Gage, acquired by William L. Clements and now at the University of Michigan; his comments in the informal report, *General Gage's Informers,* are still a provocative guide to later inquirers. Mr. French's wise scholarship was equaled by his generosity. Shortly after I had dealt, necessarily briefly, with the opening of the Revolution in *The Charles,* he offered to lend me his copious factual notes for use in my further investigations into the happenings of April nineteenth.

The incongruity of the decision made in the early morning on Lexington Common was first noted, incidentally and with his characteristic wit, by Mr. Murdock in a paper called "Historic Doubts on the Battle at Lexington," read before the Massachusetts Historical Society. It was this passing reflection that led me to a re-examination of the evidence resulting in the hypothesis presented in this book. His further speculations on Earl Percy's retreat, read before the Colonial Society, contained many suggestions and some determined investigations of alleged atrocities of great value to my consideration of the battle reports as propaganda.

For copies of primary source documents and illustrations, I am indebted to Miss Helen M. Brown. Copies of the silhouette of Jonas Clarke and the portrait of Lord Percy, photographed by Mr. Henry Jackson, were furnished through the courtesy of Mrs. Robert C. Merriam, curator of the Lexington Historical Society, which also owns the miniature of Major Pitcairn. The Doolittle prints of Lexington Common and of the British officers on the ridge in Concord are used through the courtesy of the Connecticut Historical Society. The Doolittle prints of Earl Percy in Lexington and of North Bridge, Concord, are reproduced through the courtesy of the Albany Institute of History and Art. The Gage portrait is in the collection of Colonel R. V. C. Bodley in Boston. The portraits of Hancock, Samuel Adams, Paul Revere, John Adams, and Dr. Joseph Warren are owned by the Museum of Fine Arts in Boston. The broadside is reproduced through the courtesy of the Essex Institute, Salem, Massachusetts. The British cartoon is reproduced through the courtesy of the John Carter Brown Library in Providence, which owns the original. The view of Boston Common is from a print in the Phelps Stokes Collection, New York Public Library, after an original water-color drawing by Christian Remick, dated 1768, in the Concord Antiquarian Society.

Arthur Bernon Tourtellot

Wilton, Connecticut

January 14, 1959

PROLOGUE

THE BEAT OF THE DRUM

"... and having met at the place of our company's parade, [we] were dismissed by our captain, John Parker, for the present, with orders to be ready to attend at the beat of the drum."

DEPOSITION OF NATHANIEL MULLIKEN
AND OTHERS[1]

In the clear chill of an early April morning in 1775, twenty-one companies of picked British soldiers—grenadiers, the tallest, most heavily armed of infantrymen, traditionally the first to attack, and light infantry, the agile flanking troops of the regiments—marched out from Boston across the softly rolling countryside of Middlesex.

After a restless night of alarms, counsels, musters and dismissals of militia, mysterious couriers, intelligence and counter-intelligence, a forty-five-year-old veteran of Rogers' Rangers in the French and Indian wars, Captain John Parker, commanding the Lexington minutemen, directed his drummer boy to go across the road to the Common and beat the call to arms. And when William Diamond, bringing the enthusiasm of his sixteen years to the beating of his gaily emblazoned drum, rolled out the call to the village's minutemen, the War of the American Revolution began.

Everyone, including Captain Parker, knew where the British

were headed: Concord, five miles to the west. To get there, the British regulars had to march right into Lexington's Common, a two-acre triangular patch that divided the road into two branches.

As William Diamond continued to beat the call on his drum, the Lexington minutemen—perhaps thirty of them—assembled on the Common. Captain Parker directed Orderly Sergeant William Munroe to form the men in ranks.

Eventually Captain Parker had thirty-eight men strung out thinly in one line and in part of a second. "I was stationed about in the centre of the company," said Sylvanus Wood. "While we were standing, I left my place and went from one end of the company to the other, and counted every man who was paraded, and the whole number was thirty-eight and no more."[2]

The rolling beat of William Diamond's drum began to drown out, in the ears of the approaching British, the soft thud of their own marching feet on the unpaved roadway. Aware that the drum was sounding a military assembly, the British officers halted their troops, the light infantry in front and the grenadiers in the rear. Orders were given to stop, prime and load their guns, double their ranks, and then to proceed again at double-quick time.

All the elements of an inevitable, if ludicrously one-sided, battle were now present in almost geometric simplicity: a little band of armed yeomen, their number perhaps swelled into the forties now, stood in one and a half straggly rows, their guns primed and loaded; up the road, headed toward them on the double, came several hundred soldiers, their guns also primed and loaded.

Now this was an odd situation, a suicidal situation, for Captain Parker and his minutemen—all of them hard and practical men —to get themselves into.

First of all, the British threat in itself did not call for a Thermopylaean stand. The British soldiers represented about one sixth of the strength of General Gage's peacetime occupation army garrisoned in Boston. The little army had been stationed there for nearly a full year—all through the summer of 1774 and the remarkably mild winter of 1774–75; in all that time they had molested no one, destroyed no property. Except for the kind of minor and isolated encounters common between townspeople and the military in garrison towns—a taunting remark, a drunken argument, a dispute over a woman—the occupation was wholly peaceful. Occasionally, during the year, battalions were marched out of Boston into the surrounding country for exercise and then, without incident, returned again. "The people swear at us sometimes," one colonel wrote, "but that does us no harm."[3] General Gage himself was probably the most peaceable occupying general in all history. He had thus far proved much more irritating to his own people than to the Americans, annoying his government at home by his passiveness and his soldiers by such unwarlike restrictions as banning the wearing of sidearms on the streets of Boston. Nicknamed "Old Woman" by his officers and men, he was dubbed "The Mild General" by George III. And now he had sent the flower of his regiments across Middlesex for the not very bellicose purpose of seizing some powder stored at Concord—and that was all. This Captain Parker knew, the colonials having already dispatched warnings to the Concord militia to hide the stores. Moreover, the British march from Boston to Lexington, three quarters of the way to Concord, had been accomplished without the destruction of any property or harm to any person.

Would Captain Parker, then, have seen this situation as one requiring a suicidal stand by his little company on the Common? The only American general who commanded later that day did not think so: "This company continuing to stand so near to the road, after they had certain notice of the advancing of the British in force, was but a too much braving of danger; for they were sure to meet with insult or injury, which they could not repel. Bravery, when called to action, should always take the strong ground on the basis of reason."[4]

Secondly, Captain Parker was not a man to have ordered a little group to expose itself directly and foolishly to enemy fire. He was a

man of maturity, well read, sensible; a working farmer attuned to
realities; a father, wholly supporting a wife and seven small children; in his youth an experienced fighter in all kinds of wilderness
battles during the French and Indian wars, well practiced in the
tactics of concealment and guerrilla warfare. No local military
martinet throwing his weight around, he was elected as their
captain by the minutemen themselves, who chose him over men
who had been older in service and higher in rank during the
earlier wars. He obviously had qualities of sense and judgment
that attracted the respect of his townsmen. He simply would not
have made, for any military reasons, the decision to line up his
slender company in the very path of British troops outnumbering
him nearly twenty to one. If he knew the approximate strength of
the British, any such military decision would have been criminally
stupid and incredibly irresponsible. And Captain Parker did know
that, even if he had got his whole company on the Common, they
would be outnumbered by at least seven to one. Indeed, if anything the strength of the British marching forces had been *over-
estimated* in Lexington that night, having been placed at twelve
or fifteen hundred men by intelligence received five hours earlier.[5]
If Captain Parker had had it in mind to challenge such a force,
he knew how to do it. Before the road from Boston leveled out to
a straight stretch before Lexington Common, it passed between
two wooded hills. In ten minutes Captain Parker could have had
his militia—out of range and out of sight of the British—raining
bullets down on the heads of the enemy. Instead, he lined them up,
hopelessly ineffective, on the Common. This decision must have
been made, therefore, for other than military reasons, or it must
have been made by someone else.

Thirdly, the Lexington minutemen were not inexperienced
youngsters. The oldest was sixty-three, a veteran of Louisburg in
1758 and the Indian uprisings of 1762, an officer of the company
and unquestionably consulted by Parker. Two others were also in
their sixties; four in their fifties; eight in their forties. Of the

seventy-seven, fifty-five were over thirty, and over twenty of them had served in the French and Indian wars. Democratic in their organization and simple and direct in their relationship with one another, the minutemen would obviously have counseled with their elected leader during the three hours between the first alarm and the fatal muster on the Common. In fact, Captain Parker, in a deposition given six days later, said that they did: ". . . in the Morning, about One of the Clock . . . ordered our militia to meet on the Common . . . *to consult what to do,* and concluded *not to be discovered,* nor meddle or make with said Regular Troops."[6] Thus, the company participated in the decision.

The decision—made at the first alarm, three hours before William Diamond was ordered to beat his drum and the minutemen to stand like tenpins in open sight on the Common, visible for a thousand yards up the road—was "not to be discovered." It was a sensible decision, one to be expected of a man of Parker's character and experience and of the clearheaded farmers and craftsmen of his company. But sometime between one-thirty and four-thirty, it was abandoned. Parker lined his men up in the rising daylight on the clear green of the Common where discovery was certain, and he began a war that ended seven years later with an effect on human history more lasting and more penetrating than any that had gone before.

1

CAPTAIN PARKER'S LEXINGTON

"The men who fell on this green, under the shadow of the village church . . . were men born and reared here, taught at the village school and from the village pulpit. . . ."

RICHARD HENRY DANA, JR.[1]

The little group that Captain Parker mustered on Lexington Common before daybreak on April nineteenth, 1775, had some of the characteristics of a family reunion. At least a quarter of those present were his own relatives or those of his wife—cousins, nephews, brothers-in-law. Among the oldest was a first cousin of the captain, a fiercely determined grandfather, Jonas Parker, there with his son, Jonas, Junior; and among the youngest was the captain's widowed sister-in-law's son, the sixteen-year-old fifer, Jonathan Harrington. There were nine Harringtons, seven Munroes, four Parkers, three Tidds, three Lockes, and three Reeds. These six families furnished twenty-nine of the seventy-seven minutemen who answered William Diamond's drum call.

This was as Captain Parker would have expected. His Lexington was a little village, sprawled out over nineteen square miles and inhabited by a little more than a hundred families. Since immigration had virtually stopped with the French wars of the seventeen-fifties, the population of the town, changed only by the births and deaths of the inhabitants, stayed unaccustomedly stable during the last half of the eighteenth century. In 1775 there were seven hundred and fifty people in the town—men, women and children, five slaves—and four hundred cows. The town consisted topographically of about ten thousand acres of fertile fields, very gentle hills, and occasional woodlands, sometimes broken by slight greenstone formations, patches of peat bog, or scores of little streams that eventually found the Charles or Mystic rivers to empty into the sea fourteen miles away.

Lexington's weather was varied, the arrival and duration of the seasons uncertain. In the little burying ground north of the Common are the cryptic evidences of long and bitter winters. But the winter of 1774–75 was so mild and short that old men, always particularly concerned with such things, noted it in their diaries; and in the parish register there were listed only a half dozen funerals. Lexington had also known long, warm summers, and yet almost all these were marred and heavy with epidemic deaths of children and young adults, probably from typhoid. All this bred a people who had learned to accept and yet to go on, and if all these vital records show anything beyond statistics it is that here were a brave people who had a kind of sturdy gallantry and who triumphed over all the successions of losses they suffered. This perhaps—as much as anything—made equalitarians of them, although there was a somewhat special position occupied by the schoolteacher and by the two physicians, Dr. Joseph Fiske (whose father practiced in Lexington before him) and his son, Dr. Joseph, Junior, who was to go away as a surgeon in the Continental Army.

By American standards Captain Parker's Lexington was an old town, many of its families having lived there, some in the same houses, for five or six generations. Captain Parker's mother's family, the Stones, had been in Lexington for four generations, the Parkers for three, but both families had been in Massachusetts since 1635, when the Bay Colony was only five years old. Every decade since the 1640s the town of Lexington had grown by perhaps a hundred people. Every decade a little more of the woodlands was cleared, and the broad meadows cultivated, and the rich peat swamps used. Most of the settlers, of course, came from the seaside port towns and were turning away from the mercantile or fishing life for the ways of the farmer, turning away from the sea to the land. For over a century now they had worked hard and prospered. They had built themselves houses of remarkably simple and enduring dignity and married among themselves so that almost all the families were in one way or another interrelated. The town burying ground was, to a considerable extent, a family graveyard, with all its stark headstones, with their fatalistic legends, tracing the marriages among the families of the town.

The gravestones told, too, of the flinty theology to which John Parker's forebears had subscribed back in the early days, when the cold persistent spirit of John Calvin hung like a pall over the town and filled it with a grim preoccupation with the eternal damnation of all but the elect. The craggy dogma of the Bible state, however, began to wane long before Lexington was a century old. John Parker's generation grew up with considerable reservations about the doctrine of the elect. Gradually, the people of Lexington became a pragmatic people, unsuited to the preservation of the Puritanism of the 1600s, and without making any great issue of it shook off the more styptic elements of the old faith while such of its last defenders as Cotton Mather were wallowing in their own absurdities.

Meanwhile, the patchwork of small but productive farms that were stretched across the town of Lexington began to be less isolated from one another, less wholly independent. A village life and a village character started to emerge. With others of the town Captain Parker's great-grandfather, Samuel Stone, subscribed in 1711 to a fund to purchase an acre and a half of land where the

Concord, Bedford, and Boston roads met, to be owned in common by all the people of the town. Even then the Common was the center of village life. Muzzy's Tavern (later Buckman's), having been licensed as a public house since 1693, stood directly across the road from it. The Reverend John Hancock's parsonage stood up the road a few hundred yards. Conspicuously adjacent to the Common was the old meetinghouse, built in 1692, which functioned also as a town hall, an armory, an assembly place, and sometimes as a schoolhouse. In 1714 a new and larger meetinghouse was built on the Common, a great barnlike structure with two tiers of galleries and the main floor made up of high-walled pews carefully sold, in the order of the desirability of their location, to members with "respect first for age, second for real and personal estate, third to have respect to but one head in the family." John Parker's grandfather was granted "the second seat"—unmistakable sign of a solid citizen. The next year, 1715, they built a schoolhouse on the Common, behind the meetinghouse some distance. There from October to March each year, a fireplace blazing at one end of the one room, the Lexington children were instructed by a succession of underpaid Harvard graduates, who courted the minister's daughters and most of whom later entered the ministry themselves. The people of the town also built stocks on their Common to punish malefactors, including common scolds, dug a well to water the schoolchildren and "the town people on Sabbath days," and erected a stubby belfry to house a five-hundred-pound bell, given to the bell-less town by John Parker's cousin, Isaac Stone. But by far the most powerful influence on the Common, as John Parker was growing up, was the outpouring of the voice of the Reverend John Hancock, for over half a century the pastor of the Lexington church.

From the tall pulpit of the newer meetinghouse Hancock dispensed a liberal and cheerful theology to the generations of Parker's parents, his contemporaries, their children, and some of their grandchildren. They listened also as he guided them through many of their temporal affairs. He was known to settle land disputes by driving a stake in the ground and simply telling the disputants that *that* was the boundary and there would be no further argument about it. And he moved swiftly to deter his parish from having elders—a variety of lay deputy clergy, usually of a meddling and troublesome nature—by stating flatly that the duty of the older elder would be to accompany the pastor on all out-of-town trips and pay all expenses and that of the younger elder would be to brush down and harness the pastor's horse when he required it.

Witty, respected, an entirely new type of native American clergy, who saw the death of the old Puritan theocracy with relief and apparently with some delight, old "Bishop" Hancock awakened on a cold December night in 1752 with an acute stomach-ache and died promptly, at the age of eighty-two, without inconveniencing even Dr. Fiske up the road at the next house. John Hancock left his mark on Lexington. At the time of his death, the parish at Lexington was sixty years old, and he had ministered to it for fifty-four of them. He brought its people out of the melancholy hopelessness of predestination, through the "new lightism" that split many of the Massachusetts churches in half as they strained at theological gnats; and, by his wise, good-humored intervention from time to time, he accustomed the townspeople to the role of the clergyman as a dominant voice in temporal affairs on the somewhat novel grounds that he might be a rational mind worth listening to instead of a priestly authority they could not avoid. This last may well have been his most significant achievement.

By the time of Hancock's death, when John Parker was twenty-three, Lexington had acquired its eighteenth-century character as a quiet, self-contained village that governed itself, elected and instructed its own representative to the Great and General Court—the colonial legislature of Massachusetts, and prized the royal charter as the mother country's irrevocable recognition of its basic rights and freedoms. During the long, scattered wars with the French and Indians in the 1740s and 1750s, as many as forty of Lexington's two hundred male adults had fought to defend the King's realm in North America, at the capture of Louisburg, at Lake Champlain, and at the fall of Quebec. Several had joined the hardy corps of Major William Rogers' Rangers; and one of them, Edmund Munroe, was the regiment's adjutant. Four of the Parker family, including John, marched off to these wars and acquired a degree of military confidence and competence that stayed with them all their days.

From his family experience John Parker also learned something of political self-determinism. His father, Josiah Parker, was selectman for twelve years and had served for repeated terms as town clerk and assessor. His cousin, Jonas Stone, was also a selectman and later a representative to the General Court and a delegate to the Provincial Congress. After the fall of Quebec and the interminable French wars drew to their close in the 1760s, the political life of the times and, indeed the political objectives of the people began to take ascendancy over the old religious life and objectives. The most articulate and influential agent of the transformation in Lexington was, oddly enough, the extraordinary and persuasive young pastor who had been called to succeed Hancock, the Reverend Jonas Clarke.

ii

Three years out of Harvard, Jonas Clarke arrived in Lexington in the spring of 1755. He was twenty-four years old, unmarried, large and impressive in appearance, neat to the point of fastidiousness in his dress, and more concerned with the practical social applications of Christianity than with its body of doctrine. Gregarious, worldly, of a literary bend, he was a gifted social and political philosopher, with a strong inclination to logic. He was one of an entire generation of Harvard men who came under the influence of the "gentle, tender, affectionate"[2] President Edward Holyoke, whose attachment to the libertarian principles of John Locke furnished the rationale of the Massachusetts patriots who led the revolutionary movement during the cold war that went on for over a decade before the outbreak of armed hostilities.

Before he accepted their call to Lexington, Jonas Clarke drove the hard bargain with the town fathers necessary to win their respect. The parish settled on him an outright payment of £133 and an annual salary of £80 but shrewdly demanded that he quit forever any "claim, title or interest in or unto any part of the ministerial land in this town." The ministerial land was a tract acquired by an assessment of the parishioners for the purpose of providing revenues for the clergy; the Reverend John Hancock had had the right to take wood from it for lumber for use on his own property and for fuel. So Jonas Clarke demanded, and got, a supply of twenty cords of wood a year in addition to his salary. However, when the expenses facing the town seemed to Clarke "not small," he sometimes gave back a part of his salary in gracious little letters to the moderator at town meetings. An excellent manager of his own affairs, he lived reasonably well, brought up a family of twelve children, and left his heirs a highly productive sixty-acre farm.

Clarke was a man of greater and more far-reaching intellect than John Hancock had been, and he possessed some of the versatility and range of interests that characterized such contemporaries as Jefferson and Franklin. He managed his farm with extraordinary skill and kept a systematic, almost scientific record of its production. Something of an experimentalist in the gaunt liturgy that his sect permitted itself, he abandoned the old New England psalm singing, threw out the atrocious versifications by the Harvard divines that had been used for a century, and even introduced hymn singing in the parish. He was interested in all the activities in the town, and his house soon became a busy gathering place for both the townspeople and for visitors from other communities. It became clear, within a few years of his settlement at Lexington, that he would be the greatest single influence in the town's history.

As the youthful successor to the octogenarian Hancock, Clarke was a compelling and attractive personality to the young people. John Parker, for example, was only a year older than the new pastor and early fell under his influence. He spent hours talking with the young cleric and always left with his arms loaded with borrowed books. Parker and his twenty-four-year-old bride, Lydia Moore, were probably the first couple married during Jonas Clarke's pastorate. A couple of years later Clarke himself married Lucy Bowes, daughter of the pastor of the neighboring town of Bedford and a granddaughter of the Reverend John Hancock, whose ancient relict still lived in Lexington. Clarke and his young wife moved into the Hancock house with the matriarch and set about raising a family, ultimately numbering six girls and seven boys, all but one of whom lived to adulthood.

By the time John Parker was back from the French and Indian wars, the Reverend Jonas Clarke was well established as the leader of affairs in Lexington. Parker's cousin, Jonas Stone, was elected deacon of the church, and Stone was also the town's leading politician, being successively assessor, selectman, treasurer, and delegate to the General Court. In due time Clarke and Stone became a team, Clarke defining policy and Stone carrying it out.

iii

Although the War of the American Revolution began when Captain John Parker lined up his handful of men on Lexington Common, the Revolution itself was not a battle of bullets but a battle of opinion that began in the early 1760s. After the distractions of the French wars, the British sought to consolidate the empire by expanding Parliamentary control over the colonies, by revoking the old charters that virtually gave them home rule, and by radical alterations in the British tax structure so as to impose upon them unfamiliar burdens—this last on the general grounds that the colonies benefited most directly from large proportions of Great Britain's army and navy expenses. All this constituted what was essentially a badly needed program of administrative reform; and if there were any economic wrongs to be redressed at the time, they were wrongs suffered by England and not by the colonies. In fact, the failure of the Grenville ministry that initiated the reforms was not so much due to errors of substance or even altogether of procedure—although errors of the latter variety came in abundance later; the failure of Grenville was a total neglect of communications. Under the old patent charters the colonies had probably the freest form of regional self-government the world has ever known, before or since. This freedom had bred in the colonies such a commanding sense of self-determinism on most all their affairs that when the administrative reforms enacted in London found expression in more positive executive actions by the colonial governors in America, it bore to the colonists a strong smack of outright tyranny. Moreover, the source of the irritation lay as much in the sudden enforcement of old laws, particularly revenue laws, as in the passing of new laws.

There was a general feeling, most acute in the port towns, that a good and free-trading era was coming to an end. The trading of the colonial merchants had made them far richer, and at a much faster pace, than their heavily taxed counterparts in England. Profits were immense, and taxes and tariffs low and often completely ignored. At the same time, the security of the colonies was the responsibility of the British, and whatever freedom there was on the high seas that fell short of piratical anarchy was safeguarded by the British navy. Meanwhile, the long French and Indian wars had left Britain with a great debt; the far-flung empire, with its vulnerabilities to France and Spain, involved heavy military and navy expenses; and there were serious doubts that domestic revenues in England could be greatly increased. Finally, with the major preoccupation of the British on the North

American continent—the boundless, drawn-out conflict with the French—concluded, it was high time that someone tried to bring about a more efficient management of colonial affairs. For the truth of the matter was that the British empire as a political entity had no existence beyond a loose federation, no political philosophy beyond a theoretic loyalty to the Crown, and no real management of its colonial interests at all. In fact, several colonial officials had served out their appointments without ever leaving London—a custom so common that when Grosvenor Bedford was turned out of his job as Collector of Customs at Philadelphia because he had lived in London all the twenty-five years that he held the post, Horace Walpole wrote the Prime Minister, protesting Bedford's discharge as unjust. As the King's First Minister, George Grenville could see nothing but disaster ahead if some order were not created out of the political, administrative, and fiscal chaos of the empire.

But if the realities of the situation were on his side, philosophy and theory and the intellectual drift of the times were on the side of the colonists. Indeed, the little village of Lexington in Massachusetts, its small population supporting itself by consuming and selling the products of their farms and of their few craft shops, had little economic stake in the conflict. It had nothing but theory to justify concerning itself with the growing squabble with Britain.

The custodian of political theory in Lexington was the Reverend Jonas Clarke. His passion for the subject sprang from many sources. For one thing, all the theology and ecclesiasticism he had been through in his young life was tied up inextricably with politics. For the impact of the covenant, a political contract as well as a declaration of faith, was a living force in the New England consciousness, which was deeply ingrained with the notion that if men could bind themselves together to manage their own spiritual lives they could do the same with regard to their temporal affairs. When all the Calvinist strictures were wrung out of Puritan thinking, the one lasting social effect was this overriding tenet of self-reliance. To Jonas Clarke and the New England clergy, however, Puritanism left other legacies. Although the Bible state of the theocrats was dead by his time, its long shadow was to fall over his own years and the history of his province far into the future; and the ministers were all the more jealous of their positions in their communities when they saw their influence as priests fading and as political tutors rising. And they still clung to their roles as magistrates. Offenders in Jonas Clarke's congregation still "stood up in meeting" and recited, to the elevated delight of their brethren in the endlessly long Sabbath sessions, the details of their errings. The reliance of Puritanism upon Judaism, with the authority of the temple and the Mosaic code, had survived the gradual diminishing of the old association of parish and town as one entity with two faces.

In contrast to the old Calvinist preachers with their vengeful Jehovah, Jonas Clarke preached the Christian virtues, but he was nevertheless fully aware that there was much to be said for the old emphasis by way of preserving the ministerial authority. Yet he was realist and social student enough to know that for the future the strength of the ministry lay in its members being with their people rather than over them. And if the Anglican clergy derived strength from associations with royal governors, the nonconformist ministers did from associations with selectmen. Throughout many New England towns, nevertheless, the waning influence of the ministers had become a real problem. The reactionary efforts of Jonathan Edwards had failed signally, and only at Yale College in Connecticut was there any longer a premium on Calvinist orthodoxy in New England. The time had long gone when the Puritan priests could hope that their influence would be restored by automatic consent that theirs was a mystical authority—absolute and pervasive. From the somewhat strained device of the "halfway covenant"—an implement that permitted those who could show no evidence of the regeneration necessary to full communion to become "half members" of the church, thus preserving its organizational strength in the face of its waning spiritual authority—the old ecclesiasticism had never recovered. Since the halfway covenant permitted the baptizing of the children of half members, infant baptism had already become an empty formalism; and with the failure of the short-lived revival movement, the "Great Awakening," the churches as a whole had serious likelihood of going the same way. The alternative, of course, was their becoming progressive social forces in a world, not of doctrine, but of tidal realities. It is not insignificant that, first with John Hancock and later with Jonas Clarke, this was the road taken by the Church of Christ in Lexington.

A less subtle and generally less powerful force that tended to unite the dissenting clergy against the strengthening of ties with Britain was the abhorrence of an American episcopate. The Church of England had grown alarmingly in New England during the eighteenth century, and it had moreover attracted an increasingly impressive following from the upper classes of the larger towns. Its position throughout the rest of the colonies was, of course, exceptionally strong. It was the established church in many places, including the thriving city of New York, and the only church of any size and influence among the aristocracy of the South. As the number of Anglican clergy grew and the inconvenience of a long voyage to London for ordination became more general, fears mounted in the dissenting minds of the nonconformists that a bishop might be sent to America. The combination of bishops and royal governors conjured up visions of twin assaults upon traditional, if in some respects illusory, religious and civil liberties. And the Puritan clergy knew enough, by way of century-old experiment of their own, of the grip that combined religious and civil authority could have on a people. Even though there was no probability of an American episcopate, the bare possibility loomed as the final blow to the local power of the nonconformist clergy in their towns and in the province: ". . . every poor parson whose head has never felt the weight of a bishop's hand will soon know the power of his pastoral staff, and the arm of the magistrate into the bargain."[8]

The fears of an episcopate were almost entirely political: the theological dispute about the practices and doctrines of the Church of England, including the necessity of bishops to preserve the apostolic succession, had long since died out from sheer lack of interest. Neither Jonas Clarke nor his predecessor Hancock showed much sensitivity to the old doctrinal disputes. Old Hancock had loved to be called "Bishop" and felt that he was fully entitled to it, because he had participated in so many ordinations, at one of which he made the startling suggestion that "He that desires the office of a bishop desires a good work."[4] And Jonas Clarke felt no qualms about restoring to the drab Calvinist services some of the very features of the Anglican liturgy that his forebears had found so repugnant.[5] But the political fears of the Anglican church were a different matter; it was enough that the Church of England, the monarchy and the Parliament were in league. The basic ingredient of the covenant, on the other hand, was the idea of the consent of the governed—the Puritan church itself holding that its authority over its members was derived only from their voluntary compact to submit themselves to its authority.

The extension of the idea of the covenant to all political institutions was not a difficult thing for Jonas Clarke and those of his generation at Harvard who had been steeped in John Locke and gone to school to President Holyoke. An enlightened cleric of remarkable and prophetic political insight, Holyoke was, like Jonathan Mayhew and Charles Chauncey, an articulate critic of the old Calvinism and the abortive attempt to revive it in the 1740s. "In whatsoever churches of Christ there is made use of external force and compulsion in these regards, so far they are gone off from the simplicity that is in Christ . . . The ministers have no right to impose their interpretations of the laws of Christ upon their flocks . . . Every man therefore is the judge for him in these things. . . ."[6] This libertarian theology, which must have had the Mathers spinning in their graves, was matched by the president's political philosophy. As early as 1736, long before there was any political conflict with England, President Holyoke had used language amazingly close to that of the Declaration of Independence forty years later: "All forms of government originate from the people . . . As these forms then have originated from the people, doubtless they may be changed whensoever the body of them choose to make such an alteration."[7]

In the pulpit of West Church in Boston, Jonathan Mayhew, two months before his death, paid unabashed tribute to the one love of a fervid life: "Having also from my childhood up . . . been educated to the love of liberty . . . I would not—I cannot now, though past middle age—relinquish the fair object of my youthful affection, Liberty, whose charms, instead of decaying with time in my eyes, have daily captivated more and more."[8]

Edward Holyoke's teachings left a permanent impression on Jonas Clarke, which became clearly visible when Clarke assumed leadership in the town of Lexington's response to the new British colonial policy. So ingrained was Clarke's idea of political freedom that Lexington's protest of the first major tax measure of Parliament, the Stamp Act, disposed of its economic effects in one vague paragraph and treated, with magnificent reasoning, its political implications, opening "a door to numberless evils, which time only can discover,"[9] in twelve precise paragraphs that anticipated by a century such political philosophers as John Stuart Mill. The Stamp Act, passed by Parliament on Grenville's recommendation in 1765, was to go into effect one year later. At the urging of Clarke the town of Lexington voted that its selectmen write instructions to its representative in the General Court of the colony for protesting the act. The instructions turned up in Clarke's handwriting.

Actually, the Stamp Act in itself would have little direct economic effect upon a village of small farmers. It was directed largely at the commercial classes who were most able to pay, and

Grenville had thought it to be by far the least obnoxious sort of tax: "It will fall only on property, will be collected by the fewest officers . . . does not require any number of officers vested with extraordinary powers of entering houses. . . ."[10] The Stamp Act provided for a tax on legal and commercial documents, few of which ever passed through the hands of a Lexingtonian, and on printed materials, hardly of decisive economic importance in a town that had no newspaper or printer. Clarke's concern with the act was almost entirely with constitutional questions, and the instructions that he wrote for the selectmen were more suggestive of a judicial opinion than a material protest, with some *obiter dicta* at the outset that appear to have been addressed less to the minister in London than to the townspeople of Lexington: "We have always looked upon men as a set of beings naturally free:—And it is a truth, which the history of the ages and the common experience of mankind have fully confirmed, that a people can never be divested of those invaluable rights and liberties which are necessary to the happiness of individuals, to the well-being of communities or to a well regulated state, but by their own negligence, imprudence, timidity or rashness. They are seldom lost, but when foolishly forfeited or tamely resigned."[11] Aside from its general validity as political doctrine, this also served to remind Clarke's townsmen that, however remote the effects of an individual Parliamentary act so far as they were concerned, it could establish a precedent, create a pattern, for the erosion of their fundamental freedoms—if they were not alert in recognizing incursions upon them.

Clarke then proceeded to anatomize the act on constitutional grounds. It violated the charter, which provided that taxes could be imposed upon the colony only by its own legislative assembly. It violated the ancient right of British subjects to be taxed only with their own consent. It was passed without a hearing, even though respectful petitions had been prepared and dispatched to London. It deprived the colonists of trial by jury, by providing that violators of the act would be tried in admiralty courts before judges only. It violated two essential principles of Magna Charta: indictments by the oath of honest men of one's neighborhood and trials by one's peers. And it spawned such evils as the inevitable rise of a class of informers, paid to report violators, and the cutting off of any means of redress against unjust accusations and convictions.

By his skilled diagnosis of the issues evoked by an act of seemingly little relevance to the lives of the people of his little community, Jonas Clarke achieved much. He drew the town deeply and creditably into a great and historic debate. He accustomed it to the idea and practice of acting on the broad political stage that extended beyond town affairs. He hit upon an effective and dramatic method of political education. He shaped attitudes and molded public opinion by addressing the papers of the town as much to its own inhabitants as to obnoxious ministers beyond the seas.

One by one, as Parliament passed new acts affecting the colonies, the town of Lexington appointed committees to deal with them. One by one, they were scrutinized by Jonas Clarke in his study and dissected in long, closely reasoned papers later adopted by the committees as constituting the opinion of the town—which indeed they did after they had been read, discussed, and endorsed at the town meetings. In 1768, though not a British soldier had appeared in Lexington, it was declared that the keeping of a standing army in the province to enforce the acts of Parliament was "an infringement of their natural, constitutional and chartered rights."[12] At the same meeting a Committee of Correspondence was appointed to work with similar committees throughout the province, particularly that of Boston. Three of the five committeemen named were deacons in Jonas Clarke's church. In 1773, when Boston resisted the effort to land tea discriminatively taxed, the inhabitants of Lexington resolved that anybody in the town who purchased or consumed any tea "shall be looked upon as an enemy to this town and to this country, and shall by this town be treated with neglect and contempt."[13] In 1774, as conditions in Boston worsened with the closing of the port and the passing of other coercive measures to enforce the acts of Parliament, although still without any material effect upon Lexington, the town concluded, under the guidance of Jonas Clarke, that the time had come to prepare for rebellion.

Revolution in the minds of the people of Lexington had already been almost fully achieved. The revolt was of a philosophic nature, skillfully and positively phrased in philosophic terms and on the whole neither inflammatory nor overly emotional in either content or language. The public papers of Lexington, tracing the evolution of the town's opinion, are great state papers, written in the neat orderly hand of Jonas Clarke; and they paralleled, when they did not actually anticipate, the great papers of the colonies as a federation. In the opinion of Lexington there was little doubt left that Britain by her acts had shattered her own traditions, dating from the barons at Runnymede, of a free society. In the Coercive Acts of 1774 (which, in addition to closing the port of Boston, revoked the Massachusetts charter, transferred trials to England or to other colonies, and quartered soldiers on the inhabitants without their permission) the people of Lexington saw the revolution as really one launched by the British Parliament against a wholly British heritage. And in their minds the movement in the colonies, all their acts and resolves, was a counterrevolution to restore centuries-old freedoms and safeguards against tyranny. There was much to be said both historically and logically for this view, with its striking similarity to the original Puritanic anti-separatist attitude toward the Church of England. Puritans were reformers, by nature and conviction, and not revolutionists.

But it was clear to Jonas Clarke and thus to his townsmen, as events progressed, that no debate of the issues was to lead to any final solution. The ministry of Lord North was proceeding as if it had nothing but contempt for colonial opinion and was bankrupt of any expedient but force. The reaction in Lexington was inevitable. Having already concluded, "We shall be ready to sacrifice our estates and everything dear in life, yea and life itself, in support of the common cause,"[14] they voted at last, abandoning faith in the power of reason for the comfort of practical measures, to strengthen their arms and militia with "a suitable quantity of flints . . . two pieces of cannon . . . a pair of drums . . . bayonets."[15] Then they elected a delegate—John Parker's cousin, Jonas Stone—to the First Provincial Congress, an extra-legal body, formed without authority, after General Gage had canceled the stated meeting of the General Court, to serve as a forum and an agency for united action by all the towns of the colony.

iv

Skilled as he was in political theory and in its articulation, the Reverend Jonas Clarke was also enough of a realist to have known from the beginning that reason did not always prevail. And though there was little militancy in Lexington's attitude all during the war of opinion against Britain, Clarke had carefully laid the rationale for military preparedness, if it ever became a necessary or prudent step. As early as 1768 he pointed out significantly that "where courage, valour or fortitude has reason for its basis," it enables men "to face the greatest dangers, to stand the severest shocks, to meet undaunted and serene the charge of the most formidable enemy and all the horrors of war."[16] He counted upon the men of Lexington, under appropriate guidance, to rise to the occasion.

The men of Lexington did. There were about a hundred and seventy males over sixteen in the town, and they organized themselves into alarm list, militia, and minutemen.

In the colonies, from the time of the first settlements, all able-bodied men were required to bear arms. During the seventeenth century this was such an obvious necessity to guard against marauding Indians that it was assumed to be a normal and automatic concomitant of growing up. Ordinarily, the men simply kept a watchful eye only on their own houses and lands; but they were organized, with officers commissioned by the King, were required to stand inspection at least once a year, and were subject to calls for active duty in expeditionary forces in the Indian wars and later in the wars with the French. The annual musters became festive local holidays in the eighteenth century, since every family was involved. They all came to town from the surrounding country-side, lined up with their muskets and powder horns, executed some awkward drills, listened to the pastor preach a sermon, and spent the rest of the day in eating and drinking. Any efficiency in marks-manship that they acquired they developed on their own, and as fighters they were a wholly individualistic breed, not accustomed to volley firing and used to finding their own vantage points, selecting their own targets and priming, loading and firing at their own pace and discretion. The nature of the warfare against both the Indians and the French in the North American wilderness encouraged the preservation of such practices even when the militia was incorporated into the British field armies. For the most part, when at home the men furnished their own arms and ammu-nition, and the wearing of uniforms would have struck them as both unnecessary and of no practical use whatever.

Their officers had been commissioned by the royal governor on behalf of the crown, but except when the men of the militia were off to the wars the officers meant nothing to them. Military titles, therefore, were not scarce in Lexington. John Parker's father was known as Lieutenant, although his political activities seem to have been more considerable than his military services. Some of the officers had participated in the campaigns of the French and Indian wars and, in addition to being resourceful fighters, had shown impressive qualities of leadership. The Munroe family was particularly noted in Lexington for its military achievements and furnished several officers in the French wars. Edmund Munroe was adjutant of the regiment in Rogers' Rangers; Robert Munroe bore the standard at the capture of Louisburg; and Abraham Munroe served as a lieutenant.

Whenever it had taken to the field, the Lexington militia had fought in the service of the King. But when General Gage canceled the legislative session of the General Court in the fall of 1774, the militia considered itself dissolved. It was succeeded by the military organizations set up by the Committee of Safety on the recommendation of the Provincial Congress, which by some legal straining declared itself the lawful successor of the General Court.

In carrying out the Provincial Congress's aim to create an armed force outside the jurisdiction of the British authorities, Lexington and the other towns of Massachusetts took a poll of their manpower and divided it into two bodies: the alarm lists and the militia. Somewhat eclectic in its references to old laws, the Congress concluded that the ancient legislation requiring all able-bodied men to bear arms gave it sufficient authority for creating this general pool of manpower. At first the alarm lists consisted of all men able to move and to assume responsibility. Later only the older men, young boys, and the less agile were in the alarm lists. The rest were in the militia, the combat forces. From this an elite company of the more active men, called minutemen, was formed to be ready, at a moment's notice, to march on orders of the Committee of Safety or, in cases of emergency, on those of their own officers. Meanwhile, the militia was a reserve force, and the alarm list furnished manpower for watch duty and other chores at the sound of an alarm. Often, however, they acted simply as guerrilla fighters whenever they felt like it and unquestionably took part in the very early fighting of the war.

Captain John Parker's Lexington company of minutemen numbered slightly over a hundred men and officers. During the winter of 1774–75, the town had acquired powder, musket balls, and some muskets. William Diamond had learned how to beat the battle calls on the town's newly purchased drum. The company had elected its officers, headed by Captain Parker, "a stout, large-framed man of medium height." His chief aide, also elected by the company, was Lieutenant William Tidd, thirty-eight, who was married to the daughter of Robert Munroe, the old veteran of the French wars who had carried the standard at Louisburg. Robert Munroe himself, despite his sixty-three years, was elected third in command with the title of ensign. The second ensign was Joseph Simonds, thirty-five, who had served on some of the town committees that dealt with the oppressive acts of Parliament. All three of his commissioned officers were kinsmen of Captain Parker, and so was about one third of his company. The clerk of the company was Daniel Harrington, whose house faced on the Common and who, like Lieutenant Tidd, was a son-in-law of old Ensign Munroe.

Of Captain Parker's non-commissioned officers, Orderly Sergeant William Munroe, the young proprietor of Munroe's Tavern on the road to Cambridge and Boston, was the most enterprising: he was to have the busiest and most ubiquitous time of all the military men in Lexington on the night of April eighteenth. He appears to have felt himself authorized to make decisions independently of the commissioned officers. Eventually he became a colonel, and apparently he well deserved it. There were two other sergeants of the company: Francis Brown, who was to succeed Parker as commander of the company, and Ebenezer White, the thirty-three-year-old father of four children, the youngest of whom was born the week before the muster of April nineteenth. Four corporals were also chosen by the company: Joel Viles, the town's hog reeve; Samuel Sanderson, who was married to one of the Munroes; John Munroe, the youngest son of the ensign; and Ebenezer Parker, at twenty-four the youngest of the officers.

Nearly all of Captain Parker's minutemen were farmers, although some of them also practiced trades—blacksmiths, wheelwrights, clockmakers. Among the hundred and four were a dozen father-and-son combinations. There was one slave in the company,

Prince Estabrook, said to have been the son of an African tribal chief. There were also two men who owned slaves, including Lieutenant Tidd. Although slavery was dying in Lexington, largely because it was not hereditary in Massachusetts, it was still not uncommon in 1775. The town had voted in 1728 to give the Reverend John Hancock £85 to buy a slave, and Captain Parker's mother's family were slaveholders.[17] Several slaves, like Prince Estabrook, served long in the Revolutionary armies, many of them like him winning their freedom for their service.

In the spring of 1775, Captain Parker had little that he could do to make a military unit of his company of minutemen. Spring had come early to Lexington, and the plowing was already underway. This kept the men at home and busy from sunrise to sunset. There was no guard duty to perform in Lexington, because the town contained no military stores, had no loyalists or Tories in it, and was in no danger of riots or internal uprisings. Gunpowder was in such short supply and used so sparingly that musket practice was out of the question. And there would have been little purpose and less grace in Captain Parker's marching his men around the Common in close-order drill. Consequently, musters of the minutemen were limited to one or two occasions in the spring, mainly to see how long it took the minutemen to get to the Common. Once there they cocked their unloaded muskets, snapped the flintlocks once or twice, and then adjourned to Buckman's Tavern for some rum before the trek home again.

The central military problem of the province in the spring of 1775 was not manpower but powder. In the previous September, General Gage had moved most of the powder stores from Cambridge, where they would have been readily accessible to the colonists, to the comparative safety of Boston. What the several towns had already drawn from the stores before Gage got around to their removal was pitifully small in amount, but enough, if carefully used, to give the provincial militia some effectiveness. The amount and distribution of the colonists' supply of powder and arms were reported regularly to Gage by Dr. Benjamin Church, a member of the Provincial Congress and of its directorate, the Committee of Safety, who sold the information to finance an expensive mistress in Boston. Meanwhile, however, the colonists had been smuggling munitions out of Boston under the very noses of Gage's troops. They simply loaded the stores into wagons, covered them with hay or manure, and drove out over the Neck to the countryside. Church told Gage about this, too, and a stop was put to it before much had been gained. Powder was still critically scarce in the provincial towns.

If Captain Parker had any special problem, then, as April came, it was not with his men, all of whom he knew very well and on whom he could fully rely. It was gunpowder. However, even this was of little immediate concern, for, so far as he knew, the Lexington minutemen were going nowhere. He had received but one order, dated March 30, 1775, from the only authority behind the existence of his company, the Provincial Congress, meeting five miles away in Concord. ". . . whenever the army under command of General Gage, or any part thereof to the number of five hundred, shall march out of the town of Boston, with artillery and baggage, it ought to be deemed a design to carry into execution by force the late acts of Parliament, the attempting which, by the resolve of the late honourable Continental Congress, ought to be opposed; and therefore the military force of the Province ought to be assembled, and an army of observation immediately formed, to act solely on the defensive so long as it can be justified on the principles of reason and self-preservation. . . ."[18]

Back on his farm, some two miles from Lexington Common, Captain Parker went about his main business, preparing the fields for the spring planting. Jonas Clarke undoubtedly kept him generally informed on the proceedings at Concord, where the Provincial Congress remained in session until April fifteenth, discussing the thorny question of how to get the other colonies to show more spirited resistance to the British and align themselves more actively with Massachusetts. Captain Parker was to do more to accomplish this in a few hours than the Provincial Congress was able to achieve in weeks.

2

THE VISITORS

"The liberties of all alike are invaded by the same haughty power."

SAMUEL ADAMS[1]

In April 1775 the Reverend Jonas Clarke was forty-four years old and had been pastor of the Church of Christ in Lexington for twenty of them. If, in the minds of the sixteen members of the congregation who had voted against calling him to Lexington, there had been doubts about the likelihood of his ever filling adequately the shoes of old Bishop Hancock, they were by now thoroughly dispelled. Jonas Clarke was in 1775 an impressive presence indeed. A great man in size with a massive head, he attired himself in a gown, cassock, and band for his pulpit appearances and wore a huge white wig that gave him a magisterial aspect. Eloquent and endowed with a voice of thunderous volume, he could be heard on Sundays across the Common in the rooms of Buckman's Tavern and in the surrounding meadows. Although he never ignored his ecclesiastical duties, he had become more and more immersed in the political conflicts of his time, and he was a respected confidant of the leaders of the Provincial Congress.

The old Hancock house, up the Bedford road a few blocks from the Common, was no longer dominated by old Mrs. Hancock who had died in 1760, three years after Clarke had moved in with her granddaughter as his bride. It was now dominated by Clarke. His first son had died in infancy, but ten other children had followed in good order—all of them healthy and active. Every morning Clarke's voice boomed throughout the house, as he stood at the foot of the stairs and bellowed, "Polly, Betsey, Lucy, Liddy, Patty, Sally, Thomas, Jonas, William, Peter—get up!"[2] Having organized his populous household and his farm as efficiently as his parish, he found the time to write prodigiously. In addition to producing some three thousand sermons, each of an hour's length, he kept a long and detailed journal and wrote scores of public papers. He must also have imposed a stern discipline on his host of children. The Hancock-Clarke house had altogether only eight rooms, and the children ranged from sixteen years down to five months in age—a fertile situation for the development of complete chaos if there had been no firm rules.

Clarke also took the leading part in the education of his older children and helped to prepare some of the Lexington boys for Harvard. The little school on the Common was temporarily closed in 1775 for economy reasons, and the town's "women schools," which the younger children attended, taught only elementary reading, writing, and arithmetic.[3] This left the town without a schoolmaster, a void into which the energetic Clarke willingly stepped so far as candidates for Harvard went. His house also contained the town's most extensive library, which he made freely available to all who wanted to borrow books. Often, the Hancock-Clarke house's usual population of twelve was swollen to a score or more by townspeople there on public business or to advance their learning, political or clerical visitors from Boston or Cambridge, or by Clarke's father and mother, who journeyed the twenty-five miles from Hopkinton for long visits.

Presiding over the functional aspects of this busy household was

Clarke's competent wife, Lucy. During an age in which the burying grounds were full of tiny headstones memorializing the deaths
of small children—one of Captain Parker's minutemen, Abijah
Childs, lost six in twelve days—Lucy Clarke was to rear twelve
of thirteen. Cooking over the open fires of an incredibly small
fireplace in the great kitchen of the house, she prepared meals for
thirty-six a day, laundered for at least twelve people, made clothes
for most of them, kept the house clean, and, during the long
hours of her husband's writing in his small study off the kitchen,
kept the children quiet.

Into this sufficiently quiet household in the spring of 1775 there
came in pairs a quartet of distinguished visitors, not just to call, but
to live for an unpredictable period. Before they left, there was a
population of twenty in the house and an armed guard of ten
around it. And the home of the Reverend Jonas Clarke, one of
the most persuasive apologists of the Revolution, became a center
of great public affairs, much to the satisfaction of Clarke, who
shortly found himself participating in discussions of the most
critical importance with the political leaders of the province in
his own study.

To one of the visitors, however strained the circumstances, it
was a homecoming of sorts. John Hancock, thirty-eight, Treasurer
of Harvard College, President of the Provincial Congress, Chairman of the Committee of Safety, richest merchant in Boston and
probably the richest man in Massachusetts, was—like Jonas
Clarke's wife—a grandchild of old Bishop Hancock. Of the
bishop's three sons, two—John the second and Ebenezer—had
been graduated from Harvard and entered the ministry. Ebenezer
was settled at Lexington as associate of his father, with the promise
of succession on his father's death, according to terms arrived at
after some rather rough bargaining with the parish by the bishop;
but the son died twelve years before his father did, so that it all
went for nothing. The other clerical son, the second Reverend
John Hancock, served three years as librarian of Harvard College

and then became pastor of the church at Braintree, where the venerable bishop also made the financial arrangements. Unlike the Reverend Ebenezer, the Braintree Hancock married, and he sired three children, one of whom was John Hancock, the future patriot; but like the Reverend Ebenezer, the Reverend John also died before the bishop, leaving young John orphaned at the age of eight.

The boy was taken in charge by the bishop's third and surviving son, Thomas Hancock, a childless Boston merchant of immense wealth and flexible ethics. The Hancock mansion stood on Beacon Hill overlooking Boston Common, and it was the most elaborate establishment in Boston, for Thomas Hancock was inordinately fond of extravagant display. Thomas Hancock had left his father's Lexington parsonage at the age of fourteen to become apprenticed to a Boston bookbinder and drifted after a while into the export-import business. Bred to the toughest mercantile practices of his era, Thomas Hancock was a smuggler, a profiteer who sold contaminated meat to the army during the French wars, and a shrewd and merciless destroyer of competition. Although he amassed enormous riches, there was something missing from his life—the respect of his fellows so manifestly enjoyed by his reverend father and brothers. This Thomas Hancock sought to achieve by display. His agents in London were instructed to get him the finest coaches, clothes, house furnishings, and even a coat of arms—all of which ostentation accomplished the exact opposite of what Thomas Hancock had had in mind and made him a somewhat ridiculous figure. Because he inherited his uncle's egregious sense of display along with his fortune, young John Hancock was to be dogged all his days by a total lack of prudence in exhibiting his wealth.

Young John Hancock was graduated from Harvard, learned the finer points of the free-booting trading of the eighteenth century, and basked agreeably in the surface elegance of his uncle's establishment. He was superficial, impressionable, self-centered, and always excessively concerned with whether or not other people valued him sufficiently highly. During his boyhood he had made regular visits to his grandfather's Lexington parsonage, the major part of which had been built by his rich uncle, probably as a penance but ostensibly as a gift to his father. After the old bishop's death and while his grandmother was still alive, young John Hancock made periodic duty pilgrimages to Lexington; but later he seldom saw the provincial towns. His was the life of a rich young man in Boston, where he alternated between life in his uncle's mansion under the watchful eye of his possessive Aunt Lydia and the waterfront where he kept a middle-aged mistress. Then, when he was twenty-six, his uncle died and made him heir designate to a fabulous fortune and the immediate object of the unshakable matriarchal rule of his aunt, Lydia Henchman Hancock.

After his uncle's death Hancock, known widely and solely as Thomas Hancock's favored nephew, sought a character of his own. Without the acumen and drive of his uncle, he was a man of more varied endowments, genuinely generous in nature, and of a flexibility that was often his salvation. Although his intellectual capacity was limited and his impressionableness almost childish, he was aware of other worlds than the noisy turmoil of the Boston trading circles. He started to practice a certain amount of spontaneous philanthropies, including wholesale relief for the homeless after the great Boston fire of 1767; the purchase of church pews for widows; bells, pulpits, and Bibles for meetinghouses; a collection of books for Harvard, and a concert hall for Boston. In good time he became the Treasurer of Harvard College, a trust not conferred lightly by the canny guardians of the college funds. He also became captain of the Independent Corps of Cadets, with the rank of colonel, and thus commanded the honor guard of the royal governors. This furnished him not only with a title but with an opportunity to indulge his love of elegant dress. He had his tailors in London devise the most magnificent regimentals the colony had ever seen, bought new uniforms for the entire corps, and hired two master fifers to play at drills. For the rest, he managed the business left him by his uncle with only moderate competence. His towering vanity brought about recurring breaks with his agents overseas. His speculations turned out to have none of the diabolic genius of his late uncle. His interest in commerce kept flagging as he sought new ways to impress himself upon the people of Boston as a great man. In this he was more successful than he had been in the commercial life, for public events were on his side and a man named Samuel Adams could use him.

When John Hancock, at the age of thirty-eight, and Samuel Adams, fifty-two, presented themselves at Jonas Clarke's house for their indeterminate stay in March 1775, while the Provincial Congress met in Concord, they offered a dramatic study in contrasts that a decade of working together and occasional squabbles had not diminished. Hancock was handsome and elegant; Adams was dumpy and palsied. Hancock was so splendidly attired it took several trunks to carry his clothes; Adams was so seedy that his friends had to buy him decent clothes for public appearances. Hancock was capricious, shortsighted; Adams was clearheaded, farsighted. Hancock was in vacillating search of fame; Adams was in consecrated pursuit of a cause. Hancock was the most important thing in his world; Adams the least in his. With Hancock the political life was a way to achieve a popularity he desperately needed; with Adams politics was a means of bringing about the salvation of the new world. Hancock—urbane, vain, shallow, irresolute, a little frivolous; Adams—simple, plodding, astute, determined, somewhat somber. Hancock, the splendid poser; Adams, the stolid true believer. Hancock, the used; Adams, the user.

When they arrived on Clarke's threshold, the major thing they had in common was a problem: where did the Revolution—still a revolution of opinion and not of action—go from there? The Provincial Congress was sitting in Concord passing resolutions and urging actions that had little hope of being carried out generally in the colony. The Committee of Safety was functioning

as a sort of executive cabinet, but it had no real authority or power
except through whatever persuasion it could exercise. There was
not the remotest semblance of a united spirit throughout the
colonies. The First Continental Congress—since the Stamp Act
the first united forum of the colonies, which Adams had attended
in Philadelphia six months earlier—seemed to him infested with
"half-way patriots" intent on reconciliation with Great Britain,
until he himself, by some masterly stratagems, had wrested it
from the control of the "conservatives"; but the colonies at large
were nevertheless startled by its mildly separatist economic conclusions, and there were some wide fears that what the Bostonians
wanted was separation from England so that they could run all the
colonies themselves. Samuel Adams had returned to Boston quite
dissatisfied with the general feeling of the Continental Congress
that by purely economic measures the colonies could bring about a
reversal of British policy.

A mere reversal of British policy was not what interested Adams.
Born into a family of means, Samuel Adams was himself a failure
in commercial life, dissipating his legacy from his father and
making an insoluble mess of his job as tax collector of Boston.
His sole genius was in political manipulation, and he rose to
commanding power during the early days of the struggle with
Britain. He managed to give direction and purpose to popularist
groups in Boston, who had previously just been against the wealthy
classes who were running things. And as the gap between the
colony and Britain widened, he cemented these groups, many
of whom had battled each other literally in the streets of
Boston, into the nucleus of a liberty party. Into them he
had breathed the spirit of revolution. For ten years he had neglected even to support his family in order to labor to keep that
spirit alive, and he had no intention of seeing it puffed out by
the cautions of the first Continental Congress. The economic
paralysis brought about by the Coercive Acts in Boston, the
financial burden of novel taxes, and the other economic troubles

of the times were to Adams only symptoms of a deeper, more important rift involving the essentials of political morality. He was firmly convinced that Great Britain was a depraved society, corrupt in religion, corrupt in politics, corrupt in values. Unlike some of his countrymen's, his concept of the issue was never so particularized that it could be reduced to slogans. Taxation without representation was abhorrent enough to him, but he could never see it as the crux of the matter, and the cure of colonial representation in Parliament never interested him. At Philadelphia he wrecked completely the scheme of Joseph Galloway, Speaker of the Pennsylvania Assembly, to establish a kind of domestic parliament in the colonies that would legislate jointly with the British Parliament on colonial affairs. Although he bided his time in announcing it, he was interested only in total, complete independence.

Fanatic as he undoubtedly was, Samuel Adams was also a political realist of the keenest insight. He knew a great deal about men's minds, and he was easily the most gifted man of his times in understanding and manipulating the group mind. He knew that when all the oratory was done and all the great thinking expressed, all that they achieved was the definition of objectives. To achieve the objectives themselves, it was necessary to consolidate in one line of action groups that had little in common but could be made to have a common intent. The accomplishment of this strategy of revolution was Samuel Adams' single-minded purpose and his everlasting monument.

ii

In his long and persistent effort Samuel Adams made use of every person, every prejudice, every element, every fear, and every aspiration in colonial society. By patient, skillful, strong-minded, and often ruthless work he finally welded together forces of such dynamic drive that it is difficult to believe that any of his contemporaries fully understood them. Into these forces he drew the young merchant prince John Hancock at an early date, encouraging and flattering him when it was desirable and cracking down heavily on him when it was necessary, but always using him. To Hancock it was enough that he was becoming more than a merchant: he was becoming a statesman in time of crisis.

Up until the March meeting of the Provincial Congress in Concord, to which Adams and Hancock were commuting from Jonas Clarke's house, the road to revolution had been full of barriers, bumps and detours. Hancock was so uncertain that at times he gravitated toward the Tories, and he could never get over a feeling of awe toward royal governors. But Adams always got him back on the road again and finally down it so far that there could be no turning back. By 1775 he was the only man singled out by the ministry in London as the equal of Samuel Adams in obnoxiousness, and Gage had been sent orders to arrest both Hancock and Adams.

To Adams the distinction was hard-won. A decade, sometimes turbulent and sometimes so somnolent that only Adams seemed to care, had gone by since Samuel Adams first came into alliance with any considerable groups in Boston on the passage of the Stamp Act, and from then on he never let the issues evoked by the act lapse from public awareness for a moment—even though at times there were few listening. Elected to the General Court during the economic uneasiness of 1765, he put little faith in the slow, legislative route to political reform. When a Continental Congress was proposed in 1774, he said that "from the length of time it will take to bring it to pass, I fear it cannot answer for the present emergency."[4] He saw his seat in the General Court as useful chiefly as a spot from which to hurl harpoons at the royal governor. He put far greater faith in the Boston mobs, who were ever ready to attack authority, colonial as well as royal. Adams, in bringing the mobs together, gave them a sense of responsible and creditable purpose and saw to it that they concentrated on such worthwhile objectives as the new "stamp masters" and resident officers of the crown. It is no exaggeration to say that Adams' mobs nullified the Stamp Act by scaring the stamp masters out of town. He then blandly announced in the General Court that obviously the life of Boston could not come to a halt just because there was no one around to furnish the stamped papers for legal and commercial documents; so the British Parliament repealed the act as unenforceable.

Adams had hit upon a technique of dramatic violence that he never abandoned. He used it again and again, always at an opportune time and always with masterful effect—not least of which was the mobs' inciting the British troops to fire on a group of mobsters in 1770, creating the long politically useful Boston Massacre. Although Samuel Adams' cousin, John Adams, the most disciplined of the minds of the period, could not stomach that episode and served as defense counsel for the soldiers, the Boston Massacre was the longest lived myth in American history. Moreover, it gave a fiery emotional content to a dispute that had until then been economic and theoretic. Its anniversary was observed in skillfully stage-managed ceremonies, which took broad liberties with the facts, in churches and assembly places of the colony for a decade until independence was won. Throughout the immediate pre-Revolutionary period, Boston was indeed virtually controlled by the mobs. And the mobs were controlled by Samuel Adams. He understood their members as individuals, and he had mastered the strange alchemy by which the mob becomes both more and less than the sum of the individuals.

As Adams took the low road to political leadership, Hancock, whose business interests were having a hard enough time without tax innovations, took the high road. He was elected to the General Court, too, and Samuel Adams, recognizing him as an ideal symbol of respectability and broad commercial interests to identify with the revolutionary movement, got him introduced to the mobs and lionized by the two leading mobs, once deadly rivals, at a peace feast, for which Hancock paid the bill. Hancock, in turn, got Adams a reprieve on the old default charge that had hung over him since he left the collectorship some £8000 in arrears on his accounts, saving him from almost certain imprisonment. During the long struggles over all the issues, from the oppressive taxes to the quartering of troops, Hancock and Adams supplemented one another admirably. The outward and visible implications of Hancock's association with the revolutionary faction were of inestimable importance merely on the surface; for while Samuel Adams and his old associates had nothing to lose by the revolutionary path on which they were set, John Hancock had tremendous assets and interests to lose and nothing predictable to gain. At the same time, the essential differences in character and values of the two men repeatedly boiled to an explosive point, and more than once Hancock was almost sent flying into the arms of the Tories, to whose company he was more attracted socially anyhow. Hancock was extremely sensitive about his personal status before the public, and Adams did not think that anything, including reasonable political behavior, let alone personal position, was as important as the cause. On the whole, therefore, while Adams labored at every conceivable task, some risky, some grueling, all demanding of ingenuity and energy, Hancock became the well-bred front man. But whenever Adams seemed to be going too far, to be bordering on treason, Hancock pulled back and even engineered the defeat of some of Adams' projects. For long periods, too, Hancock walked a middle path between Adams at one extreme and the royal governor at the other. Nevertheless, whenever a real crisis arose, he was back with Adams again.

The plans of Adams could easily accommodate the temporary deflections of Hancock. In fact, it is probable that if Adams did not encourage such occasional deflections, he welcomed them as conveying to the public generally that Hancock was no man's creature. His greatest use of Hancock was to present him, at suitable times and in suitable posts, as the well-dressed, polished, substantial gentleman that stood as a living answer to the charges, not so much in England as in the colonies, that the revolutionary movement was the irresponsible work of mobs. Meanwhile, Adams had other work to do. He forged the dissenting clergy, for example, into a powerfully influential revolutionary warhead by constantly identifying religious rights with political rights and by repeated reminders of the continuing threat of an American episcopacy. Among less individualistic classes than the clergy, Adams created and put into operation the first political machines known in America, which became both central agencies of action and incredibly efficient and rapid sources and channels of intelligence. He also devised techniques for influencing public opinion that still seemed innovations when used nearly two centuries later. Not the least effective of these were the communications from the colonial assemblies to British officials, drafts of which often appeared in American newspapers weeks before they had a chance of reaching the designated recipients. James Otis once protested this practice to Adams, who snapped, "What signifies that? You know it was designed for the people and not the Minister."[5] He thought, too, of the need to influence British opinion, long before he ever had any hopes of armed revolt, and he made certain that every action of the ministry was balanced by an unmistakable exposition of the American point of view to Englishmen. In 1768, Adams invented the American newspaper syndicate, for he was convinced that the best and most effective way of mobilizing the sympathy of other colonies for the plight of Boston in being occupied by British troops was by reporting to them in detail what it was like for a free town to be occupied. Distributed to newspapers all the way to South Carolina, the column, "Boston Journal of Occurrences," reported in considerably exaggerated news items how the townspeople suffered from the troops—all to suggest that this could also happen to Philadelphia or Baltimore, Richmond or Charleston.

Yet despite his vast skill and undoubted genius in molding public opinion and in mobilizing group action, Adams had much

too sound a sense of history not to know that the whole revolutionary movement was at the mercy of events. In the past, as in the
case of the Boston Massacre, he had occasionally inspired the
event. In his almost religious fervor for the cause, he saw this
as nothing more than the acceleration of historic trends that were
inevitable. He had also seen fit, from time to time, to meet events
halfway, as he did in the case of the Boston Tea Party, when he
abruptly terminated a public meeting to deal with the tea issue
by stating flatly that "this meeting can do nothing further to save
the country"—upon which his mob of Mohawks took off to throw
the disputed tea into the harbor. In the shrewd judgment of
Samuel Adams such stimulation of events was, from time to
time, a necessary element in the strategy of revolution. Another
such time was approaching when he came with Hancock to Jonas
Clarke's house.

The long dispute with Great Britain had brought the situation,
by the spring of 1775, to a tense stalemate. Everyone knew that
it could not continue indefinitely, but it was by no means assumed
that it would inevitably culminate in armed revolt. As punishment
for the destruction of the tea shipments the Boston Port Bill had
closed the port of Boston tight. Parliament had sought to make
violation of its laws unpopular in the colonies by making an example of Massachusetts. It rushed through a petulant and highly
impolitic assortment of acts to put teeth in its tax measures. Among
these were acts prohibiting the calling of any town meetings except
to elect officers and transferring to the Crown the appointment
of all local law-enforcement officials. Since May 1774, General
Gage, with his five thousand bored troops, had occupied Boston
to enforce the acts; and all commerce in the town was suspended.
Samuel Adams spent the year trying to keep the spirit of revolution
alive, to unite the colonies, and to create an American army that
would absorb the various militia. Despite his distrust of the slow
legislative process, the Provincial Congress was the agency that
he expected to accomplish these things within Massachusetts, and

the Continental Congress within the colonies as a whole. But he was well aware that these bodies, with their constant need for compromise, might require an occasional goading. Adams had had enough experience with them to know that they were less apt to rise to greatness than to have greatness thrust upon them. After the lukewarm session of the First Continental Congress he used every means, fair or foul, to broaden and intensify a sense of urgency.

Adams had got Hancock installed as President of the Provincial Congress and as chairman of the Committee of Safety, but he seemed unwilling to let him out of his sight. With Adams firmly in charge Hancock was enjoying hugely the sensation of a leadership that he did not have. Both men were, of course, the sole exemptions in a general offer of pardon that was made by the British in an effort to break the Boston stalemate. Hancock wore the honor in his usual theatrical way, strapping on his colonel's sword as though ready to duel with any soldier who came to get him. But Adams had no dramatic illusions about it; he knew very well that a country parsonage would be an unseemly and a very unpopular object of a military raid and that Gage was not likely to try it.

For his part, Adams could see the stalemate's breaking in either of two ways: reconciliation with Britain, with the colonies, chastened but given relief, remaining in the empire; or outright and complete separation, won by forcibly throwing the British out. He could see the former as nothing but total defeat and the moral collapse of the colonies. The latter he saw as possible only if all the colonies were united in such furious indignation by a dramatic event that they would never be reconciled. Unprepared and almost barren of ammunition as the colonies were, Adams nevertheless feared the war far less than a drift toward reconciliation. The North ministry, despite the warlike aspect of Gage's Boston army, had spent the winter of 1774–75 holding out olive branches to the other colonies. Adams knew that there were economic, social, and political pressures within the colonies that made it not at all unlikely that in due time they might be seized by eager colonial hands. Moreover, he was fully aware that many of the influential colonies outside New England, and some factions within, found the prospect of government by Sam Adams no more palatable than government by British Tories.

Adams unquestionably found Jonas Clarke a sympathetic and wise counselor on these matters. During his prolonged stay at Clarke's house, conversations far into the night could enlighten Adams on the attitudes of the Lexington farmers. Expert as he was in town mobs and their behavior, Adams, who had lived all his life in the heart of Boston, was weak in his knowledge of country people. Hancock knew nothing of them. On the other hand, Clarke knew them intimately, had taught them all the politics that they knew, and had written their official town correspondence and resolutions for them all through the dispute with Britain. Nobody could give Adams a more reliable appraisal of the capacity and willingness of the country people to resist any coercion from Gage. Moreover, Samuel Adams was a dourly religious man, a profound believer in the force and sanctity of the covenant, and it would be only from such a man as Jonas Clarke that he would willingly seek guidance.

From March twenty-second to the end of the month, the Provincial Congress in the Concord meetinghouse held rather pointless and long-winded discussions on "the rules and regulations for a constitutional army." But there was no "constitutional army." This fondest dream of Samuel Adams had got nowhere at the Continental Congress five months earlier, and the Congress had also made it perfectly clear that the majority of the delegates wanted no war of aggression against the British troops in Boston. So there was no army and little broad sentiment in favor of one. Even the little town militia surrounding Boston—a quarter of whose number were enrolled as minutemen—were inadequately supplied, uncertain of what they were supposed to do, and not very well drilled. And the session of the Provincial Congress at Concord was sagging badly, with several members not even bothering to attend and others going home before the session was over. There was also bad news from other towns. The Tories of Marblehead, north of Boston, and of Marshfield, south, had applied to General Gage for British troops to come to their towns to ensure order. The troops had gone and stayed there, and nothing happened—no brush with the townspeople, no clash with the local militia, not even bitter resolutions. To Samuel Adams, such serenity meant trouble to the cause.

Adams tried at the Concord sessions to rouse the delegates to the establishment of a provincial army of eighteen thousand men, outnumbering Gage's troops over four to one, but the cautious country delegates were not swarming to the support of the notion. They gave reasons that Adams considered inadequate, such as the exorbitant costs involved or the danger of British reprisals; or else, as Adams pressed the matter, they simply suffered sudden diplomatic illnesses and went home. As the sessions droned on, the number of delegates attending had so dwindled that Adams made a motion that all sick delegates resign and more vigorous substitutes be sent in their places. This made any further sick reports too brazen to be tried, but the session had accomplished nothing concrete and was shrinking to a halfhearted end.

In a desperate, and characteristic, effort to redeem it, Adams seized upon some intelligence received from Dr. Joseph Warren, a member of the Congress and also of the Committee of Safety, who had been left in Boston to take charge of affairs during Adams' absence. Dr. Warren had news to report from Arthur Lee, the colony's agent in London. Lee's letter was over three months old when it got to Boston, having come on a slow winter passage, and it did not have much of importance to communicate anyhow. But it was enough, under Adams' skillful use, to stir up the delegates and shake them from their deadly apathy. It reported that Parliament had resolved to support the Crown fully in the

Jonas Clarke (1730—1805), for half a century pastor and first citizen of Lexington, was the author of the town's major political papers from the condemnation of the Stamp Act in 1765 to the condemnation of Jay's Treaty in 1794. LEXINGTON HISTORICAL SOCIETY

Samuel Adams (1722–1803) was most effective as an agitator, kept the Revolutionary spirit alive for a decade before Lexington, after which he steadily declined in influence. He and Hancock became intensely antagonistic in local politics in Massachusetts, Adams succeeding Hancock as governor on the latter's death in 1793. MUSEUM OF FINE ARTS, BOSTON

John Hancock (1736–93), embittered by the choice of Washington over himself as commander in chief, was a man of theatrical vanity and limited intellect. After 1777 he confined his activities to local politics in Massachusetts, where he refused as governor to welcome President Washington in 1789 unless the President first called on him. Washington sent him a sharp note which changed his views of protocol. MUSEUM OF FINE ARTS, BOSTON

Paul Revere (1735–1818) was in 1775 a forty-year-old silversmith. Employed as a courier for the Boston Committee of Correspondence, Revere was also a self-starting patriot who often undertook patrolling duties on his own initiative. MUSEUM OF FINE ARTS, BOSTON

effort to maintain authority over the American colonies (which was hardly exceptionally grave news, since the Parliament had been rather more fretful in determining a policy for America than the King had); that henceforth rebellious Massachusetts was prohibited equal access with His Majesty's loyal subjects in Canada to the great fisheries; and finally that General Gage, who had been asking for reinforcements for months, would at last get them. Adams leaped eagerly upon all this intelligence as the salvation of the tepid session. A proclamation, full of mystery, immediately went out from Hancock, as President, to the recalcitrant delegates:

In Provincial Congress, April 3, 1775
Whereas several members of this congress are now absent by leave of the congress, and as the important intelligence received by the last vessels from Great Britain renders it necessary that every member attend his duty,—
RESOLVED, *that the absent members be directed forthwith to attend in this place, that so the wisdom of the province may be collected.*[6]

The strategem worked, and the absent delegates came rushing back to Concord, their illnesses all providentially cured. But the only business that they transacted was an attempt to strengthen steps already taken but never wholeheartedly carried out throughout the province. On April seventh the Congress prepared a circular urging that the towns of eastern Massachusetts make certain that their militia were ready in case of need for emergency action. It also enjoined them from taking any action except defensively— which hardly seems to have been necessary except for the delegates' hearty respect for Samuel Adams' ability to create crises. On April eighth a resolution was passed to send delegates to Connecticut, Rhode Island, and New Hampshire to solicit participation in raising a provincial army. On April thirteenth it was resolved to create six companies of artillery, though there were neither field pieces to arm them nor money to pay them. On Saturday, April fifteenth, having exhausted the list of actions even remotely possible to achieve, the Provincial Congress proclaimed a date for fasting and prayer and then adjourned.

All this flurry of activity with which Adams sought to rescue the session from characterization as a failure did not erase from his own mind the fact that the people of the colonies were generally far from being in a hostile mood. They were not even convinced that it was necessary to be watchful or prepared. Of the £21,000 the Provincial Congress had requested for munitions six months earlier, less than a quarter had been received. The militia were still without bayonets and armed for the most part only with their own hunting muskets. They did not have enough field pieces even to train the militia in their use, and they also lacked such ordinary equipment as spades, pick axes, wheelbarrows, and mess gear. The Committee of Supplies was instructed to correct the situation but given no suggestions on how to do it. Finally, even after Adams' effort to scare the Provincial Congress into venturesome action with the news from London, there was still indifference and a lack of concern among the delegates. When Dr. Church, attending the Congress, sent his espionage report to Gage on the last day of the session, he reported, "There was great division among the members of the Congress and great irresolution shown in the course of their debates this week. Many of them opposed raising an army and though it was motioned to take under consideration the appointment of officers for said army they would not enter upon it at all. The Committee on the State of the Province have now under consideration the means of procuring a fund for the subsistence of the army but find so many insurmountable difficulties that they can come to no determination."[7]

There was no doubt that the third week of April 1775 saw the revolutionary movement at a very low ebb. Adams, who had been through thick times and through thin in his crusade, saw no chance of any considerable improvement until the people's mood was changed from apathy to militance. No resolution, no speeches, could accomplish this. It would have to depend upon events.

The Concord session over, Adams and Hancock concluded that, in view of the repeated assurances from London that Gage was now under orders to arrest them as ringleaders and send them to England for trial, they had better stay in the sanctuary of Clarke's house until they set out for the meetings of the Second Continental Congress in Philadelphia a week later. The major thing on Adams' mind was how to inspire action in that fledging quasi-national body when the Provincial Congress had just fallen so flat. By any means, the impotent and irresolute wranglings of the First Continental Congress, the memory of which after six months still gnawed at his own crusading spirit, must be avoided. Meanwhile, in the Reverend Jonas Clarke he found congenial, informed, and sympathetic company. Hancock had other matters to occupy him.

iii

On April seventh, a week before the Provincial Congress adjourned, Dr. Joseph Warren's brother James reported on affairs in Boston to his wife Mercy: "The inhabitants of Boston are on the move. H. and A. [Hancock and Adams] go no more into that garrison. The female connections of the first come out early this morning. . . ."[8]

The females connected with Hancock were his Aunt Lydia and her protégée, his fiancée, Dorothy Quincy. They headed, fully equipped for an indefinite stay, for the house of Jonas Clarke in Lexington, and there they had been installed comfortably, if not with the luxury they were accustomed to, while Hancock and Adams were winding up the business of the Congress and waiting to go on to Philadelphia. It was probably Aunt Lydia who decided on the Lexington retreat—with a fine indifference to what must have begun to be an acute space problem in the little house. She was determined that her late husband's nephew and heir was to marry her own favorite niece. But Dorothy Quincy, whose family connections were more distinguished than the Hancocks' and who was popular, self-confident, and somewhat spiritedly independent, enjoyed giving Hancock, ten years her senior, an uneven time of it. Aunt Lydia thought that the more the two were together the sooner their marriage could come about, and the last major business of her life would be done. She had no intention of letting wars or rumors of wars interfere with this serious matter. She and Dorothy were given the big upstairs bedroom in the Clarke house, close to the big bedroom occupied by Hancock and Adams. Aunt Lydia probably took over as much of the management of the house as she could, for distinguished patriots from out of town kept coming to the house for dinner.

Among these was one of Hancock's ghost writers (Samuel Adams was the other), Dr. Samuel Cooper, militant and politically minded pastor of the Brattle Street Church, who had written Hancock's most famous oration, the 1774 anniversary speech on the Boston Massacre. Cooper, whose church in Boston was attended regularly by Adams, was the clerical firebrand of the revolution and a kind of chaplain at many of Adams' meetings with the mob leaders during the early days. It is written[9] that the Sunday before his visit to Lexington "Dr. Cooper, a notorious rebel, was officiating at his meetinghouse, and, on notice given him, protested sudden sickness, went home, and sent to another clergyman to do his duty in the evening. He, with every other chief of the [revolutionary] faction, left Boston before night and never returned to it. The cause, at the time unknown, was discovered on the fourteenth of said month [April], when a vessel arrived with Government dispatches, which contained direction to seize the persons of certain notorious rebels. It was too late. They had received timely notice of their danger, and were fled."

Cooper, Clarke, and Adams, drawing Hancock into the discussions so much as the attention required by Dorothy Quincy's presence allowed, had ample opportunity to discuss possible courses of action. It was still certain that public opinion would not tolerate any aggressive attack on the troops in Boston, even if an army could be improvised for the purpose. And Adams had all Sunday, Monday, and Tuesday—the sixteenth, seventeenth, and eighteenth—to consult with Clarke.

In addition to paying some attention to his fiancée and his aunt, Hancock had other matters on his mind as well. He had brought his secretary, John Lowell, to Lexington with him, and lodged him with a trunkful of papers to be attended to in Buckman's Tavern, a few minutes' walk from the Clarke house. Among the papers was a disturbing letter from President Langdon of Harvard. It reminded Hancock that the Corporation had written him four times since November 1774 for a statement of his accounts as treasurer of the College, that he had twice made appointments for meetings to present them and had failed to appear on both occasions, that the College couldn't very well function without its funds, and, finally, that the Corporation would now like him to turn over the money, bonds, and papers that he held for the College since he was obviously too busy with more pressing matters to handle them. Hancock wrote a steaming letter back, saying that he resented the Corporation's action and that he would do something about the College's funds that he was holding when he got back from Philadelphia. But he was so furious with Harvard that he never did give the College its funds (his estate did after his death), and he waited eleven years before he gave it even an accounting. Although his business affairs were muddled that April and the Boston port closing had left him somewhat short of cash, if Hancock had used Harvard's funds, he had probably done so mistakenly. Embezzlement is much less likely to be the explanation of his behavior than wounded feelings at the Corporation's request for its own moneys, for there was never a day in John Hancock's life when his assets were as low as his pride was sensitive.

On Sunday the sixteenth there was further excitement at the Clarke house, which by now was the busiest place in Massachusetts. Paul Revere, a Boston craftsman who had long been the most trusted messenger of the Boston Committee of Correspondence, rode the sixteen miles from Boston with urgent news: there were unusual and highly suspicious movements of the British troops within the Boston garrison. Revere had joined with some thirty other Boston mechanics in setting up a voluntary, self-appointed patrol to watch the troops around the clock. "In the winter, towards the spring," he later wrote, "we frequently took turns, two and two, to watch the soldiers, by patrolling the streets all night. The Saturday night preceding the nineteenth of April, about twelve o'clock at night, the boats belonging to the transports were all launched and carried under the sterns of the men-of-war. (They had previously been hauled up and repaired.) We likewise found that the grenadiers and light infantry had all been taken off duty. From these movements, we suspected something serious was to be transacted."[10]

Revere first took this intelligence to Dr. Warren, who seems to have adopted Revere as a chief aide. They decided that the intent of Gage was probably to use the transports' boats to ferry the grenadiers and light infantry across the Charles and out to the countryside on a raid of the colony's military stores, or to seize Adams and Hancock (for which the number of troops would appear excessive), or to do both. They then agreed that on the next day, Sunday, Revere had better ride out to Lexington and take his report directly to the Clarke house.

For Revere, who had been employed by the Boston selectmen to ride all the way to New York with news of the Boston Tea Party, the chore was a routine one. The ride was so uneventful that he recalled nothing of it in later years. But to Adams the news that he brought was far from routine. The month of April that had opened so dull showed promise of delivering the kind of events that Adams and the cause so badly needed.

The obvious decision of Gage to make some sort, *any* sort, of a move was to Adams the beginning of the real dawn of a new era.

Repeatedly he had been held back, the whole revolutionary movement stranded, by the faint of heart who were always qualifying and undermining plans for action with such phrases as "defensive moves only" and "in the event that Gage's troops with artillery and baggage move out of Boston." Now let them move. Samuel Adams had sublime confidence, amply justified, in his ability to make events work for him and to manage the effect that they had on men's minds. Here, with the news that Revere brought, then, was nothing but opportunity.

Consulting with Hancock, he first got out of the way the details that had to be handled before he could contemplate further the grander implications of the intelligence from Revere. As chairman of the Provincial Committee of Safety, Hancock sent orders by messenger to Concord, five miles away, to direct the local committee to hide the arms, munitions and supplies in widely scattered places throughout the town and to move what they could to other towns in the area. Additional messengers were dispatched to other communities to give advance warning to the minutemen that they might soon be called upon to live up to their names. A special meeting of the Committee of Safety was also called for the next day, Monday.

And now Samuel Adams could ponder the suddenly bright turn in the prospects of the revolutionary movement, so lately almost dead of inertia. There could be no doubt that the British were about to make an excursion in force out into the countryside. As a result, anything could happen. Adams saw all history, all wars, all politics as simply action and reaction. He was reasonably certain now of getting from the British the kind of action needed by the cause. His only remaining concern was to get the right kind of reaction from the colonists. He had two days to think about this, in the company of the most influential man in Lexington, the Reverend Jonas Clarke, and at a place not more than a few rods from the parade ground of the Lexington militia.

3
THE MIDNIGHT RIDERS

"We rid down towards Lexington, a pretty smart pace. . . ."

PAUL REVERE[1]

If Samuel Adams had problems in the spring of 1775, his arch-foe, General Thomas Gage, "Captain-General and Governor-in-Chief" of Massachusetts, had even more. Adams' illegal government, the Provincial Congress, was ineffective enough, but Gage's legal government in Boston was merely a ghost, governing no one but the occupation troops. His effective command also extended to the loyalists who had moved into Boston, but the towns outside paid no attention whatsoever to his government. He had no legislature, the General Court having changed itself into the Provincial Congress, and no courts, for the royally appointed judges were afraid to hold sessions. Most of the clergy refused to read his proclamations, and most of the inhabitants ignored them.

During the winter of 1774–75, Gage could please no one. The Tories and his own troops thought him so mild in his government that they openly ridiculed him. The patriots thought him a monster, up to the work of the devil, and beneath contempt. Actually, Gage was a man of exceptional patience and strong democratic instincts, of noble lineage, married to an American wife, and of far less rigidity than the average military man. Altogether, in the Boston of 1775 he was in an impossible and, in some respects, a silly situation. He was not ruling Boston with an iron hand, although with over four thousand well-armed troops in the little peninsular town of seventeen thousand and with men-of-war in the harbor capable of blasting it from three sides, he could easily have imposed martial law. Instead, he permitted perfect freedom. He let the radical press insult him unmercifully, permitted public meetings to be held for the sole purpose of inspiring opposition to his government, and so often took the side of the townspeople in their run-ins with the soldiers that one of his officers complained that, while the townspeople were never blamed for offenses against the troops, "if a soldier errs in the least, who is more ready to complain than Tommy?"[2] He imposed no censorship, no curfews, no regulations impeding the personal liberties of the inhabitants.

His reasons for the restraint he showed were sensible: "I have been at pains to prevent anything of consequence taking its rise from trifles and idle quarrels, and when the cause of Boston became the general concern of America, endeavoured so to manage that Administration might have an opening to negotiate if anything conciliatory should present itself or be in a condition to prosecute their plans with greater advantage."[3] Moreover, he put little faith in the ability of four thousand troops to put down any determined rebellion in any case: "If force is to be used at length, it must be a considerable one, and foreign troops must be hired, for to begin with small numbers will encourage resistance, and not terrify; and will in the end cost more blood and treasure. An army on such a service should be large enough to make considerable detachments to disarm and take in the counties, procure forage carriages, etc., and keep up communications, without which little progress could be made in a country where all are enemies."[4]

Throughout the winter of 1774–75, Gage presided with flexibility and prudence over a highly incendiary set of circumstances. The Port Bill had thrown almost all the laborers in what was entirely a shipping town out of their jobs, on the one side. On the other, there were four thousand soldiers with virtually nothing to do. That the idlers and the soldiers did not have a major conflict was as much tribute to Gage as an administrator as some of his later military ventures were a rebuke to him as a general. In the spring, however, Gage, who was far less militant than the Boston Tories would have liked, began to receive rumbles of dissatisfaction with his command in London. On April sixteenth he received a letter from Dartmouth, the Secretary of State, in which the earl cast doubt, in no very uncertain terms, on the wisdom of Gage's general course. He told Gage that the King and his ministers wanted action, particularly in the form of the arrest of the leaders of the Provincial Congress—who, at the time of Gage's receipt of Dartmouth's letter, were sitting in Jonas Clarke's study in Lexington. The earl rejected Gage's sound judgment that four thousand troops could never subdue the colonies and added that the prospects of Gage's getting an army that he considered adequate for such a job were so dim as to be out of the question. Dartmouth went on, comfortable in the certainty of his knowledge of affairs three thousand miles away, that Gage had been altogether too lenient anyhow and concluded with ministerial sarcasm, "In reviewing the charter for the government of the province of Massachusetts Bay, I observe that there is a clause that empowers the governor to use and exercise the law-martial in times of actual war, invasion or rebellion."[5]

Gage got this long and reproachful letter from the Secretary of State on April sixteenth, four months after it was dispatched on a sloop of war. This was the day after he had Dr. Church's final summary of the session of the Provincial Congress and a detailed report of the distribution of the military stores at Concord. Despite Dartmouth's order to put top priority on the seizure of the leaders of the Congress—an idea that Gage apparently recognized as outrageous, and that would furnish the one certain incentive for a provincial attack on the troops in Boston—Gage determined that the one thing that his troops could accomplish was the destruction of the few central depots of colonial military supplies. He had exact intelligence on the volume and location of these supplies from Dr. Church, and he had further intelligence that specified what stores were in what places. He also had Church's reports on the difficulty the Congress had encountered in trying to raise a provincial army. Nothing that Dartmouth said in his scolding letter to Gage struck the latter as sufficient grounds for changing his plans to seize the Concord stores in favor of seizing Hancock and Adams. He knew where the stores were. He knew the provincial militia were weakly organized. And he probably had the usual field general's contempt for the omniscience and bland assumptions of government ministers who sat thousands of miles away.

It was a sound enough decision for Gage to make: armies without ammunition were powerless; political leaders always had successors lurking in the background ready to make capital of their martyrdom. That Gage seriously considered seizing the stores at Concord long before he received Dartmouth's letter on April sixteenth is clear not only from his ordering the boats out the night before but also from his instructions almost a month earlier to Ensign Henry de Berniere of the Tenth Infantry: "The twentieth of March Captain Brown and myself received orders to set out for Concord, and examine the road and situation of the town; and also to get what information we could relative to what quantity of artillery and provisions . . . The town of Concord lies between hills that command it entirely; there is a river runs through it, with two bridges over it; in summer it runs pretty dry; the town is large and covers a great tract of ground, but the houses are not close together but generally in little groups. We were informed they had fourteen pieces of cannon (ten iron and four brass) and two cohorns; they were mounted, but in so bad a manner that they could not elevate them more than they were, that is, they were fixed to one elevation; their iron cannon they kept in a house in town, their brass they had concealed in some place behind the town in a wood. They had also a store of flour, fish, salt and rice; and a magazine of powder and cartridges. . . ."[6]

Although Gage had already received the information on the military stores, he obviously sent Brown and de Berniere to get the report of infantry officers on the conditions of the roads. Gage also knew, from another letter from his informer, dated April eighteenth, that many of the munitions stores had been moved following Revere's Sunday trip to Lexington, some of them out of Concord altogether but most of them to new places in the town, and that the provisions for the projected provincial army were still in their original places.

The first overt action of Gage—the launching of the boats from the transports—came on the night of Saturday, April fifteenth, the same day that he issued the general orders relieving the light infantry and grenadiers from their regular duties. He told no one his purpose in issuing the orders—not even the man he had chosen to command the force. But just as Revere and Warren had guessed what he had in mind and brought about the hurried shuffling of the stores in Concord, so did Gage's own officers. In his journal for the fifteenth, Lieutenant Barker, who never approved of anything that General Gage, or for that matter any of his senior officers, did, wrote: "General orders. 'The grenadiers and light infantry in order to learn grenadiers' exercise and new evolutions are to be off all duties until further notice.' This, I suppose, is by way of a blind. I dare say they have something for them to do."[7] How a man of Gage's military experience could assume that there would be nothing transparent in the orders, particularly when issued the same day that the boats were being readied on the Charles, is baffling. But it was characteristic of a kind of operational impracticality from which Gage suffered grievously as a field officer. Over and over again his military actions fell far short of his perception and judgment. On March fifth he had written to Dartmouth that much was to be feared from the provincial militia's "forming ambushments, whereby the light infantry must suffer extremely in penetrating the countryside."[8] Yet on April eighteenth he was preparing to send the best units in his army, amounting to perhaps a sixth of its total strength, to run just such a gantlet.

Still confident that his intentions were a total secret, Gage stuck resolutely to his policy of secrecy even throughout the day of April eighteenth, the day the expedition was to leave. Lieutenant Colonel Francis Smith of the Tenth Infantry was summoned by Gage, told that he was to command the expedition but not where it was going, and then given sealed orders to be opened only when he was on the way that night. At eight o'clock in the evening the regimental officers were called to Gage's headquarters and told to have their companies of grenadiers and light infantry "on the beach near the magazine guard exactly at 10 o'clock this night,"[9] according to Lieutenant Frederick Mackenzie of the Royal Welch Fusiliers. Mackenzie added that quiet was emphasized and the men were to be marched in small groups to the rendezvous, which was at the foot of Boston Common on the Back Bay. The regimental officers were told nothing of the purpose or the ultimate destination of the troops. Shortly before ten o'clock the men were awakened by their sergeants' shaking them, stole silently out of their barracks by back doors, and marched in total silence in little groups to the obscure beach on the Back Bay—a tidal flood completely barren of any buildings or people. "A dog, happening to bark, was run through by a bayonet."[10]

By nine o'clock on the evening of April eighteenth, then, Lieutenant Colonel Smith knew that he was going to lead an expedition but did not know where. The regimental officers knew that they were supposed to have their grenadiers and light infantry companies on the beach by ten o'clock. But the soldiers themselves had not yet been wakened. At nine o'clock Gage sent for his brigadier, Hugh, Earl Percy, and told him that he was sending an expedition to Concord to seize the stores. He said, further, that it was still a secret, even to Lieutenant Colonel Smith, who was to command. Lord Percy left in a little while and walked across Boston Common back to his own quarters. He noticed a group of townspeople talking in a huddle and, concealing his identity by his cloak in the total darkness, overheard them discussing a British march that night. They mentioned the arms stored at Concord as the specific objective, and Percy turned around and went back to report the incident to Gage. By then the troops were presumably embarked across the river, and all Gage could do was to issue orders that no townspeople were to leave Boston that night.

ii

The only patriot leader left in Boston on the night of April eighteenth, Dr. Joseph Warren had a busy time while all this stealthy mobilization of the British was going on. In the afternoon information started to flow into his surgery: the British were to march that night. Virtually all the information originated with British officers, for, careful as Gage was to conceal the destination and objective of the march, he all but published the fact that *some* march was intended. So all during the afternoon the gossipy little town, where all normal business had ceased, fairly bristled with rumors—not just a grapevine but a jungle web of information that kept meeting itself. A British officer told a gunsmith; the gunsmith told Colonel Josiah Waters, a member of the local Committee of Safety; Waters, of course, told Dr. Warren. At the same time, one John Ballard heard a Province House groom discussing the news in a stable; Ballard told William Dawes, an energetic cordwainer, who had recently endeared himself to Dr. Warren by smuggling two cannon out of Boston; Dawes told Paul Revere, "who told him he had already heard it from two other persons."[11]

As the afternoon wore on and long before Gage told even Lord Percy, his brigadier, the plan of the night, Revere and Dawes had all their own plans made for getting the word to Lexington and Concord—they were certain that Adams and Hancock at Lexington or the stores at Concord must be the objectives of any major British move. The only thing that they were unsure of was the line of the march the troops would take (the boats in the Charles could have been a feint) and the time of their departure. In those days Boston was connected to the mainland only by a thin isthmus called Boston Neck. The troops could march out across the Neck, although somewhat conspicuously, and thence in a great arc all around the Back Bay or else westward through Watertown to Waltham and then north to Lexington and Concord. Or else they could be ferried across the Charles in boats, landed in East Cambridge and then march in almost a straight line through Cambridge to Menotomy (now Arlington) to Lexington. The "sea" route was about sixteen miles to Concord and the land route was over twenty-one miles. All the evidence thus far known to Warren suggested that Gage planned to ferry the troops across the river. But Warren had also had information about Gage's scouting party of Captain Brown and Ensign de Berniere and their visit to Concord of a few weeks earlier. He knew that they had gone out the longer "land" route and come home the shorter "sea" route, obviously to give Gage road reports on both routes. Revere had also anticipated that the actual route taken by the British would not be known until the last minute. Accordingly, on his way back from his intelligence ride to Lexington the previous Sunday, he had stopped at Charlestown, across the Charles from Boston, and arranged a signal code with Colonel Conant of the Charlestown Committee of Safety that "if the British went out by water, to show two lanterns in the North Church steeple; and if by land, one as a signal, for we were apprehensive it would be difficult to cross the Charles River or get over Boston Neck."[12] Between them, however, Revere and Dawes managed to do both.

Dawes left by land as soon as Dr. Warren got word, in the early night, that the troops were being marched in small groups down to the shore on the Back Bay. His instructions were to go to Clarke's house in Lexington and tell Adams and Hancock that the British were on the way. Although Gage always had a guard at the only entrance and exit to the town on the narrow Neck, it was not particularly efficient. Dawes, who was of a humorous and genial temperament, had often delighted in seeing how often he could pass in and out of the town without being stopped. He sometimes disguised himself as a country produce peddler and once spent all day posing as a drunk following British officers around and continuing to follow them as they marched past the guard on the Neck. Dawes had also invented a smuggling strategem, a buttons game, for getting contraband gold coins out of the town to his family in Worcester. In an age when everyone wore brass or gilt buttons he made himself conspicuous by wearing cloth-covered buttons on both his coat and waistcoat. When he was accepted for this peculiarity, he put gold coins inside the cloth buttons and wore the contraband out of Boston to Worcester, where his wife removed the gold coins and replaced them with ordinary button molds. Dawes had also, from the beginning, taken the precaution of befriending any of the guards at the Neck who looked approachable. On the night of the eighteenth he had the good fortune to find one of his friends on duty. He was too discreet and too disinclined to presume upon the friendship to ask the guard to open the gate. But when the guard had to open it anyhow for a squad of soldiers on routine patrol, Dawes had his chance: "attending their motions apparently as a spectator, [he] was allowed by the connivance of the guard at the gate, who was privately friendly to him, to pass out with them."[13]

Paul Revere, meanwhile, had a more complicated exit from the town and a less casual one. First of all, he was well known to the British as a patriot express rider. Secondly, he had to get across the Charles River in the shadow of a British man-of-war just as the British troops would be crossing. And finally, unbeknown to him, Gage had that afternoon posted mounted officers, with their sidearms concealed as though they were on pleasure jaunts, along the Cambridge roads, just in case messengers should try to give out alarms that night. It was ten o'clock—the rendezvous hour of the troops on the beach—when Dr. Warren sent for Revere. As in the case of his instructions to Dawes, Warren's concern was with Hancock and Adams at Clarke's house in Lexington and not with the supplies at Concord: "I would immediately set off for Lexington where Messrs. Hancock and Adams were, and acquaint them of the movement and that it was thought they were the objects."[14] (In his deposition, however, Revere mentioned the stores at Concord as also a possible objective.)

In accordance with his Sunday agreement with Conant in Charlestown, Revere stopped long enough to get the sexton of the North Church to go up and display the lanterns for a long enough time—perhaps a couple of minutes—to be seen by Conant across the Charles but not long enough to attract British attention to them as a signal. Revere then went to get two friends to act as oarsmen to row him across the river, on the bank of which he had long been accustomed to keeping a boat. They proceeded to cross the Charles downstream some distance from the troops' rendezvous and separated from them by the *Somerset* man-of-war. They muffled the oars and stayed seaward of the *Somerset,* well out of sight of the British troops and hopefully also beyond sight or hearing of the man-of-war. "It was then young flood, the ship was winding, and the moon was rising."[15]

Having concluded what should have been the most difficult part of his mission, Revere walked from the Charlestown shore into town, where he met Colonel Conant, Richard Devens, a member of Hancock's Committee of Safety, and a few others. They had seen the signal lanterns in the North Church steeple, and Devens had already sent an express rider to warn Adams and Hancock. Devens told Revere that on his way home from a meeting of the Committee of Safety in Menotomy he had met several British officers riding out on the Lexington road. Some of them apparently had intercepted Devens' messenger, for he was never heard of again that night. Revere borrowed a horse—"a very good horse," he said—from Deacon John Larkin, who was never to see it again, and started off to Lexington, it now being close to eleven o'clock. By the route he was taking, it was about eleven miles to Lexington—a ride, on a fast horse, of well under an hour.

At Charlestown, Revere met two British officers on horseback. They had been in the shade of a tree, out of the moonlight, and by the time Revere saw them he was so close to them that he could see their holsters in the soft light. When they saw him, they separated, one coming toward him and the other racing up the road to stop him there in case he eluded the first. Revere stopped, turned, and hurried back to the intersection he had just passed, where the roads to Cambridge and Medford forked to the west and north. Having originally taken the Cambridge road, Revere now turned up the Medford road. One of the officers, following him and seeing his intention, took his horse across a field to cut Revere off on the Medford road. The officer rode right into a clay pond, where his horse became mired in the oozy bottom, and Revere got away. The other officer followed him about three hundred yards but gave up when his horse was evidently being outdistanced by Deacon Larkin's fast runner. The incident added some mileage to Revere's course, however, because instead of going directly to Lexington through Cambridge he now had to take a long swing to the north around Cambridge. As long as he was in Medford, he stopped at the house of the captain of the Medford minutemen and gave him the news. He got back on the main road from Boston to Lexington beyond Cambridge. On this road Dawes, having taken the long road out over the Neck, would also be riding. Revere, despite the detour, got there first, and not long after midnight he was riding past Lexington Common to Jonas Clarke's house.

iii

Besides the dozen or so British officers, Revere, Dawes, such other horsemen as Richard Devens' messenger from Charlestown, and Ebenezer Dorr, who took the news over Boston Neck to Roxbury, local town militia and Committees of Safety started to send out *their* scouts. At times it appeared that there were more riders abroad than there were soldiers; many of them were meeting each other, dodging each other, or capturing each other. The general confusion of this whirl of communications and espionage was further augmented by the casual attitudes of many of the riders. Just as the British officer didn't bother about Revere after chasing him three hundred yards, other officers that night caught scouts, chatted with them, and let them go. The early spring had apparently stimulated a certain amount of nocturnal wanderings among many provincials, for the accounts of British advance officers were full of amiable conversations with people they met on the road. Certainly the officers had been under orders from Gage to treat the colonists they encountered with respect, but they carried it to such extremes that they nearly defeated the whole purpose of their being out at all.

Richard Devens, of Charlestown, had passed British officers on the Lexington-Cambridge road as he rode home in a chaise with Abraham Watson. Both men were known members of the Committees of Safety and Supplies, which had been meeting that day at Menotomy. The British officers did not even bother to stop them. Devens and Watson then turned around and "rode through"[16] the officers in order to go back to Menotomy and warn three other committee members, Elbridge Gerry, Charles Lee, and Azor Orne, who were lodging in Menotomy overnight, that the British were out. Although the British officers must have thought this conduct of the men in the chaise unusual, they again did not stop them. As a result, when Elbridge Gerry got the news, he sent yet another rider out to Jonas Clarke's house in Lexington with the information about the officers. This messenger got there in good time, waited for Hancock to write a polite little note of acknowledgment to Gerry, and rode back unmolested to Menotomy.

Meanwhile, some Lexingtonians were also abroad on the highways. Solomon Brown, the eighteen-year-old son of one of Jonas Clarke's deacons and a minuteman, was returning from market in Boston in the late afternoon when he passed some of Gage's leisurely riding officers on the road to Lexington. Brown noticed that although it was one of those clear, warm April days occasionally visited upon New England, the officers were wearing their greatcoats. The reason was apparent to him when, as their coats fell back, he saw that they were wearing side arms—which was strictly forbidden by Gage when the officers rode into the country for their own exercise and pleasure. The officers, furthermore, looked to the observant young Solomon as if they were killing time before taking up their posts on the Lexington-Concord road, and "they did not care to reach there until the shades of the evening had set in."[17] The officers paid no special attention to Solomon, sometimes passing him and then lingering while he passed them. Finally, Solomon spurred his horse and raced into Lexington, where he stopped at Munroe's Tavern, some distance south of the Common, and told William Munroe, the orderly sergeant of the minutemen, about the armed officers.

Lexington's excitement began with the prompt action that Munroe took, apparently on his own initiative but certainly with the approval of Clarke, Adams, and Hancock. Since Solomon Brown had told him that there were nine officers, Munroe assumed that it was Adams and Hancock whom they were after, nine officers being about what Gage might send to take two dignitaries into custody. So with a sergeant's precision he posted an armed guard of nine men, including himself, around Jonas Clarke's house on the Bedford road. Word of this action, of course, spread immediately all over the town. By nine o'clock about thirty minutemen, intending perhaps to relieve the guard in shifts, were gathered in Buckman's Tavern. Soon they were joined by others who came to the tavern after seeing the officers ride into Lexington. As the officers disappeared down the road to Concord on the opposite side of the Common from Buckman's, the minutemen decided, in a spontaneous conference of war with Jonas Clarke, that the officers ought to be followed, lest they double back to Lexington, although what the followers were supposed to do about it isn't clear. Three minutemen were chosen for this ambiguous assignment: Elijah Sanderson, Jonathan Loring, and Solomon Brown. The latter was perfectly willing to go himself but flatly refused to take his horse, which he had exhausted on the ride home from Boston. Jonas Clarke promptly offered his horse, and so three more riders dashed off into the night, these in pursuit of Gage's nine riders.

Around ten o'clock—just when Gage's troops were rendezvousing on the Boston shore of the Back Bay and Paul Revere, still in Boston, was setting out for Dr. Warren's—the three Lexington riders, who were totally inexperienced spies, were captured by the nine British officers they were following. When they heard the approaching horses, the British officers had lined themselves up across the road. The officers remained mounted. "One rode up and seized my bridle," Elijah Sanderson deposed, "and another my arm, and one put his pistol to my breast, and told me, if I resisted, I was a dead man. I asked, what he wanted. He replied, he wanted to detain me a little while. He ordered me to get off my horse. Several of them dismounted and threw down the wall, and led us into a field. They examined and questioned us where we were going, etc. Two of them stayed in the road, and the other seven with us, relieving each other from time to time. They detained us in that vicinity till a quarter past two o'clock at night. An officer, who took out his watch, informed me what the time was. It was a bright moon-light after the rising of the moon, and a pleasant evening. During our detention, they put many questions to us, which I evaded. They kept us separately, and treated us very civilly. They particularly inquired where Hancock and Adams were; also about the population. One said, 'You've been numbering the inhabitants, haven't ye?' I told him how many it was reported there were. One of them spoke up and said, 'There were not so many men, women and children.' They asked as many questions as a yankee could."[18]

While the nine British officers were conducting their somewhat aimless interrogation of the three young minutemen, back in Lexington the armed guard still surrounded the Clarke house with its swollen population of fourteen Clarkes, Adams, Hancock, his Aunt Lydia, and Dorothy Quincy. When the three scouts did not return, Sergeant Munroe was apparently convinced that they were caught as the officers returned toward Lexington to nab Adams and Hancock. Safe behind the guard, the Clarkes and their distinguished but now-troublesome guests retired around midnight.

Shortly after they had all gone to bed, Paul Revere pulled up to the Clarke house and was intercepted by Sergeant Munroe, who had apparently never heard of him. Revere, not used to dealing with underlings, demanded admission to the house. "I told him," Munroe said in his deposition, "the family had just retired and had requested that they might not be disturbed by any noise about the house." This apparently irritated Revere, who had had a busy day and a long and tense ride. " 'Noise,' said he. 'You'll have noise enough before long. The regulars are coming out.' " Munroe then let him pass, and Revere rapped on the parsonage door. A window flew up, and the massive head of the Reverend Jonas Clarke emerged to ask who was there. Still irritated, Revere refused to answer and demanded to see Hancock, who by this time heard the commotion and shouted out merrily, "Come in, Revere; we're not afraid of *you*."[19] Revere gave Hancock a written statement from Dr. Warren, in which he estimated that Gage was sending out "twelve or fifteen hundred men"[20]—about twice the number actually sent—but otherwise correct in its details.

Revere refreshed himself and Deacon Larkin's horse at the

Clarke establishment, which was now thoroughly aroused for the rest of the night. Captain John Parker was sent for and came the two miles from his farm. A messenger was sent to Buckman's to get some of the minutemen there to act as couriers to rouse others who lived some distance from the center of Lexington. Parker himself went to Buckman's later and made it his headquarters for the night. Finally, William Dawes arrived at the Clarke house with the duplicate message from Dr. Warren.

There evidently being a shortage of horses in Lexington by now, Revere and Dawes took their briefly rested mounts and set out for Concord. Since neither knew the road well and since their horses were still tired and there seemed to be plenty of time anyhow, they started out at a relaxed pace and were soon overtaken by one of the few riders of the night who seemed to be about normal activities. It was Dr. Samuel Prescott, youngest of a long line of Concord physicians, who was going home after courting his girl, Lydia Mulliken, who lived in Lexington near Munroe's Tavern on the main road to Cambridge. Lydia's brother, Nathaniel, was a minuteman, and Prescott undoubtedly found that the evening was destined to other things than courting. He mounted his horse, when Nathaniel Mulliken was alerted, and rushed off—yet another courier—to take the news to Concord. When he caught up with Revere and Dawes, the two express riders talked to him and found him to be "a high son of Liberty."[21] When Dr. Prescott pointed out that he knew almost everybody in Concord and that they were much more apt to believe him than a couple of strangers, Dawes and Revere adopted him as a partner.

About halfway to Concord, while Dawes and Prescott were alarming a household, Revere spotted two British officers on the road ahead. He called to Dawes and Prescott that the three of them could capture the officers, for although he knew that nine officers had gone through Lexington, he was convinced that they had broken up into teams. Revere was wrong. Before Dawes and Prescott could reach him, he was surrounded by four officers, and

as Dawes and Prescott came up they were corralled, too. The trio
were then forced into a pasture. Dr. Prescott said to Revere, as
they were being herded through an opening in the stone wall into
the pasture, that he was going to make a run for it. He jumped his
horse over another wall on his flank and, knowing the terrain well,
got away. Revere broke away and made for a woodland, intending
to dismount from Deacon Larkin's horse, which must have been
near exhaustion by now, and to run on foot into the woods. But
Revere guessed wrong again. More officers poured out of the
woods, capturing both Revere and his weary horse. Dawes meanwhile galloped his horse to a nearby farmhouse, at which he
stopped so suddenly his watch flew out of his pocket. Although he
lost both his horse and his watch, he eluded capture, and a few days
later he went back and found the watch. Dawes considered that his
night's work was done, and he went back on foot to Lexington,
where he kept out of sight.

Revere was taken in hand by an officer "who had appeared to
have the command there and [was] much of a gentleman."[22]
Although Revere was completely alone now and surrounded by
British officers, the interrogation session out in the pasture in the
moonlight was amiable enough, even polite. Revere was asked his
name ("Sir, may I crave your name?"[23]), where he came from,
when he left Boston, and whether he was an express rider. Revere
"replied that I esteemed myself a man of truth"[24] and answered
all the questions truthfully. But when it came to the night's oper-
ations, Revere stretched the truth a little, and so did the officer. The
officer told Revere that he and the other officers were out to catch
deserters. "I told him I knew better. I knew what they were after;
that I had alarmed the country all the way up; that their boats had
catched aground, and I should have five hundred men there soon;
one of them said they had fifteen hundred coming. He seemed
surprised and rode immediately off up the road to them that
stopped me . . . They came down on a full gallop. One of them
(whom I since learned was Major Mitchell of the 5th Regiment)

clapped his pistol to my head and said he was going to ask me some questions, and if I did not tell the truth he would blow my brains out." Revere gave the same answers. He was then searched for arms (he had none) and told to mount. When he took the reins, the major, who knew all about Revere's riding career, grabbed them out of his hand. "By God, sir, you are not to ride with reins, I assure you."[25] So another officer led Revere's horse.

When Revere and his captors got into the Lexington-Concord road again, they were joined by other officers with four prisoners. Three of them were the Lexington minutemen, Solomon Brown, Sanderson, and Loring. The fourth was a one-armed peddler, who seemed to have wandered into all this activity innocently, when he had merely set out to Concord to get an early start in the morning. It was now two o'clock in the morning, when the officers marched their prisoners, all mounted, back toward Lexington. After a while they cut the bridles and saddles loose on the horses of the three minutemen and the peddler, drove the horses away, and set all the prisoners but Revere free on foot. (Why the British officers turned these men loose before their own soldiers were near is a mystery, particularly since the officers had taken pains to tell them that "four or five regiments of regulars"[26] were on the way to Lexington.) A little later, outside Lexington, they took Deacon Larkin's horse away from Revere and gave it to a heavy sergeant of grenadiers whose own horse was tired, and set Revere free. He headed across the burying ground, north of the Common, and back to Jonas Clarke's house.

iv

Matching the comedy of errors that General Gage's advance officers were achieving on their mission was the conduct of his expedition from its start. From the time that Percy disabused Gage of his illusion that it was to be a highly secret expedition that would quickly and quietly accomplish its purpose and then get back to Boston, everything went wrong.

His orders to Lieutenant Colonel Smith were sound enough:

Boston, April 18, 1775

Lieut. Col. Smith, 10th Regiment foot,
Sir

Having received intelligence that a quantity of ammunition, provision, artillery, tents and small arms have been collected at Concord, for the avowed purpose of raising and supporting a rebellion against His Majesty, you will march with the corps of grenadiers and light infantry, put under your command, with the utmost expedition and secrecy to Concord, where you will seize and destroy all the artillery, ammunition, provisions, tents, small arms and all military stores whatever. But you will take care that the soldiers do not plunder the inhabitants or hurt private property.

You have a draught of Concord, on which is marked the houses, barns, etc., which contain the above military stores. You will order a trunnion to be knocked off each gun, but if it is found impracticable on any, they must be spiked, and the carriages destroyed. The powder and flower must be shook out of the barrels into the river, the tents burnt, pork or beef destroyed in the best way you can devise. And the men may put balls or lead in their pockets, throwing them by degrees into ponds, ditches, etc., but no quantity together so that they may be recovered afterwards.

If you meet with any brass artillery, you will order their muzzles to beat in, so as to render them useless.

You will observe by the draught that it will be necessary to secure the two bridges as soon as possible; you will, therefore, order a party of the best marchers to go on with expedition for that purpose.

A small party on horseback is ordered out to stop all advice of your march getting to Concord before you, and a small number of artillery go out in chaises to wait for you on the road with sledge hammers, spikes, etc.

You will open your business and return with the troops as soon as possible, which I must leave to your own judgment and discretion. I am,

Sir,

Your most obedient
humble servant,
Thos. Gage[27]

These orders reflected much of Gage's policy from the beginning, including absolute abstention from injuring the person or property of any of the inhabitants. They were, moreover, extremely specific, leaving nothing but the method of destroying some pork and beef to Lieutenant Colonel Smith's judgment. But they failed in one important particular: they gave the commanding officer, who was apparently of a notoriously slow nature, no time table, using only such phrases as "the utmost expedition" and "as soon as possible." However suggestible these might have been to an energetic officer, to Lieutenant Colonel Smith they meant only "when you get around to it."

Lieutenant Colonel Smith was a portly professional officer of the type, frequently caricatured in British lore, who settle into comfortable ruts as soon as they reach regimental command level and, having given up any thought of becoming generals, never extend themselves. Physically a slow-moving man of conspicuously generous bulk, Smith had no concept of time at all. His command of the whole expedition when it was in his charge was characterized by lateness and delay, as if he regarded Gage's emphasis of speed as rhetorical language that always appeared in orders but did not really mean anything.

Smith's command was made up of about seven hundred men, all of them light infantry and grenadiers. Altogether there were twenty-one companies, eleven of grenadiers and ten of light infantry. These troops were not formed into regiments of their own. Each infantry regiment had its own company of light infantry and its own company of grenadiers. Each of the ten infantry regiments in Boston and the one marine regiment furnished its company of grenadiers; and all, except the Sixteenth Regiment, whose light infantry had not yet arrived in Boston, furnished their companies of light infantry. Although the British army often formed temporary expeditionary forces by using the specialized troops from several regiments, they were in a way mongrel forces. They always posed a command problem and, to some extent, a morale problem, particularly in an army that traditionally put the greatest emphasis and distinction on the regiment. The system also required the commanding general to put together a command for the expeditionary force from the officers of the various regiments.

For the assignment on April eighteenth, Francis Smith of the Tenth Regiment was chosen for the command because he had seniority (he applied for retirement the following August), long experience in the American colonies going back at least twelve years, and a long association with Gage. Probably, as far as Gage was concerned, the choice of Smith avoided problems in the garrison; his seniority made reaction of a political nature unlikely —which would have been of some importance to a man of Gage's temperament. For second in command Gage selected Major John Pitcairn, of the Second Marines Regiment. An able and enterprising officer, Pitcairn was a man of considerable character, respected as much by Whigs as by Tories, by the patriots as much as the loyalists. The patriot propagandist Ezra Stiles, the minister of Newport and later President of Yale, referred to Pitcairn "as a good man in a bad cause." It is probable that Gage thought of Pitcairn as a guarantor of the two things that he considered most urgent about the night's business, speed and taking care that there was no plundering of the inhabitants. By assigning Pitcairn, Gage also side-stepped garrison grumbling. There were nine regiments of infantry besides Smith's. Eight of them would have been disgruntled if an infantry major were chosen. There was only one regiment of marines. It would, of course, be complimented.

When the British soldiers rendezvoused at the foot of Boston

Common on the banks of the old tidal basin of the Charles, at ten o'clock, there was time enough for them to be rowed across the river, march out to Concord in the night, pass through Lexington in the darkness, and arrive in Concord before daylight—if Smith had conducted the operation with "the utmost expedition." But Smith was so slow that he wasted half the time—some three hours —that it took to march to Concord. He was late from the very beginning and did not even get to the rendezvous on time. An old regimental officer of his limited enthusiasm was probably of the opinion that the embarkation should be handled by underlings, who would send to notify him when it was accomplished. The brisk competent adjutant of the Twenty-third Regiment, Lieutenant Frederick Mackenzie, was highly critical of the sloppiness of the operation's beginnings. Mackenzie was not attached to the light infantry or grenadiers, but as adjutant it was his job to see that his regiment's companies reported for the rendezvous. Gage had told the regimental officers that this was to be "exactly at ten o'clock this night." To a soldier of Mackenzie's sober ability this meant in no uncertain terms exactly at ten o'clock. "The companies of our regiment marched accordingly," Mackenzie wrote in his diary, "and were the first, complete, at the place of parade; here we found a number of the men-of-wars' and transports' boats in waiting."[28] After noting that everybody else was late, Mackenzie had his professional conscientiousness jolted again by the increasingly apparent fact that no one had appointed an embarkation officer, and the men just stood around the boats. Mackenzie himself, having got the approval of some navy officers present, loaded the two companies from his regiment into the nearest boats and had them wait offshore for orders to cross the river. The companies from the other regiments followed his example and boarded the boats until they were all filled. Then all the boats, the bayonets of the soldier passengers flashing in the moonlight, floated idly around until Lieutenant Colonel Smith got there.

Not only Smith but the companies of his own Tenth (Lincoln-

shire) Regiment got off to a bad start. Ensign Jeremy Lister of
the Tenth, although he was not in the light infantry or grenadier
companies, went down to the rendezvous anyhow, "being anxious
to know the reason of this order."[29] He had his youthful pride in
his regiment severely shaken by the failure of its light infantry
company's lieutenant to report at the rendezvous. The lieutenant,
James Hamilton, was sent for repeatedly but still failed to show up,
finally pleading illness, which "was supposed by everybody to
be feigned which 'twas clearly proved to be the case afterwards."[30]
"Thinking it would be rather a disgrace for the company to march
on an expedition, more especially it being the first, without its com-
plement of officers," Lister begged to be permitted to go in Hamilton's place "for the honor of the regiment." His offer was
accepted, and he went back to his lodgings in the town to get his
field equipment.

Finally, Lieutenant Colonel Smith arrived and ordered the
boats to cross the river. But since the boats required two trips to
take all the men across, it was between midnight and one o'clock in
the morning before they were ferried across the few hundred yards
of the Charles' tidal backwash, the soldiers having been ready at
ten o'clock. Lieutenant Barker, the cantankerous officer of the
King's Own who disapproved of General Gage, Lieutenant
Colonel Smith, and all his superiors so heartily, found nothing right
in the operation, even after the long delay in getting the troops
over the river. "After getting over the marsh," he complained in
his diary, "where we were wet up to the knees, we were halted in a
dirty road and stood there until two o'clock in the morning, waiting
for provisions to be brought from the boats and to be divided, and
which most of the men threw away, having carried some with
'em."[31] In his eager disapproval of things Barker probably made
everything a little worse than it was, in order to prove his superiors
a little less competent than they were; but his chronology of all the
wasted time is accurate. Lieutenant William Sutherland, of the
Thirty-eighth Regiment, an altogether different type of young

officer, who had no complaints about anybody and who was on the expedition as a volunteer to go in advance of the troops, reported in his account that they had to wait for two hours in the Cambridge marshes and "the tide being in we were up to our middles before we got into the road."[32] Apparently, when the troops were landed on the Cambridge shore from the boats, they were on fairly dry land, but during the long delay the tide (Paul Revere said "it was young flood" when he crossed an hour or so earlier) had come in and filled the marshes around them. By the time they were finally given the order to march, it was two o'clock in the morning. After four hours from the time of the rendezvous they were about a quarter of a mile from where they started.

The little army of seven hundred passed the Newell Tavern in Menotomy, north of Cambridge, about three o'clock. The alerted members of the Committee of Safety, Gerry, Lee, and Orne, peered curiously out of a darkened upstairs window at the troops marching by on the road below. The three dignitaries were startled to see a sergeant's patrol turn into the path leading to their door. Clad in nightshirts, they hurried to the nearest exit, which happened to be the door the soldiers were approaching. The landlord shouted to Gerry, "For God's sake, don't open that door,"[33] and took the three committeemen out through a rear door. They hid from the patrol by throwing themselves flat in the corn stubble of the field behind the tavern—an experience from which old Mr. Lee, in his nightshirt and unaccustomed to the cold earth on an April night, took cold and never recovered.

v

Back in Lexington the delay of the expeditionary force was so considerable that there arose some doubt—probably much to Samuel Adams' distress—as to whether it was coming or not.

The first alarm to the minutemen was given immediately after Paul Revere's arrival at Jonas Clarke's house. Sergeant Munroe kept the guard at the parsonage, for his hunch that the British were after Hancock and Adams seemed now confirmed by the letter that Revere brought from Dr. Warren. Munroe sent another horseman out into the night—this one in the direction of Cambridge to check the size of the British force and the rate of march. Captain Parker had his minutemen, a hundred and thirty of them, mustered on the Common, and Daniel Harrington, the clerk of the company, whose house and blacksmith shop were across the road from the Common, read the roll. This was probably done at one o'clock. If the British had not wasted three hours in embarking and starting their march, they would have been well on their way by then, probably entering the southeastern part of Lexington. At one o'clock, however, they were still standing in the Cambridge marshes and were to wait another hour before marching.

The night was chilly in Lexington, and some of the minutemen were old men. Having loaded their guns with powder and ball, they had nothing to do but stand there, looking at the candlelights flickering in the warm comfort of Buckman's Tavern across the road. They began to grumble as the time passed. There was no word from Munroe's couriers who had gone to find the British army and none from the three minutemen who had set out earlier in the night after the British officers who went to Concord. So Parker sent out another rider. This one came back to the Common at about two o'clock and reported that there was no army on the way to Lexington. At that hour, of course, the British were still getting into formation in the Cambridge marshes. So Parker dismissed the company, subject to the drum call of William Diamond in case the British should show up after all.

The minutemen who lived nearby went home, and the rest went to Buckman's Tavern, where they talked, dozed, and probably drank a little to take the chill out of their bones. At intervals Parker sent couriers down the road toward Cambridge—four in all—but none of them came back. The disappearance of these horsemen permanently into the night bothered no one. It was apparently assumed from their failure to return that they could find no trace of the British or else that the latter were so far away that the couriers had to go all the way to Boston to find them. Lexington now had seven official couriers riding around the Middlesex roads in every direction; in addition Revere, Dawes, and the resourceful young Dr. Prescott, who had come to Lexington to spend a quiet evening with his fiancée, were bound for Concord; and there were also numerous individuals, including the one-armed peddler, riding around. But nobody had yet seen any British army.

Back at Jonas Clarke's house, a five-minute walk from Buckman's, where the remaining minutemen waited, there had been some activity. Paul Revere, horseless, had tramped across the old burial ground, where all the ancestors of the minutemen had been sleeping peacefully for a century and longer. He had stayed out of sight of the Common by going through the fields behind the Harrington houses, north of the Common, and thence through pastures and wood lots to Clarke's house. In contrast to his earlier visit that night, the house was bright with light, and all but the smallest Clarkes were wide awake. The leaders, Adams and Hancock, were in conference with Jonas Clarke. Hovering around in the background were Aunt Lydia and Dorothy Quincy.

Hancock was being difficult. Seized by one of his periodic yearnings for the dramatic, he was all for taking to the field personally and, not forgetting that he was lately a colonel commanding the Independent Corps of Cadets, stopping the British army. If he was seeking to impress his young and not easily impressed fiancée, he was wasting his time. Years afterward, when Hancock was in his grave, his widow, full of irreverent memories and with an old lady's liveliness, recalled the night of April eighteenth to William H. Sumner: "Mr. Hancock was all night cleaning his gun and sword and putting his accoutrements in order, and was determined to go out to the plain by the meetinghouse . . . to fight [along] with the men who had collected . . . but partially provided with arms, and those that they had were in most miserable order."[34] While Hancock was busy with his warlike gestures, Clarke and Adams consulted with Captain Parker of the minutemen and apparently also drew Sergeant Munroe into their deliberations.

When Revere arrived with his report of his capture by the British officers and their conversation, it was agreed that the British meant business. It was hastily concluded that Adams and Hancock had better get away from Lexington before the British troops arrived. But up until their departure, Dorothy Quincy told Sumner, Hancock insisted on fighting the British himself. "It was with very great difficulty that he was dissuaded from it by Mr. Clarke and Mr. Adams."[35] He nevertheless went down to the Common to see the minutemen and came back to the Clarke house to repeat his desire to fight. Adams finally stopped his protests by pointing out the importance of Hancock, and incidentally of himself, to the leadership of the cause. With his own fanaticism characteristically tempered by prudence, Adams declared flatly, "It [fighting] is not our business. We belong to the Cabinet."[36] This convinced Hancock finally. But, according to Sergeant Munroe's deposition, he had one last military threat to make as he left the Clarke house, Aunt Lydia and Dorothy Quincy remaining behind. "If I had my musket, I would never turn my back on those troops."[37]

Samuel Adams hated to ride horseback, and so a carriage was brought. Sergeant Munroe led the party, consisting of Adams, Hancock, Revere, and Hancock's secretary, John Lowell, to the north of Lexington. There he left them concealed in a clump of woods. Shortly after Munroe's departure it occurred to Hancock that the trunkful of papers, many of them dealing with the business of the Provincial Congress and the Committee of Safety, had been left behind in Lowell's room at the Buckman Tavern, right beside the Common where the British might easily capture it. Revere and Lowell went back to get it before the British appeared.

So the long visit of Samuel Adams and John Hancock to the little village of Lexington came to an end early on the morning of April nineteenth—although from all the evidence later available, particularly General Gage's orders to Colonel Smith, they could have stayed in Jonas Clarke's house until they left for Philadelphia. For four weeks Adams, Hancock, and Clarke had been together. For three days, since Revere's Sunday visit, they knew that a British march into the countryside, probably through Lexington to Concord, was likely. For four hours, they knew that it was certain. Since Hancock's behavior, brave or simply foolhardy as it may have been, during those last four hours, ruled him out as a serious adviser on the military situation (he apparently saw nothing unwise and useless in the President of the Provincial Congress standing with sword drawn and pistol cocked in the line of march of British soldiers supposedly intent on arresting him), Adams and Clarke unquestionably made up a policy between themselves. Adams knew the broad strategy of the resistance, because he was at this point its sole architect. Clarke knew the men of Lexington and, what is more, could control them as no outsider could. The policy obviously determined upon between the time of Revere's first alarm and of the minutemen's first muster and the time of the actual arrival of the British troops, was for the minutemen, however outnumbered, to make a conspicuous stand but not to fire.

As for Captain Parker, he was a simple farmer, of some military experience but with no pretensions to wisdom in grand political strategy. There were only two sources of counsel that he would be apt to heed on such matters. One was his only formal source of authority, the Provincial Congress, whose real leader, Samuel Adams, was five minutes' walk from Parker's headquarters at Buckman's all that night of alarms. The other was the Reverend Jonas Clarke, Parker's pastor and friend, the real political leader of Lexington and the draftsman of its statements of public policy in provincial affairs. It is inconceivable that in all those hours of waiting, Parker would not have had the counsel of Adams and Clarke if not their directives. And it is the only explanation of Parker's conduct as commander of the minutemen on Lexington Common.

Now, "between daylight and sunrise," as Sergeant Munroe, who had returned from showing Adams and Hancock to their retreat in the woods, put it, Captain Parker got his first definite word that the British were indeed coming. It was four-thirty in the morning now. All Captain Parker's minutemen, except for the twenty-five or thirty at Buckman's Tavern, had gone home. And the British force of seven hundred light infantry and grenadiers was a mile and a quarter away. Captain Parker aroused William Diamond and sent him out on the Common to beat the drum call to arms.

vi

After all the inefficiency of Lieutenant Colonel Smith and the British and after all the efficiency of Dr. Warren in Boston and Revere and Dawes, Captain Parker and the Lexington militia ended up with about fifteen minutes to prepare for their gallant but absurdly hopeless appearance against the British. This was due to the fact that, unlike the British officers who had been sent out in advance of the troops the previous afternoon and who caught provincial messengers only to let them go again, there were two highly competent junior officers moving somewhat in advance of the force itself: Lieutenant Sutherland, the last-minute volunteer, and Lieutenant Adair, of the Second Marines Regiment. One of them on each side of the road, Sutherland and Adair captured the Lexington scouts in a systematic and rapid way as soon as they came within reach. The first two—the one sent out by Sergeant Munroe and the first of Captain Parker's four—they encountered an hour after their march began, that is, about three o'clock. "I heard Lieutenant Adair . . . call out, 'Here are two fellows galloping express to alarm the country,'" Sutherland reported; "on which I immediately rode up to them, seized one of them, and our guide [a Boston Tory who accompanied the British] the other, dismounted them, and by Major Pitcairn's direction, gave them in charge of the men."[38]

A little while afterward Major Mitchell and his fellow officers who had captured Paul Revere, the three Lexington minutemen, and the peddler on the Concord road and let them all go, approached Sutherland and Adair. Apparently having swallowed Paul Revere's story that there were five hundred militia on Lexington Common to intercept the British, Mitchell told Sutherland that the whole country was alarmed and that he and his eleven brother officers "had galloped for their lives"—a remarkably imaginary exposition for a military report, since the only provincials they had encountered, all without weapons, were a courier, three Lexington scouts, and a one-armed peddler. But Mitchell's dramatic story further alerted Sutherland and Adair, who shortly saw another rider approaching them at a crossroad. They shouted for him to stop, but he spurred his horse and took off. A surgeon's mate of the Forty-third Infantry took up the chase and caught him. This accounted for Captain Parker's second scout.

Sutherland and his companion, who were having a singularly gregarious time of it for a country ride at three o'clock in the morning, then met a mysterious "very genteel man, riding in a carriage they call a sulky, who assured me there were six hundred men assembled at Lexington."[39] Who this respectable bluffer, who had a story matching Revere's, was, nobody knows; but his information obviously strengthened the British conviction, originating with Major Mitchell's preposterous tale, that they were in for a battle.

No sooner had the busy Sutherland got through with the genteel man in the sulky than another rider came charging out of another crossroad. Mitchell seized the bridle of his horse and dismounted him—Parker's third scout. As daylight began to break faintly in the eastern sky, Sutherland met "some men with a wagon of wood who told us there were odds of one thousand men in arms at Lexington and added that they would fight us."⁴⁰ The accumulation of all this arithmetical information on the size of the provincial force, which at the time consisted of twenty-five or thirty men dozing in Buckman's, had a sobering effect on the already sober Sutherland. He and Adair decided that they had better turn around and find their own main forces, of whom they were now quite far in advance, having already reached the southeastern fringes of Lexington. But instead of finding the British troops, they came upon "a vast number of the country militia going over the hill with their arms to Lexington." Sutherland captured one of them, Benjamin Wellington, a Lexington minuteman, who was locally famous as "the first man to carry milk as far as Boston." Sutherland disarmed him and told him to go home. (Wellington went to the meetinghouse instead, got another gun, and joined the other minutemen.) Sutherland then continued to go back down the road toward Boston until he reached the advanced section of the British force under Major Pitcairn.

Earlier in the march Lieutenant Colonel Smith had detached six companies of light infantry, about two hundred men, from his main force and sent them ahead under the command of Pitcairn to seize and hold the two bridges over the Concord River. This was in accordance with the orders that he had from Gage, who apparently had it in mind that the action would cut off militia from the back country from molesting the other British troops while they went about the main business of destroying the provincial stores in the town of Concord. As soon as Pitcairn was advised by Sutherland that there were apparently militia to the number of a thousand men swarming all over the countryside, he ordered his troops to stop and prime and load their guns. Lieutenant Colonel Smith, meanwhile, had dispatched a messenger back to Boston to tell General Gage that the whole expedition was not going as well or as simply as planned and to urge upon the general to send out additional forces to help him.

From all the information that the British now had, their situation was not very happy. They were not only three hours behind schedule and would be marching into Concord in broad daylight, but there was a force of anything from five hundred to a thousand militia waiting for them at Lexington. And from what the British officers knew of colonial fighting, the militia would be firing from concealed positions—behind stone walls, trees, farmhouses, and barns. The officers had to assume a vigorous attack and prepare for it. What they were to come upon, of course, was Captain Parker's little band of no more than forty or fifty lined up like targets on the open plain of Lexington Common.

As far as Captain Parker knew, on the other hand, there were twice as many British troops on the march than was actually the case—twelve to fifteen hundred as opposed to six or seven hundred. Parker's fourth scout of the night, Thaddeus Bowman, had eluded Sutherland, who had rejoined the main forces. Bowman saw the British forces when they were a mile and a half away from the Common, and it was his news that sent William Diamond out to beat the drum call.

With the British only about twenty minutes away Parker had little time to lose, but there was still time to send the men already in Buckman's out behind walls or trees to keep the British under observation and to make them convenient targets if necessary. There was time to send his corporals to outposts on the roads approaching the Common to disperse the minutemen arriving in response to William Diamond's drum at concealed spots all around the Common. Instead, Parker told Munroe to line up the handful of minutemen present in rows on the Common. New arrivals were shunted into the two thin rows, as they reached the Common, and those who were unarmed went into the meetinghouse to get guns.

Down the road, which was straight and level for a thousand yards before it reached the Common, the steady beat to arms of William Diamond's drum was final and indisputable proof to the

British that their march was to be contested within a matter of yards.

From the vantage point of an upstairs room in Buckman's Tavern, where he had gone with John Lowell for Hancock's trunk, Paul Revere looked down the Lexington road, almost a quarter of a mile, toward Cambridge. "I saw the ministerial troops from the chamber window, coming up the road," Revere recalled. His only concern now was to get Hancock's trunk away. "We made haste and had to pass through our militia, who were on a green behind the meetinghouse, to the number, as I supposed, of fifty or sixty. It was then daylight." Revere, whose role was of such dramatic dimensions earlier in the night, had degenerated by now into a general utility man. By the time the battle launching the war of the American Revolution began, he was so occupied in lugging a trunk up Bedford Road from Lexington Common that he did not witness the event. "I could not see our militia for they were covered from me by a house at the bottom of the road."[41]

4

THE BATTLE: LEXINGTON

General Thomas Gage (1721–87), married to an American, was a gentle occupation commander. He was recalled to England six months after Lexington and never returned to America. COLLECTION OF COLONEL R.V.C. BODLEY, BOSTON

Major John Pitcairn (1722–75) of the Royal Marines, second in command of the British forces, was disgusted with the conduct of his troops. He died two months after Lexington at the Battle of Bunker's Hill, in the arms of his son, Lieutenant Pitcairn. LEXINGTON HISTORICAL SOCIETY

The firing on Lexington Common was sketched two weeks after the event by Ralph Earl, a Connecticut militiaman, whose company joined the provincial forces at Cambridge. Earl drew his sketch from the northwest side of the Common. British light infantry are firing at the scattering minutemen, while the grenadiers march along the road in the background. The buildings are, left, Buckman's Tavern and its stables, the meetinghouse on the Common, and the belfry. The engraving, made by Amos Doolittle, was widely circulated. CONNECTICUT HISTORICAL SOCIETY

*Earl and Doolittle's version of the British at Concord showed Major Pitcairn, left, and Lieu-
tenant Colonel Smith, right, looking from a ridge in the center of town toward the provincial
militia on another ridge. The British troops are in the road below the ridge. At the left is the
Concord meetinghouse.* CONNECTICUT HISTORICAL SOCIETY

"We shall be ready to sacrifice . . . life itself."

THE INHABITANTS OF LEXINGTON[1]

Lexington, April 25, 1775

I, John Parker, *of lawful age, and commander of the Militia in* Lexington, *do testify and declare, that on the nineteenth instant, in the morning, about one of the clock, being informed that there were a number of Regular Officers riding up and down the road, stopping and insulting people as they passed the road, and also was informed that a number of Regular Troops were on their march from* Boston, *in order to take the Province Stores at* Concord, *ordered our militia to meet on the common in said* Lexington, *to consult what to do, and concluded not to be discovered, nor meddle or make with said Regular Troops (if they should approach) unless they should insult us; and upon their sudden approach, I immediately ordered our Militia to disperse and not to fire. Immediately said Troops made their appearance and rushed furiously, fired upon and killed eight of our party, with out receiving any provocation therefor from us.*

John Parker

Middlesex, ss., April 25, 1775:

The above named John Parker *personally appeared, and after being duly cautioned to declare the whole truth, made solemn oath to the truth of the above deposition, by him subscribed. Before us,*

Wm. Reed
Josiah Johnson
Wm. Stickney
JUSTICES OF THE PEACE[2]

This is all that Captain John Parker ever said of the affair, and it all leads up to a giant contradiction. He telescopes time a little bit; it was "one of the clock" when he got the news and, shortly after that when he ordered the muster of the minutemen on the Common "to consult what to do," and then he dismissed the company. Three hours, at least, passed before he mustered them again—three hours during which he had time to talk with Hancock, Adams, and Clarke. His first instinct—not to act like an authoritative military commander but to "consult" with his neighbors and friends "what to do"—was a perfectly natural one. The minutemen were not easy men to order around. They were less a military company than a voluntary, self-governing unit—resourceful, responsible, unafraid, but a collection of men who had no bosses in their ordinary daily lives and who did not lend themselves very readily to the mechanical response to orders snapped at them by someone else. If Parker hadn't known this, they would never have elected him their captain. They knew that he was the kind of man who *would,* in an emergency involving them as much as him, "consult what to do."

For his part, Parker, having lived all his life in Lexington, knew these men who constituted his little militia well. He had gone to school with them, went to church with them, fought alongside some of them in the French and Indian wars, and was related either directly or by marriage to many of them. The last thing that would have occurred to him was that the relationship between him as their captain and them as members of his company could be as brisk and cold and automatic as that between a regular officer and his troops. And Parker knew enough also about war in the still heavily wooded American countryside to understand that, if war came, the cause of the colonies would be less dependent upon the parade ground discipline of the militia than upon those very characteristics of individualism, independence, and resourcefulness that made them unlikely exhibits on a parade ground but hard men to beat in country warfare.

So John Parker consulted with these men, this varied assortment who had paid him the compliment of electing him their captain. They concluded not to make themselves conspicuous or to "meddle" with the British troops; and then they went home, or dozed around Buckman's, until they were called again. Parker obviously kept busy. He sent one messenger after another to find out and report to him whether the British troops were on the Lexington-Cambridge road and how far away. Dorothy Quincy remembered that Hancock went down to the Common. It can be taken as certain that, if he went, so did Samuel Adams, who would never have let him out of sight in the midst of such promising events; and Clarke would have guided them down the road from the parsonage, around the corner of the Common to Buckman's. The captain of the militia would have discussed the night's affairs with the President of the Provincial Congress and with the Delegate to the Continental Congress and with his own pastor. And it was concluded, from the evidence of what happened afterward, that the minutemen would make a show of strength on the open Common, but that they would not fire. Apparently they would just stand there, as seven hundred British soldiers, on their first expedition after a year's dreary occupation of an isolated peninsular port town, marched harmlessly by a few feet away. Whatever anyone else thought of this placid picture, Samuel Adams, who had a profound understanding of the abrasive qualities inherent in such a situation, knew better. All his ten years' experience with the

Boston mobs, all his careful manipulation and channeling of the prides and prejudices, strengths and weaknesses, capacities and limitations of human beings as parts of a group would have gone for nothing if he hadn't known better. And, what was worse, so would have the unbelievably singlehanded success of Samuel Adams, thus far, in keeping the issue of revolt against Great Britain alive in the colonies.

Parker's men took a suicidal stand, and the issue burst fully into life. When the approach of the British was unmistakable, he had sent young William Diamond to beat the call to arms. He met the assembling men on the Common and told Sergeant Munroe to draw them up in the two long thin lines to make them look more formidable in numbers than they really were. Having perhaps twenty minutes from the time that Thaddeus Bowman came to him with the last intelligence of the morning until the British were upon him, he made no effort to get his men into the readily available positions in adjacent pastures and woodlands from which they could have both observed the British and had the advantage of surprise and mobility in case of conflict. But he lined them up on the Common, with orders not to fire.

All this was as it should be if one understood Adams' growing problem of unifying the colonies behind some incontrovertible event that would make it clear to any American colonist that life under the British was utterly impossible. Adams, of course, was familiar with all the rabble-rouser charges against him and knew also that many of the Middle Atlantic and Southern colonists, sympathetic and active in the colonial cause, regarded him as an inciter of mob actions when it suited his political purposes. But this time he had something to go on. He was fresh from a meeting of the Provincial Congress that had just decided, not without his guidance, "that should any body of troop with artillery and baggage, march out of Boston, the country should instantly be alarmed, and called together to oppose their march to the last extremity."[3] Adams would be willing to take a chance on the ex-

peditionary forces of the nineteenth having artillery or baggage
with them.

If—after his original consultation with his minutemen on the
Common at the first alarm—Parker was advised by the high
leadership concentrated by chance in Lexington that night, not
having any other authority over him and no military superior
present, he would have seen it as appropriate and fitting to
acquiesce. His own military experience would have made him
realize that a company captain is not a general or a strategical staff.
But once the British started to move toward his men, from the
road on to the Common, he felt as any company commander and
ranking officer present would: the situation, including their safety,
was entirely his responsibility. And he ordered them, not to stand
their ground and not to fire, but to disperse. It was the only battle
order that he said he gave; and it was the only one that any officer
in his situation could have given. As it turned out, it served Adams'
cause just as well.

ii

Full of bloated intelligence that had from five hundred to a
thousand militia concentrated in Lexington to mow them down,
the five British advanced light infantry companies, with Major
Pitcairn in command, moved into the straight stretch of the road
from which the Common was in sight. Their guns were primed
and loaded. They expected a fight. Pitcairn, with some of his
mounted officers, rode up to the head of the column.

The Lexington Common that Pitcairn saw that April sunrise
was a two-acre triangle, not wholly open but somewhat cluttered
for its size with the ungainly three-storied oblong meetinghouse
facing down the road toward the oncoming British. On the left
was the belfry that looked as if it had been plucked off the top of
the meetinghouse by some gargantuan child and left incongruously
at its side. Behind the belfry was the little schoolhouse and to its

left the well put there for the townspeople's use. Behind the meetinghouse was a large tree, but the Common was otherwise almost entirely cleared. On the road to the right, as Pitcairn approached the Common, was Buckman's Tavern, a pleasantly proportioned building with two massive chimneys and already nearly a century old. Stretching along the Bedford Road toward Jonas Clarke's house was the tavern's string of stables and outbuildings. Almost directly across the Common from Buckman's, on the left road leading to Concord, was the house of Marrett Munroe, married to Captain Parker's sister, whose son, Nathan, was among the minutemen assembled on the Common. And facing the Common from the north side, looking down across it to the road from Boston were two other houses—both, like Marrett Munroe's, with that sensitive regard for proportions that distinguished the buildings of villages all over New England in the eighteenth century. In one of these lived Daniel Harrington, the clerk of Captain Parker's company, who had read the roll earlier that night, his wife, and their seven young children. In the other lived young Jonathan Harrington and his wife and small son. Between the houses, set back a distance, was David Harrington's blacksmith shop, as handsomely proportioned as the houses. For the rest, surrounding the Common, there were only pastures and woodlands and, a little off toward the west off the Concord road, the old burial ground.

On and around the little Common stood perhaps a quarter of the town's population. Sergeant Munroe had got some forty of his minutemen in line; perhaps thirty more were milling around, going to the meetinghouse for ammunition, coming in across the meadows and pastures from their houses, crossing the road from Buckman's. Other townspeople, unarmed but curious, stood around the Common, in the yards of the three houses or behind the stone walls of the pastures and meadows—Jonas Clarke among them later on. From their own windows the families of Daniel and Jonathan Harrington and Nathan Munroe could watch all that went on. Seventy militia, more or less; a hundred spectators, most of whom would be getting up at this hour anyway; and, hauling the trunk up the edge of the Common, Revere and Lowell—this was the formidable force that confronted Major Pitcairn and his five companies of light infantry as they came within sight of the Common.

Primed as they were for at least five hundred and possibly a thousand armed belligerents, the approaching British must have at first got the impression that the whole number present was much larger than it actually was, and in the dawning light it would have been difficult to distinguish combatant from spectator. Yet there was no mention later by the British officers of the figures five hundred or a thousand. Major Pitcairn thought that he saw "near two hundred of the rebels."[4] Ensign de Berniere of the Tenth Infantry's light infantry company, which was in the van of the British march, said that "there were about a hundred and fifty rebels," and he also mentioned that the militia were drawn out widely separated in their lines.[5] The disgruntled Lieutenant Barker of The King's Own Regiment, who resented so much the delay at Cambridge and was convinced from the beginning that the whole expedition would fail, put the number "between two and three hundred."[6] The British official reports, in language of qualifying vagueness, used "about two hundred."[7] Only the British captured later in the day and who gave depositions to the provincials came closer in their estimates, perhaps because they did not have to justify actions of the British army any longer or perhaps because the provincial authorities saw to it that they did not over-estimate the size of their opposition. John Bateman of the Fifty-second Regiment deposed "there was a small party of men gathered together,"[8] and Lieutenant Edward Gould of The King's Own was the most nearly accurate of all: "We saw a body of provincial troops armed, to the number of about sixty or seventy men."[9]

Although little more than half of them got into Sergeant Munroe's deceptively stretched out platoons, Captain Parker did have some seventy men altogether on or near the Common. Even this small number constituted one tenth of Lexington's entire population and little less than half the adult male population. And they were, in fact, pretty much what would be found as the male population of any country village. Among the oldest was Ensign Robert Munroe, the old veteran officer who had fought other wars on the British side. At sixty-three, he could have been excused from duty as a minuteman, but old men of his type are not easy to put aside, and he joined his two sons and two sons-in-law in the field. Of the same determined bend was his fifty-four-year-old cousin, Jedediah Munroe, who armed himself with—in addition to his musket—a long sword brought by his forebears from Scotland. Another senior minuteman was the close neighbor of the pastor and a first cousin of Captain Parker, the aging Jonas Parker, who had told everyone in Lexington that, no matter what the circumstances, he would never run from the British, and whose son, Jonas, Jr., stood at his side. The oldest of all was Grandfather Moses Harrington, sixty-five, whose youngest son Caleb was with him. His nephew, Jonathan, who owned the house facing the Common, was also with him, and so were a dozen other nephews and remote cousins. There were other father-and-son combinations: old Thomas Hadley and his son, Samuel; John Muzzy and his oldest son, Isaac. Altogether there were eight father-and-son combinations on the Common. There were also very young men, twelve in their teens and a score in their twenties. Most of them were farmers, but there were also tradesmen among them.

There was the slave, Prince Estabrook, highly popular with Lexington children as a willing referee in their games. There were also some minutemen from the companies of other towns who just happened to be in Lexington by chance and who enlisted in Parker's company for the night. As a military company the whole collection would never look like much: some old men, a generous block of the middle-aged, some inexperienced youths in their teens. They had with them their old hunting muskets, or else they had to go to the meetinghouse to get one belonging to the town. Half of them had gone home and back to sleep since the first alarm and did not move too quickly, and many of them were not in a position to hear any orders that Captain Parker might give. Several, like Joseph Comee, were in the meetinghouse, out of ear-range of the orders of Captain Parker or anyone else outside.

As he saw this group on the Common, Major Pitcairn, a man of quick and sound judgment, saw clearly enough how to handle it. He ordered his soldiers not to fire but to surround the motley group and disarm it. He did not even want to capture them. In the first place, he regarded the whole thing as a civil action, involving not an army but British subjects in violation of the government's laws; in the second place, there were specific orders not to molest the inhabitants; third, the purpose of the expedition was to destroy the stores at Concord and to get back to Boston; finally, no provision was made for the taking or transporting of prisoners. On the other hand, he could not just let them go away with their arms, possibly to follow his line of march to Concord, taking pot-shots at his troops on the way. So he did what had to be done: "I instantly called to the soldiers *not to fire* but to surround and disarm them."[10]

By this time some of Parker's men had heard their own captain's almost simultaneous order to disperse: "I immediately ordered our troops to disperse and *not to fire*."[11]

There were then, so far as the testimony of both commanding officers go, only two orders given. Both included the directive "not to fire." That these were the orders given was confirmed on both sides. Lieutenant Sutherland, who was one of the mounted officers close to Pitcairn, wrote: "I heard Major Pitcairn's voice call out, 'Soldiers, don't fire, keep your ranks, form and surround them.' "[12] And Ensign de Berniere, in the first company of light infantry: "He ordered our light infantry to advance and disarm them."[13] As the light infantry moved to the right of the meetinghouse and between it and Buckman's Tavern, toward the militia, somewhat behind the meetinghouse, Major Pitcairn and his group of mounted officers galloped their horses around the left of the meetinghouse. This was a sensible tactic for Pitcairn, because it would put him to one side of both forces, in ready hearing range of either, it still being a point of some consequence to him that the colonists were as much subjects of the King as the troops were. There he repeated his order to his own troops, and he told the colonists to lay down their arms.

Those of Captain Parker's company who were on the Common had heard his order to disperse, and they started to break ranks. But they did not disperse in a very orderly or uniformly prompt manner—"many of them not so speedily as they might have done," said Jonas Clarke.[14] Men like these were not apt by training or by nature to react instantly or uniformly. Besides, some of them who had grown up with John Parker would be much more apt to consider an order from him a strong suggestion than an absolute directive. A few would do as they pleased. One such, old Jonas Parker, the captain's first cousin, filled his hat full of flints and musket balls, set it on the ground conveniently between his feet, and prepared to spend the rest of the morning there if need be to fight it out with the British. It was he who had had no intention to run. Others of the company drifted slowly toward the edges of the Common, taking their muskets with them. Some hurried away at Parker's order, but they also took their guns. No one followed Pitcairn's order to lay down his arms.

While this somewhat straggling performance was going on, the British light infantry, in the custom of the day, started shouting as they charged forward. Someone, possibly one of the provincials off the Common, fired a shot. Perhaps it was meant to be an additional alarm—a common practice since the days of Indian raids. Or perhaps a British soldier, carried away by the excitement, fired at the minutemen. Or else a young officer backed up an order to the minutemen to lay down their arms with a warning shot from his pistol. Or possibly someone's musket flashed in the pan by accident.

In any case, the tense but almost silent scene of a moment earlier on the little Common erupted suddenly into noisy, wholly uncontrolled violence. And Major Pitcairn, an officer of the Marines commanding light infantry companies, could not restrain the troops, who had long since broken ranks and were firing at random with no orders from anyone. Pitcairn rode in among them, shouting orders to stop the firing and striking his sword downward furiously in the regulation cease-fire signal. The light infantry paid no attention to him. As a Marine officer, Pitcairn's contempt thereafter for the light infantry, up to his death at Bunker Hill three months later, was withering. The official reports of all the British command officers that day made some *pro forma* comment on the courage and intrepidity of His Majesty's troops. But not Pitcairn. He said that he would "in as concise a manner as possible state the facts," and he was scathing in his conciseness: ". . . without any order or regularity, the light infantry began a scattered fire and continued in that situation for some little time, contrary to the repeated orders both of me and the officers that were present."[15]

Lieutenant Barker of the King's Own, of course, was not surprised at any of this and in his diary was just as contemptuous of his fellow infantrymen as Pitcairn was: ". . . our men without any orders rushed in upon them . . . the men were so wild they could hear no orders."[16] Some of the junior officers, however, seemed to be under the impression that the firing was ordered and certainly had none of the sense of outrage about it that Pitcairn showed. Ensign Jeremy Lister, whose company was the first on the Common, took the firing as inevitable and, perhaps with the bravado of very young officers, as a light matter; "we returned their salute" was the way Lister put it.[17] But de Berniere, who was a serious-minded and responsible young officer, said simply that "our soldiers returned the fire."[18] Lieutenant Sutherland, who had got into all this from insisting on going along as a last-minute volunteer, was a resourceful and rather sober officer, and on ar-

riving with Pitcairn on the Common immediately rode his horse
in among the minutemen, repeating Pitcairn's orders to them to
lay down their arms. He gave no information in his account on
the manner in which the British started their firing, for he had
troubles of his own. He did not have his own horse or even an army
horse. His mount was appropriated from one of the Middlesex
countrymen he had intercepted during the night's march, and the
horse took a disturbed view of all the shouts and shots and confusion on the Common. On the first exchange of shots Sutherland's
horse took off, dashing right through the midst of the dispersing
militia and then six hundred yards up the road toward Jonas
Clarke's house. By the time he got his horse turned and back,
the minutemen had all disappeared into the woods and the grenadiers had arrived.

Meanwhile, most of Parker's men were dispersing, although a
few stayed where they were. As soon as they got off the Common,
a few of the dispersers turned and fired, and apparently there was
some firing from Buckman's Tavern (which was returned, the
shot in the door still being visible) and from the meetinghouse.
Altogether there were known to be only eight minutemen who
actually fired on the British, and the engagement on the Common
was less a battle or even a skirmish than an hysterical massacre at
the hands of badly disciplined British soldiers.

Old Jedediah Munroe, who had brought the ancestral sword
along, did not even have time to use his musket, for he was shot
down and wounded early in the affray. Ensign Robert Munroe,
Lexington's local hero at the capture of Louisburg, thirty years
earlier, was killed before firing a shot. Corporal John Munroe, on
the first discharge, thought that the British were just firing powder
and told his cousin Ebenezer so. Just then one musket ball entered
Ebenezer's arm, another grazed his cheek, and a third ripped a
hole in his coat. He lifted his own musket and fired. His cousin
John stuffed two balls down the muzzle of his gun, having rammed

it with enough powder to fire a cannon, took aim, and fired. A foot of the muzzle was shot off with the balls.

The only other minuteman who fired while still in the line was Jonas Parker, the captain's old cousin, who was never going to run. He was hit before he fired, and took aim and shot from the ground. He then reached for a ball and flint from his hat that he had set so conveniently on the ground between his feet, when he was run through with a British bayonet. Along with Parker and Robert Munroe, two other minutemen were killed on the Common proper before they had much chance to fire at the British. Isaac Muzzy, who had arrived with his father, was shot down near his position in the line, and so was Jonathan Harrington, whose house stood not a hundred yards away. Ruth Fiske Harrington, the Lexington doctor's niece, who had married Jonathan Harrington nine years earlier, and their eight-year-old son watched the young minuteman crawl across the green of the Common to his own doorstep, where he died.

The rest of the dead were killed after they had left the Common but were still close to it. Samuel Hadley and John Brown were both killed after leaving the Common. Another man, Ashabel Porter of Woburn, one of the riders of the night picked up by the British and taken captive by them, saw the battle on the Common as a chance to escape, and he bolted from the British lines before the segment he was in reached the Common. He was shot and killed as he ran away.

The American fire did not come close to matching the British in volume, and it was extremely erratic and irregular. Solomon Brown, who had been the first to discover the advance British officers from Boston that morning and caused Sergeant Munroe to post the guard around Hancock's house, fired from behind a stone wall just beyond Buckman's Tavern; two British musket balls barely missed him, one ripping his coat and another hitting the wall. Brown made a wide swing around to the back door of Buckman's, to which he supposed most of the minutemen, perhaps from habit, had withdrawn. As he went through the tavern, however, he found no one except the baffled one-armed peddler, who had wandered into history by being taken prisoner with Revere and the others earlier that morning. Brown opened the front door, by which time the rear units of the British were abreast of the tavern alongside the Common. Brown picked a likely British officer as a target, aimed, and fired. He got an enlisted man of another company in the leg.

Lieutenant William Tidd, Captain Parker's second in command, got clear of the Common on Parker's command to disperse and started up the road toward Clarke's house. A mounted officer pursued him, so Tidd jumped a fence, took aim and fired. He missed, but he got away.

Jonathan Harrington's cousin, Caleb, had gone into the meetinghouse for more powder with Joshua Simonds and Joseph Comee. All three found themselves in danger of being cut off from their company by the British. Caleb Harrington and Comee decided to make a run for it. When he got outside, Comee found that he was already separated from the militia to the north of the meetinghouse by the first platoon of the British Tenth Infantry, and the second platoon on his south side. Between two enemy platoons, he made a lightning dash westward across the Common to Marrett Munroe's house, running a gantlet of musket balls all the way. One of the musket balls hit him in the arm, but he kept going into the Munroe house and, right through it, out of the back door. Caleb Harrington, headed in the same direction, did not make it and was killed in the attempt. Joshua Simonds saw Harrington fall and ducked back into the meetinghouse, sure that a British platoon would be in after him. He lay down on the floor, stuck the muzzle of his gun into a barrel of powder and, keeping his eyes on the door, waited to pull the trigger and blow the place up when the British entered.

Joshua Simonds came closer than he knew to blowing up the meetinghouse. While Pitcairn had thus far borne the whole burden

of the affair for the British, with the recalcitrant infantrymen acting like members of a mob, the portly Lieutenant Colonel Smith,
whose own regiment's company of light infantry was first on the
Common, was, of course, late. He said afterward that he was back
in the line of march somewhere and, apparently after hearing the
firing, hurried up to the head of the column. By then the men of
his own regiment were firing indiscriminately, paying no attention
to the officers or their orders. The sight of the chaotic firing,
shouting, and random running around of the soldiers, with the
officers vainly bellowing orders, seemed to have an arousing effect
upon the Lieutenant Colonel. "I endeavored to the utmost to stop
all further firing, which in a short time I effected."[19] Lieutenant
Sutherland, whose commandeered provincial horse had darted
away at the first shots, got back to the Common by the time that
Smith got there and noted how Smith got the troops to cease
firing: "On my coming up, Colonel Smith turned to me, asked
me, do you know where a drummer is, which I found, who immediately beat to arms, when the men ceased firing."[20]

Smith then noted, with some horror as though he recognized
the wild mood of his troops, that groups of them were about to try
to force their way into the dwellings around the Common,
Buckman's Tavern, and the meetinghouse, where Joshua Simonds
lay with the muzzle of his loaded gun stuck in the barrel of powder
—ready to make a resounding understatement of Smith's comment that he knew "if the houses were once broke into, none within
could well be saved."[21]

Smith unquestionably was the man who salvaged what was left
of a situation he should have avoided. The men of the Tenth
Regiment recognized their own colonel and were suddenly sobered
into listening to orders, and the impersonal beat of the drum
brought about an automatic reaction. In his analysis of the
episode, however, Smith was silly in his overeagerness to sound
like a highly successful officer merely because he finally stopped
his own troops from rioting; and he seemed not to know very

much about the real facts of the action. "The troops then near the meetinghouse and dwellings, much enraged at the treatment they had received [during the entire encounter one British soldier had been nicked in the leg] and having been fired on from the houses repeatedly [there were no armed men in any of the houses, except for the few seconds that it took Joseph Comee to race through Marrett Munroe's house *away* from the Common], were going to break them open to come at those within; though they deserved no favor . . . I was desirous of putting a stop to all further slaughter of those deluded people, therefore gave orders, and by the assistance of some of the officers prevented any one house being entered."[22]

By the time the firing ceased, the grenadiers had come up, and Smith's whole force of seven hundred men swarmed over the Common and the roads around it. Not a provincial, except those lying dead or wounded on the ground, was in sight. Probably there was some careful peering through the windows of the houses and taverns or from behind trees in the surrounding fields. But the Common and the roads bordering it was a mass of scarlet coats, as the officers attempted to get the men back in some sort of order. "We then formed on the Common," said Lieutenant Barker, "but with some difficulty . . . we waited a considerable time there."[23]

Both Smith and Pitcairn, who ought to have been aware of the vast implications of their morning's work, appeared before the ranks and dressed them down for "the too great warmth of the soldiers in not attending to their officers and keeping their ranks," and they urged "a more steady conduct to them in the future."[24] But Smith and Pitcairn were army officers and not politicians or diplomats, and their assignment was to march to Concord and destroy the stores there. So they had the troops replenish their cartridge boxes and, before marching off the Common and down the road toward Concord, allowed them to fire a victory volley and shout out the three cheers traditional in the British army after a successful engagement. This irritated the Reverend Jonas Clarke more than even the wanton destruction of life had: "how far it was expressive of bravery, heroism, and true military glory . . . must be submitted to the impartial world to judge."[25]

iii

Scurrying with John Hancock from their woodland hideout where Sergeant Munroe had taken them, Samuel Adams heard the sound of gunfire floating out over the early morning quiet of the country. His reaction was exultant, although he did not know who was being killed. "O, what a glorious morning is this," he exclaimed. Hancock, annoyed by the physical discomfort of life in the woods, said he thought it was a strange time to comment on the weather. "I mean what a glorious morning for America," Adams said, and the town of Lexington later adopted it as a legend for the town seal. The agitator was not without a sense of ceremony when the occasion called for it.

When the British moved on toward Concord, not more than half an hour after they had rushed onto Lexington Common and had shown no interest whatsoever in Adams and Hancock, the latter were on their way to their next refuge—the Thomas Jones house in Woburn. At this point, Hancock, who unlike Adams was seeing all the events of the day in terms only of his own affairs, thought of his aunt and his fiancée back at Jonas Clarke's house. He sent a messenger to them, telling them to get a carriage and join him at Woburn. He also directed them "to bring the fine salmon that they had had sent to them for dinner."[26]

Aunt Lydia and Dorothy had watched the fighting from an upstairs window in Clarke's house, though they could have seen little more than the puffs of smoke from the shots, had seen the first wounded brought in, and had helped bundle off to safer places the smaller Clarke children. Now they got the carriage and brought John Hancock his salmon. Hancock got into an argument with

Dorothy Quincy about her proposal to return to Boston, where her father was; and she was getting the better of the argument ("Recollect, Mr. Hancock, I am not under your control yet. I *shall* go to my father."[27]) when Aunt Lydia stepped in and settled the dispute.

However glorious the morning to Adams and to America, it was becoming a nuisance to Hancock. The salmon was all cooked and just being sliced, when a self-appointed messenger burst in with the misinformation that the British were marching from Lexington to Woburn. The whole party, including a now understandably silent Adams, whose agile mind must already have been planning the uses of the yet unfinished day's events, moved on to a third refuge in Billerica.

Back in Lexington there was the pressing business of getting aid to the wounded and the sad business of cleaning up after death had come. From a slight hill beyond the swampy ground north of the Common, the men, silent at first and perhaps a little dazed, came drifting back to the Common they had fled a few minutes earlier. Doors of houses opened, and the women came out, followed by puzzled children, to help the wounded, to find their husbands, to take the necessary census of the dead. Dr. Fiske and his son, Dr. Joseph, Junior, came and bandaged wounds. Eight men in all— seven of Captain Parker's company and the unfortunate chance captive from Woburn, lay dead, most of them shot in the back as they were dispersing. Nine men were wounded. Of the eight father-and-son combinations who stood together half an hour earlier, five were broken by death—two fathers and three sons killed. Of all the men who had responded to William Diamond's drum call to arms, nearly a third were casualties.

Then it dawned on all the living that sooner or later the British would have to come back through Lexington. Children were evacuated from all the houses lining the main route from Concord to Boston through the town. Family silver and the communion service from the meetinghouse were buried or hidden. Late arriving minutemen from the outlying areas began to appear on the Common. A solitary British soldier came walking by the meetinghouse. A minuteman from Woburn went up to him, demanded his surrender, and disarmed him. One by one, five other British soldiers—stragglers, willing prisoners, looters—were picked up, disarmed, and sent off to Woburn for safekeeping.

When the British marched off, of course, they left behind them the unhappy sequela of wars from the beginning—all the personal and human debris of sudden bereavement and new uncertainties.

In Jonas Clarke's house, which—except for the Common itself —was the most active place in Lexington that day, there was among the twelve children one wondering little girl of twelve. Sixty-six years later, it was all still very real to her—everything that did not get into the orations and the textbooks. In 1841, full of memories, and the last of the Hancocks and Clarkes to live in the old house, Elizabeth Clarke sent a remarkable portrait of the day, a primitive in words, to her niece:

Lexington, April 19th, 1841

My dear niece Lucy Allen:

Miss Colton offers to take a line to you, and, as your little girl did not stay or come to this house only to give us your letter which, with the sincerest joy we read and have lived on the hope you gave us that you would come up to this old House and look on us old Beings, a house and Happy, Happy *home and many worthy men and women have been the inhabitants and oh! Lucy, how many descendants can I count from the venerable Hancock down to this day which is sixty-six years since the war began on the Common which I now can see from this window as here I sit writing, and can see, in my mind, just as plain, all the British troops marching off the Common to Concord, and the whole scene, how Aunt Hancock and Miss Dolly Quinsy, with their cloaks and bonnets on, Aunt crying and wringing her hands and helping Mother Dress* the children, Dolly going round with Father, to hide Money, watches and anything down in the potatoes and up garrett, and then Grandfather Clarke sent down men with carts, took your Mother and all the children but Jonas and me and Sally a Babe six months old. Father sent Jonas down to Grandfather Cook's to see who was killed and what their condition was and, in the afternoon, Father, Mother with me and the Baby went to the Meeting House, there was the eight men that was killed, seven of them my Father's parishioners, one from Woburn, all in Boxes made of four large Boards Nailed up and, after Pa had prayed, they were put into two horse carts and took into the grave yard where your Grandfather and some of the Neighbors had made a large trench, as near the Woods as possible and there we followed the bodies of those first slain, Father, Mother, I and the Baby, there I stood and there I saw them let down into the ground, it was a little rainey but we waited to see them Covered up with the Clods and then for fear the British should find them, my Father thought some of the men had best Cut some pine or oak bows and spread them on their place of burial so that it looked like a heap of Brush . . .

The extraordinary circumstance that I should be the only one of this Family who should witness the first Burial of the first slain of the war between Great Britain and America and Be not only continued in Life but on the same spot of Earth and in the same house where the first Patriots in the Country was at that period, Hancock and Adams and Father who was known as a superior Wigg, superior minister, a Highly respectable Man, uncommon in his intellectual faculties and, above all, a Christian, who served his Lord and Master, was faithfull to his People, gave his strength to labour for his Family, his hours of Rest to his pen so that his People's soulls should not be neglected, but Lucy, I shall tire you with my relations . . . in this my long life . . .

I think of so many things that I Jumble them up in such bad writing that you will have hard work to read, my hands tremble *and my Eyes are very sore lately, do pray read with patience perhaps my Last Letter for I am full of years.* . . .

Your Aged Aunt Eliza[28]

Later on the morning of April nineteenth, Captain Parker reassembled his Lexington minutemen, to march toward Concord. Some of the wounded, now bandaged, formed in awkward but determined lines. Among them was Jedediah Munroe, the old man who had fallen on the Common before he could shoot and who had brought along the old Scotch claymore as an extra weapon. William Diamond beat his drum again. The little company marched off toward Concord, the beat of the drum and the thin music of the fife echoing briefly after them. And this was perhaps Lexington's saddest and most triumphant moment of the whole day—the sun now high in the sky, the smell of British gunpowder still in the air, their dead brothers lying on the Common behind, and the company of minutemen, knowing now what they faced, marching off to meet the enemy again.

5

THE BATTLE: CONCORD

"The thunderbolt falls on an inch of ground, but the light of it fills the horizon. . . ."

RALPH WALDO EMERSON[1]

Two eighteenth century villages, five miles apart, some eleven and sixteen miles from Boston, each with its meetinghouse, its neat and handsome clapboard houses, its pastures and farms and quiet ways—yet Lexington and Concord had stamped on them wholly different personalities.

Concord was the larger of the two—with its fifteen hundred souls, twice the size of Lexington in population—and richer. It was also somewhat freer in disposition, a little farther removed in temperament from the homogeneity and unrelieved orthodoxy that characterized Lexington, a little more sophisticated in a way, a community of lighter mood, more diverse opinion, more inhabitants who spoke their own minds and came to their own conclusions. There were Tories in Concord, too, although they were a very small and untolerated minority. One of them, Daniel Bliss, a lawyer, entertained Captain Brown and Ensign de Berniere when they went to Concord in March to report to Gage on the roads. Mr. Bliss was forced by his neighbors to leave town with the soldiers; he never returned, and his estate was confiscated. Concord's other Tories refrained from overt acts, but they let their opinions be known. The town lacked the unanimity of Lexington.

For, where Lexington had felt the unifying and also the restraining effect of two powerful personalities, old Bishop Hancock and his successor Jonas Clarke (their consecutive ministries in the village covered a hundred and four years), Concord had a seething ecclesiastical history in a day when the ecclesiastical life of a community was almost its whole life and most certainly its political, social, and cultural life. The effervescent people of Concord had thrown out some of their ministers, split into separate parishes, hauled their clergy up on charges, feuded over Whitefield's "Great Awakening" revival movement, and generally behaved as if they were running, or attempting to run, the parish instead of letting the parish run them. Indeed, as far back as the 1640s, during the ascendancy of the Puritan theocracy, when such things were extraordinarily rare, one Concord citizen of positive views, Ambrose Martin, arose and publicly declared that in his judgment the church covenant was "a stinking carrion and a human invention."[2] Martin was fined £10, a huge sum then, for expressing his opinion of the basic *mystique* of the Puritan state. Like most people of the time, he did not have any such amount of cash; so the authorities seized some of his property and sold it for £20. Martin refused to accept payment of the surplus, to which he was entitled, and even when he hit upon bad times he held out for the whole amount. It is significant of the spirit of Concord (and it would have been inconceivable in Lexington) that fifteen of his townsmen, including the two clergymen of the town, petitioned the dour Puritan Governor John Endicott to give Martin the whole £20. Endicott said that Martin's distress was due entirely to his own obstinacy and that he could get the surplus on the sale of his property, and not a penny more, whenever he saw fit to call for it.

In the following century, old Bishop Hancock spent a considerable part of his time going from Lexington to Concord to preside over emergency sessions of church councils that were convened to arbitrate some rebellion in the Concord church, which finally split into two parishes. Concord's controversies resulted in the decline of the clergy as an influence in town affairs, and Jonas Clarke's contemporary, the Reverend William Emerson, did not hold a position of any comparable authority in the town at all.

The differences of character in the towns of Lexington and Concord were clearly reflected in the happenings of April nineteenth, 1775. The outward context of events was, of course, wholly different, too. The sun was fully up, and so was the entire population, when the British started moving toward Concord. There was no secrecy, no stealth, no quiet, no wild dashing around of riders. The morning was bright and clear. The British columns of scarlet and white, its drums beating and fifes whistling, were moving, full of confidence, into the eastern part of the town. The provincials had turned out to be hopelessly irresolute or astonishingly bad marksmen or numerically insignificant. The British troops were now nearing their real objective, could readily get it over with, and get back to their barracks for a good night's sleep.

In Concord, however, events had been moving since one o'clock that morning, when young Dr. Prescott escaped the British patrol and warned the Concord militia, having paused on the way to alarm the Lincoln minutemen, too. "This morning between one and two o'clock we were alarmed by the ringing of the bell," wrote William Emerson, the Concord pastor. Unlike Clarke, however, Emerson's sole function was to grab his musket and run to the rendezvous at Wright's Tavern. Emerson's job was that of a member of the Alarm List and nothing more; his pride was in being the first to arrive, although he was by no means the nearest to Wright's Tavern. After the militia had assembled, they arranged for a signal to reassemble on the approach of the British, sent messengers to alert other communities, and dispersed to help the other townspeople hide as much of the remaining stores as they could before the British got there. Concord had two companies of minutemen, and another from neighboring Lincoln, to receive the British.

As the morning neared daybreak, a scout was sent to Lexington and returned shortly to report that there was firing on Lexington Common; but he told Major John Buttrick, then commanding the minutemen, that he did not wait to see whether bullets were being fired or just gunpowder. On this intelligence, the minutemen reassembled and held a council of war—all with complete calm and no impulsiveness at all. There were about two hundred and fifty of them, all armed. Amos Barrett said, after conferring, that "we thought we would go and meet the British."[3] The three companies fell in line, and they marched down the road toward Lexington, their drums beating and fifes playing, "to meet the British."

The British were, of course, marching from Lexington toward them—seven hundred regulars marching in one direction and two hundred and fifty provincial militia in the other on the narrow Lexington-Concord road. "We marched down toward Lexington about a mile or a mile and a half, and we saw them coming. We halted and stayed until they got within about a hundred rods," Barrett reported. Then Major Buttrick's force executed a startling movement for one of two opposing forces that had just met. "We were ordered to the about face and marched before them [the British] with our drums and fifes going and also the British. We had grand music."[4] Amos Barrett did well to note the novelty and splendor of this scene. After seven o'clock in the morning now, here along a narrow country road came a variously garbed group of two hundred and fifty countrymen, marching along with muskets and their fifes and drums. One hundred rods behind them marched the seven hundred British soldiers, their fifes and drums adding to the grand music.

As the British entered Concord, they found themselves on less felicitous terrain than they had at Lexington. Rising steeply on their right was a long ridge of varying height but of sufficient steepness to command the road all the way into the center of Concord. Along this ridge newly arrived minutemen were already peering down at the British forces and could have fired as they pleased, without any danger of return fire. Lieutenant Colonel Smith sent his light infantry off the roadway and up onto the ridge; and the minutemen who had been there hurried back along the ridge to the center of Concord. The grenadiers continued to march along the roadway. Thus the British force arrived in the center of Concord at about eight o'clock in the morning, finally ready to carry out the object of the mission that got them up from their bunks at nine o'clock the night before. Under the procrastinating command of Colonel Smith, they had taken eleven hours to come seventeen miles, and his troops had so conducted themselves that the whole point of the mission was now irrelevant anyhow. All that was left for the hapless colonel that day was so to manage what was left of it as to convert failure to disaster. This he achieved. For, unencumbered by policy decisions or, in any case, by the presence of those who could make them, Colonel James Barrett, the commanding officer of the Concord militia, Major John Buttrick, his second in command, and their fellow officers made their decisions on purely military grounds.

To begin with, they kept their militia out of easy reach of the British and always in positions where they themselves had the advantage of observation and striking power. Concord was as much a town of hills as Lexington for the most part was of plains. Before the advancing British, the minutemen moved from one ridge to another, while all the time their number was being swollen by new companies from nearby towns. When the companies of minutemen who had made up the strange procession with the British with all the music got back to Concord center, they found the Alarm Company—the men too old for the duty of minutemen—on a hill across from the meetinghouse. The combined provincial forces then withdrew from this ridge, overlooking the little group of public buildings in the heart of the town, to a second ridge, from which they could both look down on the town and see out across some meadows to William Emerson's manse, the Concord River, and the North Bridge across it that led to Colonel Barrett's farm, where some of the munitions were hidden. From this height, they watched the light infantry come down from the ridge that they themselves had just left, and the taller, heavier-armed grenadiers form at ease along the roads converging in the town. Smith and Pitcairn mounted the first ridge and, from the town burial ground, surveyed the countryside, Smith studying the map that Gage had given him and Pitcairn looking through a glass to determine the distribution of the provincial militia that might still be scattered around the town.

Meanwhile, the militia was holding a council of war on their ridge. Emerson, the young pastor, of a somewhat evangelical sort compared to the rationalist, Clarke, was all for "making a stand, notwithstanding the superiority of their number." "Let us stand our ground," he said. "If we die, let us die here." But this wasn't Lexington, and Emerson wasn't Clarke. He got disagreement from the more venturesome ("Let us go and meet them") and from the more prudent ("No, it will not do for us to begin the war"). Emerson himself reported that the prudent won: ". . . but others more prudent thought best to retreat till our strength should be equal to the enemy's by recruits from neighboring towns that were continuingly coming in to our assistance. Accordingly, we retreated over the [North] bridge."[5] This was to be the most important decision of the day by the provincial militia at Concord. It put them on the west or far side of the river, "on a hill not far from the bridge where we could see and hear what was going on."[6] It also put them where they would not be separated from the minutemen that now started streaming in from towns to the west of Concord until there were some four hundred there.

Lieutenant Colonel Smith now divided his forces. He kept the grenadiers in the town on the east side of the Concord River, and they were deployed all around, searching for the stores and destroying any that they came upon. Of his ten companies of light infantry, he sent one to guard the South Bridge over the Concord River to the southwest of the town, presumably to stop any militia from crossing it and to search for any stores that might be there. But the North Bridge was the important one, for Smith knew that considerable parts of the provincial stores were concealed on Colonel Barrett's farm beyond it. So he dispatched seven of his light infantry companies to the North Bridge, over which the militia had just withdrawn.

With all the militia across the North Bridge the grenadiers had the town to themselves, and Lieutenant Colonel Smith, who should have been in command at the key and vulnerable position at the bridge (the only possible place where there could be contact with the provincial militia), stayed with the grenadiers, directing their operation. He kept Pitcairn, his second in command, with him, too, having dispatched the infantry companies to the bridge under the command only of one of their captains.

The search and destruction of the stores in the town went along in a peaceable way. Having been lectured by their officers on the conduct of the light infantry at Lexington, the huge grenadiers went about their business almost gently and for their pains missed as much contraband as they found. Forbidden to terrify the inhabitants, mostly women and old men left in the town, they went along almost eagerly with the most specious diversionary tactics of the inhabitants.

Timothy Wheeler, whose ancestors were among the original settlers of Concord, hit upon a method of deceiving the grenadiers by telling the truth. He had stored in his barn a large supply of provincial flour for the use of the militia; near it he carefully stacked a few bags of his own flour. With the grenadiers he adopted a tone of patient forebearance as if they were particularly backward schoolboys. He put his hand on the bag of his own flour and said, "This is my flour . . . This is the flour of wheat; this is the flour of corn; this is the flour of rye. This is my flour; this is my wheat; this is my rye; this is mine." And every bag that he touched was literally his own. The grenadier left, assuring Wheeler that "we do not injure private property."[7]

At the malt house of Ebenezer Hubbard, where more flour was stored, they rolled the barrels out on the roadway, smashed them apart, and scattered the flour over the ground. This, of course, was rather picayune work to the heaviest chargers of the King's infantry, and they sought to speed the trifling job up. They threw most of the other casks of flour, the chief provision of armies, into the mill pond. All of it was later retrieved by the provincials, when it was discovered that the flour on the outer edges of the casks had swollen and, caulking the seams, had sealed the remainder up tight. The grenadiers were similarly impatient with the confiscated musket balls, which General Gage, with a curious attention to details, had suggested the soldiers put into their pockets and scatter on their way home. The grenadiers dumped hundreds of them into ponds, and the provincials just hauled them out again the next day.

At the tavern of Ephraim Jones there was some exceptional activity. In addition to being an innkeeper, Ephraim Jones, in an appropriate merger of related professions, was also the jailkeeper. Jones depended erroneously on force rather than ingenuity in handling the soldiers. There were three twenty-four pounders concealed in his jailyard. In his inn, which was conveniently adjacent, was the chest of the Treasurer of the Provincial Congress, Henry Gardner, who had seen fit to leave it in the room he had occupied during the lately adjourned session. Jones bolted all the doors of inn and jail and refused to let the grenadiers into either establishment. This was a delicate situation for the grenadiers, who were duty-bound to be gentle and conciliatory. They sent for Major Pitcairn to handle the deadlock. He ordered a door broken down and went to the jailyard. There Jones stubbornly refused to reveal where the cannon were buried. Since neither the jail premises nor the cannon were private property, Pitcairn brandished his pistol, and Jones led him to the cannon. But the inn was private property, and the grenadiers respected the distinction. They got to Gardner's room and found a young woman blocking the door. She insisted that it was her room, that the chest was hers, and told them to go away. They left. Jones was still being held at bayonet point in the jailyard, but Pitcairn was satisfied to knock off the trunnions of the cannon and destroy their carriages and then released Jones, directing him to shift to the role of innkeeper and prepare the major's breakfast. Jones served the breakfast, rendered an exact bill, and was paid by the major. It was the only show of violence among those searching for stores in the town.

The British made a point of paying for everything demanded for their personal convenience, and many a good descendant of the Puritans had a difficult choice between indignantly and patriotically scorning money and prudently accepting it with the solid respect of good New England orthodoxy for the earth's manna. Most of them resolved the dilemma by taking the money after comments to the effect that it was probably contaminated. Colonel Barrett's wife, who had the light infantry on her hands for an hour or more, served them food and drink on their demand. At first she refused payment with the remark that "we are commanded to feed our enemies." But they pressed the money on her, tossing it into her lap. "This is the price of blood," she said ruefully, and put the money in her pocket.[8] At Amos Wood's home the British even offered to pay the ladies there for the inconvenience caused them in searching the place, giving them each a guinea. The women accepted the money; and told the officer that there was only one room unavailable for the search because it was occupied by an indisposed woman. The officer sternly forbade his men to go near it. The room, of course, held the only military stores in the whole Wood house.

In general, as the morning wore calmly on, the soldiers showed more interest in food than in military supplies. If Barker was right in his observation that, after standing around the Cambridge flatlands for two hours while their rations were being brought to them, the soldiers threw them away with characteristic contempt for army food, they were really hungry by now. They had marched all day, and they had a day's march ahead of them. But as professional soldiers, they also knew that better food than army salt pork could be had from foraging. In Concord they ate well, getting heavy breakfasts of meat, milk, and potatoes from their unwilling hosts. Once in a while, however, they got stern lectures from the women or from old men on their behavior and on the general colonial policy of the British Parliament. At the gun shop of Samuel Barrett they found the ancient father of the proprietor, Deacon Thomas Barrett, who took the occasion to reprimand them seriously for the whole drift of events since the Stamp Act. The soldiers after a while said teasingly they might have to kill him for such rebellious sentiments, but the old deacon won them over by pointing out that he was so old that if they waited a little while they would be saved the trouble.

So far as the usefulness of the raid to the military security of the King's troops in Boston went, it was, of course, a fiasco. The patriots, in the three days following Revere's Sunday alert of Adams and Hancock at Lexington, had effectively removed to neighboring towns much of the material, and what was left that the British could find and destroy could not possibly determine the outcome of the occupation of Boston. Nevertheless, the grenadiers in the town did what they could. They destroyed the cannon they found, threw musket and cannon balls in ponds and wells, chopped down the liberty pole, hacked up harness, burned gun carriages, entrenchment tools, and the wooden trenchants and spoons acquired for Samuel Adams' provincial army when he got it. If they had not concluded to burn rather than just to smash the wooden carriages and utensils, they might have departed in peace for Boston, well fed and still without the loss or serious injury of a single man. After the horror of Lexington Common, things in Concord were not going badly for Lieutenant Colonel Smith.

But at North Bridge, where Smith had sent the seven companies of light infantry to hold the minutemen on the far side of the river, tension was rapidly developing. From their vantage point, on the hill beyond the bridge, the provincial militia watched the British infantry as Captain Parsons of the Tenth Regiment, in command of the detachment, deployed his men.

ii

Captain Parsons had thrust upon him decisions that his limited experience had not equipped him to make. When he first marched down to North Bridge, he had had six companies under his command; shortly after he arrived at the bridge, a seventh company, the Welch Fusiliers, joined his force. Since a British company of the time had twenty-eight men, Parsons had altogether one hundred and ninety-six men. Before him on the hill two hundred yards away was the whole strength of the provincial militia that had arrived—some four hundred, including the minutemen who had marched so gallantly down the Lexington road earlier that morning "to meet the British," only to execute the remarkable about-face and serve as the escort of the British right into Concord.

Outnumbered two to one at the bridge, Parsons was faced with an even more serious dilemma. He had two assignments from Lieutenant Colonel Smith. One was to secure the bridge, and the other was to go on to search Colonel Barrett's farm, two miles beyond the bridge, the alleged chief depository of provincial arms and stores. He had to keep enough of his troops at the bridge to hold it. On the other hand, he had to send enough men to Barrett's to fight off the militia if it followed them or to cope with any provincial forces that they might encounter on the way to Barrett's. Parsons probably thought he was avoiding a difficult decision by splitting his forces nearly evenly. First, he marched all seven companies across the bridge. One of these he left at the western end of the bridge, so that they stood with their backs to it as they faced the colonial militia on the nearby hill—twenty-eight men, their backs to a river, facing four hundred. Two more companies, fifty-six men, Parsons placed some distance apart on some low hills along the road to Barrett's and about a quarter of a mile from the bridge. He turned all three of these companies over to the command of Captain Walter Laurie of the Forty-third Regiment, and he marched away to Colonel Barrett's farm with the other four to seize and destroy the munitions.

Watching all this, the minutemen made no move to interfere with the British. They just watched and waited, two hundred yards from the British company guarding the bridge and perhaps four hundred from the two British companies stationed on the low hills down the road to Barrett's. One minuteman decided to negotiate. "James Nichols, of Lincoln, who was an Englishman and a droll fellow and a fine singer, said, 'If any of you will hold my gun, I will go down and talk to them.' Some of them held his gun, and he went down alone to the British soldiers at the bridge and talked to them some time. Then he came back and took his gun and said he was going home. . . ."[9]

The constantly complaining Lieutenant Barker, of the King's Own Regiment, at the bridge, did not like the situation at all. "During this time," he wrote, "the people were gathering together in great numbers and, taking advantage of our scattered disposition, seemed as if they were going to cut off the communications with the bridge. . . ."[10]

Then on the hill where the four hundred armed provincials—minutemen supplemented by other militia, including such venerable men as eighty-year-old Josiah Haynes of Sudbury—looked down on the three companies of light infantry guarding the bridge, the smoke from the bonfires that Smith's grenadiers had lighted in the town of Concord was noticed. The provincials held another war conference: apparently the British were setting fire to the town, and many of these men had left their families back at their houses. Joseph Hosmer, lieutenant of one of the Concord minutemen companies, acting as adjutant of all the forces, put a question to the group of officers, town officials, armed farmers, and tradesmen around him: "Will you let them burn the town down?"[11] The answer was a concerted "No," and the group agreed that they would march back over the bridge to the town and put a stop to the burning. Colonel Barrett told the men to load their guns, gave them "strict orders not to fire till they [the British soldiers guarding the bridge] fired first, then to fire as fast as we could."[12]

The four hundred provincial militia started moving down from their position toward Captain Laurie's single company of thirty-five men at the bridge. The junior officers of both this company and the two somewhat ahead of the bridge started worried conferences on what they should do next. With no one really effectively in command they acted on their own to correct the extraordinary jeopardy in which Parsons had left them.

Ensign Lister of the Tenth Regiment's company, one of the two stationed by Parsons on the hills a quarter of a mile west of the bridge, said, "We had not been long in this situation when we saw a large body of men drawn up with the greatest regularity and approached us seemingly with an intent to attack, when Lieutenant Kelly, who then commanded our company, with myself thought it most proper to retire from our situation and join the Fourth's company [the second of the two companies left by Parsons on the low hills across the river], which we did. They still approached and in that [such] force that it was thought proper by the officers except myself to join the Forty-third's company at Concord Bridge commanded by Captain Laurie." Lister objected to the withdrawing back to the company at the bridge, because of the terrain between them and the bridge: they would have to descend, under the provincials' muskets, "a steepish hill" where they could be fired upon but could not fire back. "However, I was over-ruled."[13]

Lieutenant Sutherland, the venturesome volunteer, meanwhile had left the bridge "exceedingly vexed" that Captain Parsons had gone along to Barrett's without him and started out to catch up with him. But he was too late. The provincials were coming down the hill and since "it struck me it would be disgraceful to be taken by such rascals," he raced back to the bridge, where he joined Captain Laurie.[14]

The three companies were now together at the bridge as the militia came toward them, but they were still in the indefensible position of being on the far side of the bridge with the river at their back and only a narrow footbridge over which to withdraw. The provincials were now within three hundred yards. Lieutenant Sutherland, who seemed to be one of those zealous and capable officers whom everyone trusted, was consulted by Captain Laurie, who "was kind enough to ask me, Was it not better to acquaint Colonel Smith of this. I told him by all means, as their disposition appeared to be very regular and determined, on which he sent Lieutenant Robertson to Colonel Smith; who returned to us in a very little time with Captain Lumm, who told us Colonel Smith would send us a re-inforcement immediately. Captain Lumm very obligingly galloped back as hard as he could to hasten the reinforcement."[15]

Now the provincial militia were almost upon them, and Laurie at last recognized the vulnerability of his position and recrossed the bridge, barely having time to get his hundred men across. They were now in the right position to stop the approaching provincials from crossing, but they were far too late to form properly for the job. As for the reinforcements, Colonel Smith was, of course, late in getting them there. With complete disregard for Captain Parsons and the four companies who had gone to Barrett's, Ensign Lister proposed tearing up the planks of the bridge, and Lieutenant Sutherland and some others actually did get a few torn loose; but the approach of the militia stopped them. If they had succeeded, of course, Parsons would have been isolated on the far side of the river.

While all the other officers of the three companies were attempting to improve their prospects, the disapproving Lieutenant Barker of the King's Own apparently took the view that the whole mess was no worse than might be expected. "Captain Laurie, who commanded then these companies, sent to Colonel Smith, begging he would send more troops to his assistance and informing him of his situation; the Colonel ordered two or three companies but put himself at their head, by which means [he] stopped them from being [in] time enough, for being a very fat heavy man he would not have reached the bridge in half an hour, though it was not half a mile to it; in the meantime, the rebels marched into the road and were coming down upon us, when Captain Laurie made his men retire to this side of the bridge (which, by the bye, he ought to have done at first, and then he would have had time to make a good disposition, but at this time, he had not, for the rebels got so near him that his people were obliged to form the best way they could)."[16] The fact that Barker was right made him no more helpful at the time, when Laurie needed all the help that he could get.

The columns marching down toward the disturbed company officers was the first American army under a unified commander ever to take the field. The variegated brigade was made up of six companies of minutemen—two from Concord and one each from the adjacent towns of Bedford, Lincoln, Acton, and Carlisle, the Concord militia made up of older men and others not in the minutemen companies, and individual minutemen from neighboring Westford, Chelmsford, and Littleton. They marched down to the bridge in a long line in ranks of two, the old men in the rear and the Acton company with its energetic young captain, Isaac Davis, at the head. With him was Major John Buttrick of the Concord company. In the rear, still on a rise where he could see the whole column, was Colonel Barrett, mounted, and repeating his order not to begin the firing. As this column neared the bridge, Buttrick shouted to the withdrawing British to stop tearing up the planks. They did stop, not in obedience to Buttrick, but because of the proximity of his force.

Captain Laurie, across the river, was trying to get his companies in a proper defensive position. As it was, the hundred men were all massed at the east end of the bridge, making an excellent and compact target and unable to raise their muskets to fire without bayoneting their own comrades. Laurie ordered the troops of two companies to align themselves in columns for street firing, an infantry innovation at the time, in which the soldiers seemed poorly drilled and with which even the critical Lieutenant Barker seemed wholly unfamiliar. The technique required the company to face the enemy in ranks of four or more and to the depth of eight or less ranks. After the first rank fired, it split and wheeled around to the rear, where it would prime and reload its muskets while the second and following ranks fired. In a tactical retreat the rank, after it fired, just continued marching to the rear, stopping only when it was its turn to fire again. This was what Laurie had in mind, although he failed to realize that the country road with an open meadow on each side was not a city street and offered neither reason nor advantage to street fighting. In fact, it offered distinct hazards, because in the absence of protective buildings characteristic of city streets, any enemy could easily flank and surround the street firing squads. Lister apparently thought of this, for he ordered the third company to extend their line along the river bank. Except for the first few squads who stood ready at the edge of the bridge for the street firing, however, nobody seemed to pay much attention to Captain Laurie's orders. The ubiquitous and always helpful Lieutenant Sutherland, seeing Laurie's plight, jumped over a stone wall into a meadow belonging to Emerson's house and shouted to the men of the third company to follow him. No better disciplined than they had been on Lexington Common, none of them did—except three men. Then the shooting began and—as at Lexington—no one knew who started it, although Captain Laurie, who gave no order to fire, said that "I imagine myself that a man of my company (afterwards killed) did first fire his piece."[17] Sutherland, who was hit in the shoulder, said the provincials did, and Ensign Lister also implied that the provincials did. But the probability is that three or four of the British troops, on their own initiative, fired first, and their shots fell into the river.

At this time Captain Davis and his companions of the Acton company were only fifty or sixty yards from the British. Then the British fired a volley. "God damn it, they are firing ball!" Captain Timothy Brown of Concord swore bitterly; and Amos Barrett, who enjoyed the "grand music" so much, wrote, with his customary appreciation of the phonic details of warfare, "The balls whistled well. We were then all ordered to fire that could fire and not kill our own men."[18]

On the first British volley the intrepid Captain Davis and one of his men of the Acton Company were killed and the young Acton fifer wounded. Major Buttrick immediately gave the provincial order to fire, in something less than clipped military terms: "Fire, fellow-soldiers, for God's sake, fire!"[19] Most of the provincials fired, letting loose a rain of bullets on the British troops, two of whom were killed and several wounded. After scattered return fire the British turned and ran toward Concord, "in spite of all that could be done to prevent them," according to Captain Laurie, who would have been thoroughly justified in giving up any ambition for an army career.

The retreating light infantrymen were halfway from the bridge to the center of Concord when they encountered fat Lieutenant Colonel Smith, with a company of grenadiers, coming to their assistance. He was, as at Boston Common for the embarkation, at Cambridge for the march, at Lexington for the massacre, so late in getting there that irreparable damage to the expedition was already done. He marched his grenadiers back to Concord with the unhappy light infantry and then loitered about Concord for two hours, while minutemen from all over Middlesex county swarmed to Concord to harass his eventual retreat. He did nothing at all about the three companies, under Captain Parsons, who were still across the river at Barrett's farm. For all he knew or apparently cared, the provincials could have destroyed the bridge and isolated Parsons' companies deep in enemy territory, or they could simply be waiting in ambush to destroy Parsons' men as they returned from Barrett's to cross the bridge. The British dead were left at the bridge, and some of the wounded were also left behind to get back to the village as best they could. "When I got over," Amos Barrett wrote, "there were two dead, and another almost dead. There were eight or ten that were wounded and a running and a hobbling about, looking back to see if we were after them."[20]

The provincials were not after them or any other British at the time. After routing the British at the bridge, some of them re-crossed the bridge, picked up their dead and wounded, and went to a nearby farm. Others stayed on the town side of the river but instead of following the retreating British into town went up a hill and, deploying themselves behind a stone wall, kept watch over the road. The bridge, about which all the fighting had occurred, was almost deserted. A wounded British soldier tried to crawl out of the roadway to the grass beside it, when a country boy came along and, with a hatchet, split the fallen man's head open. "The poor object lived an hour or two before he expired," William Emerson wrote a fellow cleric.[21] When Parsons with his three companies, unmolested by the victorious provincials and aban-doned by the British commander, came back over the bridge, they were startled by the sight of the bloodily hacked head of the soldier. As soon as they got to the village, a rumor started spreading all through the British forces that the provincials were scalping their captives—a rumor that was to have a heavy bearing on the long and slaughterous afternoon that still stretched out ahead.

iii

After successfully forcing the bridge, after sending three companies of British light infantry and one of grenadiers in full retreat, and after isolating three other companies on the far side of the river, the provincials did nothing to press their advantage. Their purpose in forcing the bridge, of course, was to get to the town and prevent its burning. But by now the smoke had died down and been revealed for what it was, the burning of some of the confiscated stores. Thoughts of the other ten grenadier companies still in the village may have restrained the provincials from pressing the retreat of the light infantry farther. Fear of reprisal may have stopped them from destroying the isolated companies of Parsons while the main force was still in town. Whatever their reasoning, the provincials did nothing, except to find a meal somewhere, during the two-hour interval between the end of the fight at the bridge and the British departure from Concord. Captain Parsons, unaware of the fight at the bridge and innocent of his perilous situation from the beginning, had stopped his companies at a tavern for drinks. As he returned leisurely over the bridge, he was astonished to see some planks loose and even more astonished to see the dead soldiers.

Lieutenant Colonel Smith seemed unable to make up his mind what to do and formed his troops into line, dismissed them, reformed them, marched them a few yards in one direction and then in another. Possibly he wanted to remind the provincials that his forces were still there, still a threat, while he hoped that the reinforcements that he had asked from Gage, some ten hours earlier, would get to him before he had to begin the hazardous seventeen-mile march back to Boston in what was obviously now a thoroughly aroused and belligerent countryside. Characteristically, however, he simply delayed while the steady arrival of more minutemen from remoter towns made his eventual march more and more dangerous.

Colonel Barrett of the provincials, meanwhile, no longer had a unified command. With the independence and casual attitudes that were to characterize the colonial militia even later during Washington's leadership, the minutemen all made their own decisions about what to do next, and they wandered off in all directions—not by any means abandoning the day's fighting but obviously intending to resume as occasion arose later. There is no question that their company commanders would have responded to any call for a consultation by Barrett, but there was none. They simply kept watchful eyes on the British from a distance and determined that they would see that there was no further destruction of life and property in Concord. In the meantime, as they waited for the British to move, time was on their side: their numbers would inevitably be increased, and they could have the advantage of a running fight.

6

THE BATTLE: RETREAT

"The country was an amazing strong one, full of hills, woods, stone walls. . . ."

LT. JOHN BARKER, KING'S OWN REGIMENT[1]

At noon on April nineteenth Captain John Parker was marching his company of minutemen down the Concord road. Jonathan Harrington (whose namesake and cousin had crawled dying that morning to his own doorstep) played "The White Cockade" on his fife, and William Diamond beat his drum. Old Jedediah Munroe, who had been wounded in the morning, marched along with the rest, carrying his musket and the sword of his Scotch forebears. They were going to meet the British. Although their form, if not their appearance, was that of a military unit, they marched and were to fight as individual men. Blood had been spilled on Lexington Common, and a third of their relatives, friends, and neighbors in the company were dead or wounded. Over one per cent of their little population were killed, shot down by hysterical, undisciplined soldiers. One of every twenty-three of the adult males was dead and of the heads of families one out of every twelve. And the survivors now marched, not only out of the Englishman's native and stubborn devotion to his rights, but with a mental image, not six hours old, of the charging, shouting light infantry, the acid puffs of gun smoke floating above, and the sprawled bodies scattered below.

By noon, too, the news of Lexington Common had traveled scores of miles in an ever widening circle of Middlesex, Suffolk, and Norfolk counties. Hundreds of minutemen dropped their tools in the workshops, their pens in parsonage studies, their plows in the fields, their axes in the woods, and, lining up on their village greens, went tramping off with their awkward music in unfamiliar and imperfect cadence toward Lexington. Ten, twenty, and thirty miles they marched, from Sudbury and Framingham to the south, Billerica and Reading to the north, Stow on the west, Charlestown on the east, from Danvers, Dedham, Needham, Medford—eventually from over forty towns in all. Many of them, after mustering and marching from their villages, broke ranks and went as the crow flies, across fields, through woods, over hill trails.[2] Half the time they ran, the Danvers company going sixteen miles in four hours. Before the day's fighting was over, some thirty-six hundred men, in companies of ten to forty, had poured into the area in a fifteen-mile-long strip from Concord to Lexington to Cambridge and had taken up positions on hills, behind walls and trees, in roadside houses and barns, waiting for the British.

Back in Concord, at noon, Colonel Smith's forces took some of their wounded to local physicians for treatment. The expedition had not been thought sufficiently hazardous to justify sending an army surgeon along. Several of the wounded were taken to Dr. Timothy Minot's in the center of the town, where Smith and Pitcairn had already requisitioned chairs and set up an improvised staff headquarters on the lawn. Later, while Dr. Minot and Dr. John Cuming were treating the wounded, Smith, Pitcairn, and other officers gathered at Wright's Tavern for brandy and food. A servant from Dr. Minot brought to a wounded officer a watch inadvertently left at the doctor's.

Some of the more seriously wounded were taken to private houses and quartered in bedrooms. At the shop of Reuben Brown, the harness maker who had scouted for the Concord militia at Lexington at dawn that morning, a chaise was taken, and from John Beaton another was taken, to transport the wounded back to Boston. One of the British who had died on the half-mile retreat from the bridge, was buried summarily in the middle of the town. Some of their wounded, like the man at the bridge axed by the country boy, were left wandering or lying around and were listed as missing. Meanwhile, the Concord militia had disappeared; the smoke from the burning gun carriages and stores had gone; and Captain Parsons' three companies—for all practical purposes abandoned on the other side of the river—had returned unscathed. Smith, according to William Emerson, showed "great fickleness and inconstancy of mind" during the two hours after the fight at the Bridge, when he just wasted time in Concord.[3] He probably fretted about Gage's failure to send reinforcements or even to get a messenger to him. Finally, at noon, he gave the orders to march.

Smith and Pitcairn could not have relished the prospect of parading back through Lexington and hostile countryside to Boston. Smith had botched the whole assignment badly and beyond hope of recovery. Pitcairn, the major of marines, could have nothing left but contempt for the infantry, who had stampeded, failed to obey orders, and behaved equally badly at Lexington Common and at the North Bridge in Concord. Smith was so slow and ponderous that even his junior officers were openly criticizing him. As the companies formed for the returning march, three of the light infantry companies found that half of their officers were wounded. Nobody, of course, knew where the provincial militia was, or what it had in mind to do next, or even where it would appear again.

So the uninspired procession started to move out of Concord.

The ambulatory wounded walked in the middle of the columns, and those unable to walk rode on horses. Lieutenant Gould of the King's Own Regiment and Hull of the Forty-third Regiment, the most seriously wounded of the officers, went out ahead of the march in the commandeered chaises. There were no fifes and no drums. Their only purpose now was to get back to Boston, and they wanted to be as inconspicuous as possible. Taking the same route by which they had entered Concord some four hours earlier, the grenadiers marched in the road, the light infantry in flanking columns along the high ridge on their left and the edge of a great meadow on their right. They marched for ten or fifteen minutes, and there was no incident at all to mar their limping progress. The light infantry on the ridge encountered no militia. Then they came to Meriam's Corner, where the road to Lexington bore to the right and a road from Bedford came in from the left.

At this fork, facing the approaching British columns, the house of Nathan and Abigail Meriam had stood for a hundred and twelve years, surrounded by pleasant meadows. To the east was a smaller house and across the Bedford road a barn. At the corner there was a little brook, and the Lexington road narrowed to a bridge that crossed it. Before the brook, the ridge, on which the light infantry had moved to flank the more heavily equipped grenadiers, sloped down to road level, and all the British forces were merged again along the road.

Meriam's Corner, a mile from the center of Concord, was reachable not only by the Lexington road but through the Great Fields, which lay north of the ridge and extended a mile east of Concord. The provincial militia—some five hundred, consisting of those who had forced the bridge at Concord and later arrivals from other towns—had moved across the fields as the British were marching down the road. Also coming into Meriam's Corner, from the north along the Bedford road, was the Reading company of militia, headed by Dr. John Brooks. Behind them was the Billerica company. From over the meadows to the south of the

Lexington road came the companies from East Sudbury and Framingham. Dr. Brooks led his men to cover behind the Meriam houses and barns.

As the British tightened their columns to pass over the narrow bridge, marching silently, slowly, and evenly, the militia opened fire on them. Amos Barrett, the Concord minuteman who had enjoyed the music so much in the morning, wrote of his enemy, "They were waylaid and a great many killed. When I got there, a great many lay dead and the road was bloody."[4]

To the retreating British, tired from their night march, fired on from the rear and both flanks and unable to see most of their attackers, it seemed as if there were thousands of militia surrounding them. Ensign de Berniere said, "There could not be less than 5000."[5] At first the British stood and returned the fire. But as they tried to hurry past Meriam's Corner, the truth gradually dawned upon them: they were not running just a few rods of hot fire but had a fifteen-mile march ahead through incessant fire. As they got toward Lexington into Lincoln, the little town that had been carved out of Concord on its west and Lexington on its east thirty years earlier, the minutemen of Captain Parker joined the battle. The British were now beginning to panic, as they ran a continuing shower of musket balls, leaving dead and wounded where they fell.

The minutemen were swarming along the woods on both sides of the Lexington road—though not nearly to the number of de Berniere's five thousand. Yet it could easily have seemed, from the shrewdly improvised tactics of the militia, as even more than that. The minutemen fired from behind trees, stone walls, or barn doors, ducked away through the woods or fields, and then reappeared some yards down the road. As one company used up its ammunition and went home exhausted from running over the rough, brambly terrain, other companies from more distant places were just arriving.

To the British, who had no alternative to staying on the road because it at best permitted speed and because if they ever got split up in the wilderness of woods off the road they would all be lost, the whole thing was an unspeakable nightmare. They were used to fighting in the open, where they and the enemy could plainly see one another. They were used to fixed-position fighting and to volley formations. Now they were facing or rather enduring a shower of fire from unseen marksmen in shifting positions. Lieutenant Sutherland, wounded in the shoulder at the bridge in Concord and unable to use a musket, was fiercely bitter about this innovation in infantry warfare. He accused the minutemen flatly of "making the cowardly disposition . . . to murder us all," and he spoke also of "rascals" and "concealed villains."[6] In Sutherland's formalized warfare shooting an enemy from concealed positions was murder—not just killing. Although Lieutenant Barker of the King's Own was much too liberal with complaints about his own officers to have any left for the fighting techniques of the militia, the British feeling in general was that fighting from concealed positions was dirty and dishonorable. They saw no contradiciton in this attitude and their own conduct on Lexington Common earlier that morning, when, outnumbering the militia at least fourteen to one, they cut the provincials down in five minutes. In that case, the rules were respected. They were in the open, and each side could see the other plainly.

The assault of the militia on the British columns became more intense and aggressive as the action moved eastward through Lincoln into Lexington, where the men of Captain Parker's company, now fighting in their own way, sought vengeance for the morning. "We saw a wood at a distance," said the Reverend Edmund Foster, one of the Bedford minutemen, "which appeared to lie on or near the road the enemy must pass. Many [of the minutemen] leaped over the wall and made for that wood. We arrived just in time to meet the enemy. There was then, on the opposite side of the road, a young growth of wood well filled with Americans. The enemy was now completely between two fires, renewed and briskly kept up. They ordered out a flank guard on the left to dislodge the Americans from their posts behind large trees; but they only became a better mark to be shot at. . . . Eight or more of their number were killed on the spot."[7]

Having been shot in the leg, the heavy Lieutenant Colonel Smith was put on a horse but found himself such a conspicuous target that he slid off and limped along with the troops. Pitcairn, taking command, charged up to the front of the columns and tried to get the panicky troops in some kind of order. His horse, frightened, threw him to the ground. The horse ran off, the major's pistols still in its saddle holsters, across the fields to the enemy, who with customary frugality put the pistols to use as General Putnam's side arms throughout the war and sold the horse at auction. Officers, sergeants, and rank-and-file fell under the fire, some being helped along by their comrades, some just left where they fell. The others fired aimlessly, as if in protest. One British officer complained "most of it was thrown away for want of that coolness and steadiness which distinguishes troops who have been inured to service. The contempt in which they held the rebels, and perhaps their opinion that they would be sufficiently intimidated by a brisk fire, occasioned this improper conduct; which the officers did not prevent as they should have done."[8]

The minutemen were fighting, of course, with no discipline or organization whatsoever. One of the provincial participants wrote, "Each sought his own place and opportunity to attack and annoy the enemy from behind trees, rocks, fences, and buildings as seemed most convenient."[9] Some of the more experienced light infantrymen started attempts to flush out the minutemen lining the road. Since the effective range of a musket was no more than sixty to seventy yards, only a narrow strip along the road would have to have been cleared to keep the British safe. But the terrain was so varied and so full of perfect natural barriers behind which to hide, that the weary infantrymen had only isolated instances of success. When they came up behind Captain Wilson of the

Bedford company waiting in ambush behind a barn, they shot him in the back. And old Jedediah Munroe of Captain Parker's company, who probably did not bother to conceal himself, was killed, and so was another of Parker's men, John Raymond, who had missed the morning muster.

On the eastern slope of Fiske Hill on the western side of Lexington, James Hayward, of the Acton company, approached a house, from which a British soldier, looking for hidden marksmen, emerged to get a drink at the well. Looking up, the soldier saw the minuteman, lifted his gun, and said, "You're a dead man." Hayward replied, "So are you," and the two fired simultaneously. The soldier died on the spot and Hayward the next day.[10]

The sporadic British flanking operation, however, did not last long. The light infantry was running out of ammunition and was near exhaustion after having been in the field steadily for nearly fourteen hours. The unfamiliar warfare was beginning to break their spirit, and they stopped returning the militia fire. A horse in the British columns "that had a wounded man on his back and three hanging by his sides" was shot and fell with its burden in the roadway.[11] The minutemen, still increasing in numbers as new companies arrived, stepped up their fire. At last British morale collapsed completely, and the columns broke up into a running mob. "When we arrived within a mile of Lexington," de Berniere said, "our ammunition began to fail, and the light companies were so fatigued with flanking they were scarce able to act, and a great number of wounded scarce able to get forward made a great confusion . . . we began to run rather than retreat in order . . . we [the officers] attempted to stop the men and form them two deep, but to no purpose. The confusion increased rather than lessened . . . The officers got to the front and presented their bayonets, and told the men if they advanced, they should die. Upon this they began to form under a very heavy fire."[12] Thus, as they passed Lexington Common in the early afternoon, the expeditionary force of the British, bleeding, frightened, tired, reached the lowest ebb of an unfortunate day. "We must have laid down our arms or been picked off by the rebels at their pleasure," Lieutenant Barker concluded gloomily.[13]

The battered force turned the corner at Lexington Common and stumbled down the straight stretch of the road that had brought them within sight of Captain Parker's company early that same morning. It is doubtful that they could have gone another mile, and they faced the tragical irony of coming to their end in the shadow of the Reverend Jonas Clarke's meetinghouse on Lexington Common. Instead of which, a four-pound cannon ball crashed through the wall of the meetinghouse from a fieldpiece a thousand yards away. It was the first artillery fire of the day, and it came from a cannon perched on a height on the Boston side of Lexington Common by the Right Honorable Hugh, Earl Percy. "I had the happiness of saving them from inevitable destruction," His Grace wrote, of the rescue of Smith's stampeding force, to his father, the Duke of Northumberland.[14]

ii

It was almost twelve hours earlier, shortly after leaving Cambridge on his ill-fated march, that Smith, aware that the news of his expedition was all over Middlesex County and that his secret raid was no secret, had sent his courier to Gage for reinforcements. As it happened, Gage himself had already been jolted by Lord Percy's report of the conversations on Boston Common revealing that both the fact and destination of Smith's march were generally known. Accordingly, he had given orders for Percy's First Brigade to be under arms at four in the morning, and he was undoubtedly joined by Percy in the decision to send fieldpieces with it. The First Brigade, consisting of three regiments of infantry, a battalion of marines, and a detachment of Royal Artillery, was almost twice the strength in manpower of Smith's force. Gage, obviously sensitive to the pressures of local Tories and the complaining ministry in London, did not want the expedition to fail. Altogether, half of his entire army was now involved in it.

If Lord Percy's brigade had left at four in the morning, and even allowing for the long march out over Boston Neck, it would have been in Concord not later than ten o'clock, about the time of the battle at the North Bridge, instead of arriving in Lexington at two-thirty in the afternoon. But the brigade did not leave at four. It left at nine, five hours later, due to staff work at Gage's headquarters that matched in incompetence and incredible irresponsibility anything that had distinguished Lieutenant Colonel Smith's efforts in the field.

When he was awakened by Smith's courier at five, Gage must have been gratified by his own foresight in having ordered the First Brigade to be under arms at four. By then the men must have been awakened, dressed, and on the parade ground. The officers would have been rounded up from their lodgings scattered all over town. (The next day Gage was to order "the officers to lay in their men's barracks 'till further orders" and the troops "to lay dressed in their barracks this night."[15]) But at four o'clock, and at five, too, all the regiments of the First Brigade were sound asleep, the troops in their barracks, and the officers dispersed all over Boston. The parade ground was empty.

Gage's orders of the night before had been delivered to the brigade's major. Since the major was not at home, they were simply left at his lodgings by Gage's aide, who made no inquiry about the major's whereabouts and no report on his errand. When the major did get home, his servant neglected to tell him that there was a message for him. So the major, who had probably had a fairly intense social evening by that hour, went to sleep. Shortly after five o'clock, when Gage was awakened by Smith's urgent message, an inquiry revealed that there was no brigade ready or even alerted to march. Lieutenant Frederick Mackenzie, the adjutant of the Royal Welch Fusiliers, who was so disturbed at the delay at the embarkation the night before, was considerably more upset over the delays of the morning. His regiment, which was supposed to have been under arms at four o'clock, received its orders, dated at six o'clock, at seven o'clock, directing it to be on the parade ground, with a day's provisions, at seven-thirty. With Mackenzie's no-nonsense attitude toward his duties as adjutant, no time was wasted in his regiment once the orders were received: "We accordingly assembled the regiment with the utmost expedition, and with the 4th and 47th were on the parade at the hour appointed, with one day's provisions. By some mistake the Marines did not receive the order until the other regiments of the brigade were assembled, by which means it was half past 8 o'clock before the brigade was ready to march."[16]

The mistake with regard to the Marine battalion was even less excusable than the one with regard to the entire brigade the night before. When the whole brigade, except the Marines, were on the parade ground, an inquiry was sent to their barracks, where it was asserted, in what appears to have been strong language, that they never heard of the orders. Gage's staff and the brigade's insisted that they had. "In the altercation it came out that the order had been addressed to Major Pitcairn, who commanded the marines, and left at his headquarters, though the gentlemen concerned ought to have recollected that Pitcairn had been dispatched the evening before with the grenadiers and light infantry under Lieut. Col. Smith. This double mistake lost us from four till nine o'clock, the time we marched off to support Col. Smith."[17]

Later it must have been a bitter reflection to the cumbersome colonel that the one thing that he himself did not bungle on his expedition—sending for help early enough—was bungled for him by someone else, and that the orders responding to his call for reinforcements were addressed in Boston to his own second in command, whom he had sent six hours earlier ahead of his main force on the way to Concord.

At nine o'clock the First Brigade marched out of Boston and set out the long way William Dawes had taken, over the Neck, to

Concord. From Cambridge they followed the same route that Smith had to Lexington. (The boats were still anchored on the Cambridge side of the Charles, waiting for Smith's forces when they returned.) It was broad daylight, of course, and they marched all through the morning, through the noon hour, and into the early afternoon. But in odd contrast to the strangely floating population of dashing riders of the midnight and early morning hours that Smith's force had encountered, Percy's brigade found the whole countryside deserted. "In all the places we marched through, and in the houses on the road, few or no people were to be seen; and the houses were in general shut up."[18]

Although it later had nothing but grievous troubles, the first Brigade had, at least, a good night's sleep due to its almost farcically delayed orders and set out jauntily enough, the fifers and drummers of the thirty-two companies derisively playing "Yankee Doodle," as in the bright, clear sunlight of early spring they marched through country roads and village streets to the relief of their brothers. Not until they came to the Great Bridge over the Charles, just south of Harvard College, did they encounter trouble, which, due to another episode of military inadequacy—this time on the provincial side—did not impede them much. Nevertheless, it put Lord Percy on the alert that there was organized resistance to his march. Percy, the best mind by far among the British in Boston, knew very well that organized resistance meant that war had commenced. And he commanded his brigade as if war now prevailed. He had to stop his uneventful march at the Great Bridge over the Charles, because the provincials had stripped the bridge of its planks and only the stringers stretched across the river. This was a superb move on the part of the provincials. It could have so delayed Percy's brigade that Smith's force would have been annihilated. However, having removed the planks, the provincials carefully piled them up on the Cambridge end of the bridge. Percy sent some men over on the stringers, and they replaced enough planks for the brigade with their cannon to move across without too much delay. The supply wagons with their personnel he left behind to finish the job.

Percy then proceeded to Harvard Square, where, the college being in spring recess and those students and tutors who had stayed in Cambridge having gone to Concord with arms from the college armory, there was nothing but an ominous quiet.

The brigade's advanced guards had narrowly averted another fiasco when they had the imprudence to ask some students in Harvard Square the way to Lexington and were misdirected. A tutor, Isaac Smith of the class of 1767, said "he could not tell a lie" and sent them on the right road—subsequent to which display of virtue he found it desirable to leave Cambridge to live in England until 1786.[19] The brigade met no one else in Cambridge.

And so it was all the way to Menotomy, Lord Percy complaining, "As all the houses were shut up and there was not the appearance of a single inhabitant, I could get no intelligence concerning them till I had passed Menotomy."[20] There, in the next town east of Lexington, his day's business with the provincials first began in one way or another.

In Menotomy, Percy got the first direct news of what had happened to Smith's forces. The place still suspiciously empty of provincials, he encountered a chaise coming toward him. It contained Lieutenant Edward Gould of the King's Own, who had been badly wounded in the foot at the North Bridge in Concord. Gould told Percy that Smith's force had been and was still under heavy attack and was running out of ammunition, that what was left of it was on the way back to Boston, probably not far behind him and the wounded Lieutenant Hull, who was with him. Percy quickened his march, now about to cross the town line into Lexington.

As soon as Percy's brigade left Menotomy, provincials started to appear—not the minutemen who were already harassing the retreat of Smith on the other side of Lexington, but the "exempts," the old men and others ineligible for the minute companies. First they captured Lieutenant Gould and Hull and sent them off to Medford for safekeeping. Then they intercepted Lord Percy's supply wagons. At first the grenadiers guarding them refused to take the orders of a dozen old men seriously. But the old men meant business and let loose a barrage that killed the driver and four "fine British horses," from which the good, thrifty people of Menotomy later removed the shoes.[21] At this display the six husky, armed grenadiers, true to the general values of the day, promptly surrendered to the dozen old men, and Percy never did get his supplies, for the old men took the second wagon, too. And in Menotomy, too, Percy heard for the first time the sharp report of the guns at Lexington—probably all provincial by then—and he marched his brigade down toward the Common.

But they stopped short of it, within sight of the meetinghouse, at the beginning of the long straight stretch, where Pitcairn had stopped just ten hours earlier to prime and load to meet John Parker's company. Percy sized up the situation immediately, with regard both to the plight of Smith and to the likely moves of the provincials; and this gentleman soldier, moving with poise, alertness, and assurance, took over command of all His Majesty's forces on the scene and exhibited a skill in military leadership which the day had not yet seen.

iii

Earl Percy and his First Brigade made their first contact with Smith's exhausted forces at two-thirty, when both detachments, Percy's from the southeast and Smith's from the northwest, came within sight of opposite ends of the Common at Lexington. Percy wisely chose to stop his forces a half mile south of the Common, near Sergeant William Munroe's tavern, which he made his headquarters. The site was excellent for a defensive delaying action and for regrouping. This point on the road offered an unobstructed view, and it was flanked by two hills, of which Percy took immediate possession, placing one of his fieldpieces on each. The hill on the right, about a quarter of a mile in advance of that on the left, put the cannon within easy range of the Common. The one on the left, rising abruptly behind Munroe's Tavern, commanded any approach from the Concord road over the fields to the west.

Lieutenant Mackenzie of the Royal Welch Fusiliers left an exact account of the tactical situation on the Brigade's arrival: "As we pursued our march, about two o'clock we heard some straggling shots fired about a mile in our front: as we advanced we heard the firing plainer and more frequent, and at half after two, being near the church at Lexington, and the fire increasing, we were ordered to form the line, which was immediately done by extending on each side of the road, but by reason of the stone walls and other obstructions, it was not formed in so regular a manner as it should have been. The grenadiers and light infantry were at this time retiring toward Lexington, fired upon by the rebels, who took every advantage the face of the country afforded them. As soon as the grenadiers and light infantry perceived the first brigade drawn up for their support, they shouted repeatedly, and the firing ceased for a short time.

"The ground we first formed upon was something elevated, and commanded a view of that before us for about a mile, where it was terminated by some pretty high grounds covered with wood. The village of Lexington lay between both parties. We could observe a considerable number of the rebels, but they were much scattered, and not above fifty of them to be seen in a body in any place. Many lay concealed behind the stone walls and fences. They appeared most numerous in the road near the church, and in a wood in the front and on the left flank of the line where our regiment was posted. A few cannon shot were fired at those on and near the road, which dispersed them. The flank companies now retired and formed behind the brigade, which was soon fired upon by the rebels most advanced. A brisk fire was returned, but without much effect. As there was a piece of open morassy ground in front of the left of our regiment, it would have been difficult to have passed it under the fire of the rebels from behind the trees and walls on the other side. Indeed, no part of the brigade was ordered to advance; we therefore drew up near the morass, in expectation of orders how to act, sending an officer for one of the six pounders. During this time the rebels endeavored to gain our flanks, and crept into the covered ground on either side, and as close as they could in front, firing now and then in perfect security. We also advanced a few of our best marksmen who fired at those who shewed themselves."[22]

None of these scattered fringe shootings came to much, for Percy had already concluded that his job was only to get Smith's crippled force back to Boston and his own brigade with them. He had no intention of going beyond his orders and chasing the minutemen out of Lexington. Using his fieldpieces, he simply kept them as far away as possible, while the light infantry and grenadiers that had been to Concord sprawled exhausted on the fields around Munroe's Tavern, recovering their wind and strength, in the midst of what Percy staked out as a protected zone—a great square with his soldiers forming lines to make the boundaries, across the Lexington-Boston road and up the hills on either side, down lines parallel to the road and then another line connecting them, again crossing the road.

Within the square there was, in addition to William Munroe's tavern, a settlement of seven or eight houses, most of them close to a century old. Among them was the house of the Widow Mulliken, where Dr. Prescott had spent the evening before, courting Lydia. Nathaniel Mulliken had been Lexington's first clockmaker, and his small shop still stood near the house. Mrs. Mulliken's seven children ranged from her oldest son, Nathaniel, twenty-three, who had been on the common in the morning and fought again in the afternoon, down to a ten-year-old. Like most of the households along the main roads through Lexington from Concord to Boston, the Mulliken house was evacuated of women and children. And all morning while the British were occupied at Concord, the women had buried their silverware and other valuables all around the countryside and then repaired to the remoter farmhouses until the British had left for good. Near the Mulliken house were two others: the house and shop of Joshua Bond, the saddle and harness maker, and the considerably more pretentious establishment of Deacon Joseph Loring and his family of eight.

All three of these houses were burned to the ground by the British, without doubt at the order of Percy, who had Smith's account of the provincials' invincible firing from the protection of roadside houses and who did not want his own rear guard molested as he moved out. Munroe's Tavern he used as a hospital for treating the wounded, and there he outlined to his officers the plan of retreat. He allowed the men of Smith's detachment a half hour's rest, ordered an occasional firing of the cannon to keep the provincials at bay (the cannon killed no one but seemed to have a considerable psychological effect as the militia saw the ball hit the meetinghouse, go in the front wall, and emerge from the back wall over the pulpit), and started reforming his men, now numbering about eighteen hundred, a third of whom were too battle-worn even to take care of themselves. These he put at the head of his column, the most protected place in the line as he learned from Smith's account of the flanking and rear-guard warfare of the provincials. Behind the Smith detachment he placed the Fourth and Forty-seventh Infantry Regiments, then the Marines Battalion and, finally, the Royal Welch Fusiliers Regiment as rear guard. He directed each of them to serve as rear guard in succession after every seven miles. He put flanking parties far out to the sides to uncover snipers behind stone walls, trees, and buildings. At three forty-five, an hour or so after he arrived, he was ready to march.

Percy in no way underestimated the rough path that lay ahead of him and knew also that General Gage would not, in order to send him help, dare to weaken the one and a half brigades left to hold Boston. His confidence, assurance, and command of the situation, nevertheless, had an immensely restorative effect upon both the officers, who had committed one mistake after another all day, and the men, who had as often as not paid no attention to them. Colonel Smith, with his massive weight now imposing upon an injured leg, was swallowed up in the anonymity of a protected position within the columns where he could do no harm.

iv

While all this reorganization and restoration of the British was going on within sight of the Common, the minutemen from a score of towns kept a respectable distance, and most of them also rested. They also had some military reorganization visited upon them in the person of Major General William Heath, the first general officer to take command of an American army in the field. Appointed a general by the Second Provincial Congress in February, General Heath was a thirty-eight-year-old Roxbury farmer who developed a passionate interest in military theory as he grew up and spent all his spare time reading military treatises. In his *Memoirs,* published after the war in the initial phase of a journalistic tradition now common among American generals, Heath described himself candidly as "of middling stature, light complexion, very corpulent and bald-headed." He had been a captain of Boston's Ancient and Honourable Artillery Company and Colonel of the First Regiment of the Suffolk Militia under Governor Sir Francis Bernard. After the provincials organized their own militia, he was chosen captain of the first Roxbury company. With four others he was appointed General Officer of the militia that was under the direction of the Committee of Safety, the directorate which functioned as commander in chief. On April 19th, Heath was the only one of the five general officers on the scene all day. He had spent the day before at the session of the Committee in Menotomy and had met some of the British advance officers, who had been sent out ahead of the Smith expedition, on the Lexington-Boston road. Apparently Heath paid no particular attention to them. Although he saw that they were armed and therefore not out on pleasure rides, he made no inquiries in spite of the fact that the whole countryside was astir with riders in all directions. General Heath went home and to bed. In his *Memoirs,* in which he refers to himself as "our General," he detailed his movements on the morning of the nineteenth:

"On the 19th, at daybreak, our General was awoke, called from his bed, and informed that a detachment of the British army were out. . . . Our General, in the morning, proceeded to the Committee of Safety."[23] This was a proper and necessary thing for our general to do, because he was commissioned by the Committee and was authorized to act only under its direct orders. The Committee, routed from its beds and forced to hide in the cornfield the night before, was still sitting in Menotomy. "From the Committee," General Heath continued in his *Memoirs,* "he took a cross-road to Watertown, the British being in possession of the Lexington road. At Watertown, finding some militia who had not marched, but applied for orders, he sent them down to Cambridge, with directions to take up the planks, barricade the south end of the bridge, and there to take post; that, in case the British should, on their return, take that road to Boston, their retreat must be impeded." This, of course, must have been after Percy's brigade had crossed the bridge in the morning, for there was neither a barricade nor a guard there when his men put back the planks removed earlier at the order of the Cambridge selectmen. Heath "then pushed to join the militia, taking a cross road towards Lexington, in which he was joined by Dr. Joseph Warren (afterwards a Major-General) who kept with him. Our General joined the militia just after Lord Percy had joined the British; and having assisted in forming a regiment, which had been broken by the shot from the British field-pieces (for the discharge of these, together with the flames and smoke of several buildings, to which the British nearly at the same time had set fire, opened a new and more terrific scene)."[24]

If General Heath intended to equate himself and his arrival on the provincial side with Lord Percy's on the British, he was certainly less successful "in forming a regiment." The minutemen and other militia were just not susceptible of regimentation. It is significant that General Heath, even though the ranking officer present and the only general officer, claimed to have done no more than to assist. Actually, the provincials' forces did with Heath present exactly what they unquestionably would have done without him. They waited until the British were on the move again and they could have another round of the running war to which they were temperamentally attuned and at which alone they had any chance of success. And if Heath or anyone else had formed them in regiments, they would quickly have dispersed into patrols and sniper groups anyhow.

Though the provincials were in no need of such a lifting of collapsed morale as the Smith expedition was, it had nevertheless been a day of tenseness, of tragedy to many families, of confusions, and, above all, of terrible commitment. Technically, they were all still British subjects and they were all of them guilty of high crimes in attacking the forces of their King. And there could be no turning back after the excitement of the chase died down. These farmers and craftsmen, clergymen and physicians, from little towns all over the area, had committed themselves to however long it would take to force by arms correction of the abuses to which they felt they had been subjected—or to lose even those rights of life and liberty that had not been violated. And even though not all of them might have thus perceived and defined their situation, they nevertheless knew what it was all about and that their actions that springtime Wednesday were not just the deeds of one day to be forgotten on the next. There were several long pauses in the day's fighting during which they thought and consulted with one another, listened as was their custom during crises to their

The battle at the North Bridge in Concord, by Earl and Doolittle, shows the British on the Concord side of the bridge, firing on the Colonial militia, whose approach from the hills on the left force the British companies back across the narrow bridge. Lieutenant Sutherland and one other man alone obeyed the company commander's order to the British troops to spread out in the field. Most of the British are just running back toward Concord. ALBANY INSTITUTE OF HISTORY AND ART

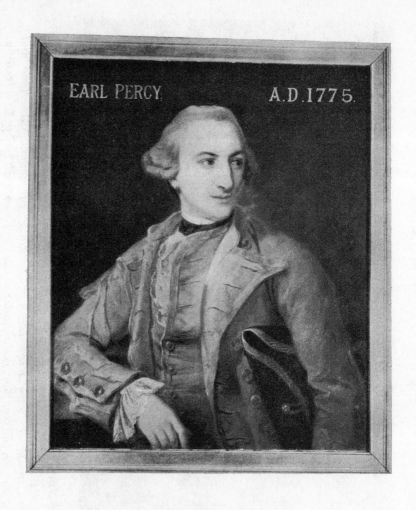

EARL PERCY.   A.D. 1775.

Hugh, Earl Percy (1742–1817), commanded the force that rescued the British expedition to Lexington and Concord. Later the second Duke of Northumberland, Percy was the only commanding officer of the day to distinguish himself. LEXING-TON HISTORICAL SOCIETY

Earl and Doolittle show Earl Percy's troops, left, who came to the rescue of Smith's force, right. In the clump of trees on the hill, right center, is a fieldpiece Percy aimed at Lexington Common to keep the minutemen away. In the background the houses of, left to right, Mrs. Nathaniel Mulliken, Joshua Bond, and Deacon Joseph Loring, probably suspected of harboring snipers, are burned by Percy's men. In the foreground are provincial militia taking ineffective shots with muskets that were seldom reliable at even a hundred yards. ALBANY INSTITUTE OF HISTORY AND ART

Dr. Joseph Warren (1741–75), a Boston physician, was probably the most versatile of the Massachusetts patriots and easily the most charming in manners. He died two months after Lexington in the battle of Bunker's Hill. MUSEUM OF FINE ARTS, BOSTON.

ministers—the learned men and the political philosophers of their times and communities—and had all the sober second thoughts that could have sent them home to their farms and shops.

It should also be remembered that the Provincial Congress, the guiding force behind all this day's fighting, although its creation was a masterful expression of the political genius of Samuel Adams and its proceedings a reflection of his skilled timing, derived whatever inherent strength and purpose it had from scores of town meetings, who debated the issues, elected their delegates, and sat down from time to time in long sessions to write them instructions. So it is not at all unlikely that during the break in the battle at Lexington in the midafternoon, the minds of these men were already turning to the implications of the day, not so much in their effects upon history, as in their bearing upon day-to-day life the next week, the next month, and the next year. There were no shouts of victory in Lexington as the thoroughly shattered corps of Colonel Smith was pursued through town to the shelter of Percy's brigade. And if there was no morale problem among the provincials, there may well have been a deeper need.

If so, it must have been met in great measure by the arrival of Dr. Joseph Warren. Adams and Hancock had disappeared before the firing on Lexington Common and were now safe in a parsonage out of town. But Dr. Warren, certainly sufficiently known to them as the boldest of all the patriot leaders, had come there to join them. Young at thirty-four, thoroughly convinced of British persecution of the colony, a gifted orator, Dr. Warren had virtually given up a large practice to devote himself to public affairs. With none of Samuel Adams' wile, or John Adams' hardheaded objectivity or John Hancock's theatrical opportunism, he was the thoroughly trusted work horse of the very early days of the Revolution and courageous to a fault. As late as the sixth of March, the fifth anniversary of the Boston Massacre, little more than six weeks before Lexington, he had stood in the pulpit of the Old South Meetinghouse in Boston and, while forty uniformed British officers squirmed in the front pews, launched upon an eloquent speech, in which he assailed the evils of lodging a standing army amidst a free people and resurrected the massacre in powerfully emotional if somewhat apocryphal terms. On the morning of the nineteenth of April, some eight hours after Warren had dispatched Revere to Lexington, a messenger came to him with the news of the firing on Lexington Common. He summoned a young colleague, Dr. William Eustis, and, turning his Boston office over to him, left for the Charlestown ferry and Lexington. On the way Warren tried to pass Lord Percy's column on the Cambridge road to Lexington but was stopped, and so he rode along behind them as far as the Black Horse Tavern in Menotomy, where he joined the Committee of Public Safety and General Heath, with whom he rode to Lexington.

While Heath "assisted in forming a regiment," Warren undoubtedly gave guiding counsel on the decision to pursue the British all the way back to Boston. A party to the proceedings of the Provincial Congress that called for the colonists to attack only to defend themselves, Warren was astute enough to realize that the episode in the early morning on Lexington Common was all that was needed to show Massachusetts innocent of any first spilling of blood and to unite the other colonies in action against the oppressors. To the conglomeration of militia that now poured into the northwest part of Lexington, while Percy was reordering his troops in the southeast sector, Dr. Warren was the Committee of Safety and therefore the only commander in chief they knew. Heath was his general officer and, as such, would naturally have carried out Warren's orders. In any case, at some time during that midafternoon hour of rest and reorganization that the British took under the shelter of Percy's cannon, the decision was made to pursue them to Boston, and Dr. Warren was the only official in town to make it.

But neither Warren nor Heath evidently gave much further attention to the military aspects of the pursuit. With Percy's men immobilized, there was plenty of time to have sent advanced units to throw obstacles in the path of his retreat or to organize and carry out a major flanking movement. But nothing of this nature was decided or done—not even a solution ventured to the most pressing problem of the militia, the shortage of powder and bullets. If there was any ammunition left in the Lexington meetinghouse, it was inaccessible, because, as Percy had established with one shot, the meetinghouse was well within range of the cannon he had perched on the hills down the road where his troops rested. It is not at all unlikely that the provincials, therefore, were spending their time on the discussion of less military and more general propositions than the distribution of powder. When the fighting did resume, there was no evidence of Heath's "regiment" or of planned strategy. Nor did Heath indicate in his *Memoirs* that he had any. The militia just broke up into small parties or individuals again, chased the British until their ammunition gave out or they got too tired or too far away from home, and then let the fighting be taken over by others nearer Boston, who were just arriving along the British retreat route.

v

After listening to Smith and Pitcairn, Percy made an assumption, and it was correct. There would be no pitched battle, with the provincials lining up in a roadway or square in a frontal attempt to halt the British. They would fight as they had on the retreat from Concord, from concealed positions along the flanks and from the rear. He issued orders accordingly. If snipers were caught in houses, kill them. If necessary, burn down the house. In case of heavy attack, disperse the provincials by using the cannon. And always keep moving toward Boston.

At quarter of four Percy gave the order, and his procession of eighteen hundred soldiers started the long and perilous road back. As soon as they moved, somewhere behind them at least an equal number of country militia scattered across the fields, through the woods, behind houses, to meet them. "Before the column had advanced a mile on the road," Lieutenant Mackenzie said in his diary, "we were fired at from all quarters, but particularly from the houses on the roadside and the adjacent stone walls, and the soldiers were so enraged at suffering from an unseen enemy that they forced open many of the houses from which the fire proceeded and put to death all those found in them. Those houses would certainly have been burnt had any fire been found in them, or had there been time to kindle any; but only three or four near where we first formed suffered in this way. As the troops drew nearer to Cambridge, the number and fire of the rebels increased, and although they did not show themselves openly in a body in any part, except on the road in our rear, our men threw away their fire very inconsiderately and without being certain of its effect: this emboldened them [the provincials] and induced them to draw nearer, but whenever a cannon shot was fired at any considerable number, they instantly dispersed."[25]

The most efficient fighting of the British was done by the flanking parties, who proceeded along the inside boundaries of the stone walls and raided, as they went, the houses from which shots came or were suspected to be coming. Whenever they tired, or the roughness of the terrain forced them to pull in toward their own marching columns, the militia came in closer, with deadlier fire. As the column moved across the flat plain of Menotomy, however, the troops in the main line of march could fire, and the exchange of shots got brisker. As the militia from the larger peripheral towns around Boston now took up the battle, Percy had to set up his fieldpieces again, and gained a little respite as the militia scattered before the cannon fire. Without stopping, he was able to get his flankers reorganized and, fanning out again, the flanking troops got some of the provincials between the British main column and the flankers. Here at Menotomy the British flanking tactics were at their most effective and the provincial militia probably at their most careless.

A party of seven minutemen from the Danvers company got in advance of the British march and, barricading themselves behind walls, trees, and piles of shingles, waited to open fire on the column as it marched by on their right. But British flankers, coming up behind them on their left, made a wide sweep and killed all seven from the rear. A musket ball from other flankers knocked a pin out of Dr. Warren's hair. Another medical man, Dr. Eliphalet Downer, got into a bayonet duel with a British soldier, after both had missed their shots, and finally killed him by knocking him out with the butt and then stabbing him with the bayonet. Three Cambridge men were killed in one spot by flankers who came upon them, and another group of four or five were killed in a hot exchange with flankers. But the shots of the unseen militia still peppered the now-tiring column of Lord Percy. His flankers, with increased desperation, probed the houses along the way to flush out the snipers.

At the fork in the Lexington Road, where the left branch turns to Medford on the east and the right continues southeasterly to Cambridge, was the tavern of Benjamin Cooper. Nearby, along the Menotomy River, was the prosperous farm of Samuel Whittemore, seventy-eight, father of nine children, including one daughter who gave him thirty-six grandchildren before she died at forty-eight. In his youth Whittemore had been a captain of dragoons in the service of George III's grandfather. Now, in his seventy-ninth year as he heard the Percy troops marching along the road, he grabbed his old musket, a brace of pistols, and the sword of his captain days and went forth alone to do battle with a brigade. He took shelter in an advantageous position by Cooper's Tavern. Within the tavern sat two known topers of Menotomy, Jason Winship and Jabez Wyman, who, at forty-three and thirty-nine, were over three decades Whittemore's juniors. With them in the bar were the innkeeper Cooper and his wife Rachel, both of whom fled to the cellar as the British approached. But the convivial brothers-in-law, Winship and Wyman, refused to budge: "They were drinking flip. Wyman was warned of the danger but says he, 'Let us finish the mug, they won't come yet.' "²⁶ Outside the tavern, from behind his stone wall barricade, the well-armed Whittemore, meanwhile, aimed his musket and killed a British soldier; he then took one of his pistols and killed another. By then, of course, the British had discovered his position, and several soldiers converged upon him. A part of his cheekbone was shattered by a musket ball, and a couple of flankers charged and beat him with the mercilessness that they bore to all hidden snipers. Satisfied that they had "killed the old rebel"²⁷ (Samuel Whittemore survived and died eighteen years later at ninety-six), they turned their attention to the tavern, a famous Whig resort and a likely place for more snipers. Inside they found Winship and Wyman at their drinks and left them dead, for under the heavy fire that was raining on the British they took no time to interrogate able-bodied men along the line of their retreat. If they looked as if they could have fired, they were killed.

Such a fate also overcame a Cambridge man of limited mental development, William Marcy, who had been "warned out of town" by the selectman in 1770 as "a man of very poor circumstances" but who stayed as a hired man of Dr. William Kneeland.²⁸ Marcy was accustomed to watching the British on their occasional exercise parades out of Boston. He thought that the retreat was merely another practice march. To improve his view he perched on a fence and noted to his delight that the exercise had the added attraction of sham firing. A bullet killed him.

Nearby, John Hicks, an avid patriot and attendant at the Boston Tea Party, was shot through the heart as he blasted at the British, and so was Moses Richardson, who was also an active combatant. Not far away Jason Russell had barricaded himself behind his gate with bundles of shingles, "from which to fire on the enemy."²⁹ When a patrol of Essex militia sought refuge in

his house from some flankers who had found them, Russell left
his barricaded gate and joined them, ready to fire from the house.
But the flankers caught up, and Russell fell in his doorway. Later
in the afternoon, Hicks, Marcy, and Richardson, and Russell,
Wyman, and Winship were buried in common graves and, in due
time, memorialized on a granite shaft for falling "in defence of
the Liberty of the People"—the poor idiot, Marcy, and the
drunken lingerers, Winship and Wyman, were immortalized along
with their less serene contemporaries.

Behind all these episodes in Menotomy and Cambridge was an
increasingly desperate British brigade in full, and now once again
thoroughly wearying, retreat and a provincial militia that seemed
to be more numerous and less visible as the day wore on. In a
determined attempt to stop the concealed firing, the British
flankers inspected every house along the road. When they came
to the house of Deacon Joseph Adams, who "knew that his life
would be in danger, both on account of his name and also for his
reputation for patriotic zeal,"[30] which however did not include
shouldering a musket, they found only the deacon's wife with her
eighteen-day-old infant and three other children. The deacon
himself had run across the fields to hide in the hayloft of the
Reverend Samuel Cooke's barn. His nine-year-old son, Joel, took
over the management of the household and saw his mother and the
baby leave safely. He struck up a conversation with the soldiers,
warned them against stealing the church silver, and used his
father's ale to extinguish a small fire that they set on leaving.[31]

Meanwhile the British limped frantically on toward Boston.
Lieutenant Mackenzie noted that the all-important flanking
parties were getting less and less efficient, eventually causing more
harm than good as they became mere plunderers.

"During the whole of the march from Lexington the rebels kept
an incessant irregular fire from all points at the column, which
was the more galling as our flanking parties, which at first were
placed at sufficient distances to cover the march of it, were at last,

from the different obstructions they occasionally met with, obliged to keep almost close to it. Our men had very few opportunities of getting good shots at the rebels, as they hardly ever fired but under cover of a stone wall, from behind a tree, or out of a house; and the moment they had fired they lay down out of sight until they had loaded again, or the column had passed. In the road indeed in our rear, they were most numerous, and came on pretty close, frequently calling out, 'King Hancock forever.' Many of them were killed in the houses on the road side from whence they fired; in some of them seven or eight men were destroyed. Some houses were forced open in which no person could be discovered, but when the column had passed, numbers sallied out from some place in which they had lain concealed, fired at the rear guard, and augmented the numbers which followed us. If we had had time to set fire to those houses many rebels must have perished in them, but as night drew on Lord Percy thought it best to continue the march. Many houses were plundered by the soldiers, notwithstanding the efforts of the officers to prevent it. I have no doubt this inflamed the rebels, and made many of them follow us farther than they would otherwise have done. By all accounts some soldiers who staid too long in the houses, were killed in the very act of plundering by those who lay concealed in them. We brought in about ten prisoners, some of whom were taken in arms. One or two more were killed on the march while prisoners by the fire of their own people."[32]

Battered as his forces were, Lord Percy won the only tactical duel on a command level that day. General Heath had ordered the taking up of the planks of the Great Bridge across the Charles, over which Percy's brigade had marched that morning, and the use of them to barricade the bridge on the south or Brighton side of the river. The Charles at that point was not fordable; and if Percy had attempted to return to Boston by the same route that he left, his brigade would have been driven into the river or annihilated by the militia. However, if he turned off the Cambridge road, to the east, north of Harvard, he could get to Charlestown, directly across from the rest of Gage's army in Boston and within the protection of the guns of the man-of-war *Somerset* in the river basin. Heath anticipated this, and for the first time that day Percy saw some of the militia in the open in a group. They stood bravely across the Charlestown road, ready to force the British to take the road to the Great Bridge. Percy stopped and ordered the cannon to the fore and fired a shot. The militia scattered immediately to their hidden positions. Percy resumed his march, and the militia "came down to attack our right flank in the same straggling manner the rest had done before. . . ."[33]

It was dark when at last Percy got his unhappy brigade on the hills of Charlestown at eight in the evening. He had taken four hours to march his hobbling, frustrated army the twelve miles from Lexington. His ammunition was almost entirely spent. He had left behind the dead and many of his wounded. Some of his soldiers, lingering too long as they pilfered the raided houses, were taken prisoner by the provincials. A few appeared to have been voluntary captives. Just before Percy's columns marched over the thin neck of land between the Charles and Mystic rivers leading to Charlestown, they were saved from the last and perhaps most hazardous threat of the day by the miscalculation of the only militia officer who took an unexcited view of the day's affairs.

Colonel Timothy Pickering, commanding the three hundred men in the militia of Salem, fifteen miles north of Boston, was brought the news of the firing at Lexington between eight and nine in the morning: Pickering reasoned that if the British troops had fired at six, then they would be almost back in Boston by nine and that since Salem was farther from Boston than Lexington was, there was no point in marching his company. With the minutemen from other Essex county towns on the march, the Salem citizens started exerting pressure on Pickering, and he finally suggested a meeting of the selectmen to discuss the situation. Finally, "to satisfy our fellow citizens," Pickering ordered his company to march.[84] He still thought it a futile business, however, and stopped the march a few miles out of town, expecting a messenger to come along to say that the British were already back in Boston. None came, and the minutemen of his company began to urge him on. At last he yielded and started his march in earnest, getting to Charlestown in time to see Percy's brigade—just out of his reach—get to the protection of Bunker's Hill, where any provincial attempt to dislodge him would have to survive the sixty-four guns of the man-of-war *Somerset*.

Of the effect of Timothy Pickering's procrastination on Percy's retreat, Washington wrote, May 31, 1775, "If the retreat had not been as precipitate as it was,—and God knows it could not well have been more so,—the ministerial troops must have surrendered or been totally cut off. For they had not arrived in Charlestown (under cover of their ships) half an hour before a powerful body of men from Marblehead and Salem was at their heels and must, if they happened to be one hour sooner, inevitably intercepted their retreat to Charlestown."[85]

"As soon as the British gained Bunker's Hill, they immediately formed in a line opposite to the neck," wrote General Heath; "when our General [i.e., Heath] judged it expedient to order the militia, who were now at the Common, to halt and give over the pursuit, as any further attempt upon the enemy in that position would have been futile."[86] Lieut. Barker, who had been with the British expedition since the embarkation the night before, saw it differently: "The rebels did not choose to follow us to the hill, as they must have fought us on open ground and that they did not like."[87]

When the last shot was fired, the British had suffered 273 casualties (73 killed, 174 wounded, and 26 missing), a rate of very nearly twenty per cent. The provincials, including militia and such accidental presences as the drunks at Menotomy and the feeble-minded Marcy, had 93 casualties (49 killed, 39 wounded, and 5 missing)—a rate of about two and a half per cent of the total militia participating. In addition, the British had destroyed at Concord a wholly insignificant amount of gunpowder, arms, and ammunition, burned three houses at Lexington, and damaged a few others. Lieutenant Barker of the King's Own completed his indictment of the entire affair, with one last and solid grumble:

"Thus ended this Expedition, which from beginning to end was as ill planned and ill executed as it was possible to be; had we not idled away three hours on the Cambridge Marsh waiting for provisions that were not wanted, we should have had no interruption at Lexington, but by our stay the country people had got intelligence and time to assemble. [Barker was, of course, wrong in this: Parker had his men assembled three hours before the British arrived, dismissed them, and recalled them. But in general, Barker was right about the price that the British paid for Colonel Smith's constant slowness.] We should have reached Concord soon after daybreak, before they could have heard of us, by which we should have destroyed more cannon and stores, which they had had time enough to convey away before our arrival; we might also have got easier back and not been so much harassed, as they would not have had time to assemble so many people . . . Thus, for a few trifling stores the Grenadiers and Light Infantry had a march of about fifty miles (going and returning) through an enemy's country, and in all human probability must every man have been cut off if the brigade had not fortunately come to their assistance."[88]

Lord Percy ended the day full of admiration for the provincial militia and permitted himself a prophecy: "Whoever looks upon them as an irregular mob, will find himself much mistaken; they have men amongst them who know very well what they are about, having been employed as rangers against the Indians and Canadians, and this country being much covered with wood and hilly, is very advantageous for their method of fighting . . . You may depend upon it, that as the rebels have now had time to prepare, they are determined to go through with it, nor will the insurrection here turn out so despicable as it is perhaps imagined at home."[39]

Night came, after the long day, to the British now lying exhausted on the Charlestown slopes, to the minutemen who encamped on the other side of Charlestown Neck, and to the little towns of Lexington and Concord, now forever plunged into history. It was a day full of mistakes. But it was a day also that made its point.

7

THE USES OF ADVERSITY

"I would wish to have all the impartial and reasonable world on our side. I would wish to have the humanity of the English nation engaged in our cause. . . ."

SAMUEL ADAMS[1]

As an example of military skill the nineteenth of April, 1775, spoke poorly indeed for the Anglo-Saxon people. The British army and the British command came close to providing a new standard of incompetence on every level and in every respect: headquarters staff work was inconceivably bad; except for Percy the field commanders were slow, unimaginative, and consistently wrong in their decisions; the junior officers didn't know what to do, and what they did do, they did badly; the private soldiers were disgraceful in their conduct—disobedient, hysterical when they were winning, and hysterical when they were losing. Yet there is something to be said for the spirit of the soldiers once they had a knowledgeable commander in Lord Percy. They endured an unfamiliar guerrilla war all the way from Concord to Boston, heavily outnumbered and after a long march out of Boston, "without the intermission of five minutes altogether, I believe, upwards of eighteen miles."[2] And except for the flanking parties it was only occasionally that the troops could see their enemy, most of whom were behind walls—although Benjamin Franklin, not much impressed when the British complained to him about all the firing from behind walls, asked quietly "whether there were not two sides to the walls."[8]

As for the American militia, it could have destroyed most of Smith's forces before they ever returned to Lexington and the shelter of Lord Percy's relief brigade with its fieldpieces. It could have inflicted much more disastrous losses upon the combined British forces between Lexington and Cambridge. And it could have shut off Percy's retreat, not only by way of the bridge over the Charles, but also by way of Charlestown Neck. Totally without strategy and only with improvised tactics and with every man in command of himself when he got into the battle zone, the provincial action of the day amounted, in military terms, primarily to a long harassment of a retreat that Percy ran his own way. The inefficiency of the musket at more than sixty yards rendered the overwhelming majority of the provincial firing harmless, and there was no planning of the use of manpower to make the militia any more effective.

If the day's battle was far from an exemplary military performance, however, it was close to perfect for the colonial cause in a much larger and more important sense. In the first place, it shut the British up in Boston so that they never again ventured far out until the evacuation nearly a year later. This cleared the atmosphere considerably, because it forced the colonial Tories to take refuge in Boston and it moved the Whigs in Boston to get out into the country. Secondly, it brought to an end the specter government of Gage, who was reduced by seven o'clock on the evening of April nineteenth to the position of the commanding officer of a small garrison army occupying a single town three thousand miles from home. Far greater in significance than either of these was its immediately unifying effect, first, upon the province of Massachusetts Bay and, second, upon all the colonies. And this was the achievement of probably the most skillful propaganda and political strategy in all American history.

For this purpose the events of April nineteenth, 1775, were ideal. The British had marched out of Boston in force and "with baggage and artillery." The British had fired to kill first. The British had destroyed property. There had been bloodshed and death—the fact that there were more British than American lives lost was insignificant in view of the eight provincials killed at dawn on Lexington Common. All this established beyond any doubt that the Americans had been the victims. At the same time—and this was equally important—the Americans were also the victors. The half-believed arguments of two years' standing that the American colonists would never stand up to British regulars was thoroughly shattered. The irresolution of the Massachusetts people was gone in fourteen hours. The longed-for but thinly rooted chance of permanent reconciliation was devastated.

Yet on the morning of April twentieth there were two wholly different pictures of the preceding day in the minds of honest men. To General Thomas Gage, still the legal and nominal Governor of Massachusetts, it was a picture of subjects of the King in a rebellious and treasonable uprising against His Majesty's troops in the execution of their duties, resulting in the killing of seventy-three of them. It was an action encouraged if not inspired by men who had formed themselves, in contempt of all law and loyalty, into an illicit government created to destroy the only duly constituted government. But to the provincial leadership the picture was one of a patient and oppressed people, finally put to the ultimate injustice of suffering the loss of their lives and property because they would not cower before the brutal enforcement of unjust and immoral laws. Which of these pictures would endure in the minds not only of the people of the colonies but of many of those in Britain would have a determining effect upon the years ahead.

ii

The provincial leadership moved swiftly and effectively to win this decisive propaganda battle. Adams and Hancock set out for Philadelphia and the Continental Congress, the scheduled meeting of which was now to become the first critical national forum of the Revolution. The propaganda uses of Lexington and Concord were left in the competent hands of Dr. Joseph Warren.

During the British retreat from Lexington, Dr. Warren was conspicuous as the only political leader who followed Percy's force with the militia all the way to Charlestown, exposing himself to enemy fire constantly. One bullet, during the brisk fighting on the flat stretch through Menotomy, shot a pin from the doctor's wig. His action—as a fighting man, as an inspirer of the other men, and as a physician rushing in under fire to aid the wounded—won the wholehearted admiration of all the militia, and the story of his participation in the battle was spread all through eastern Massachusetts. There is no question that on April twentieth the thirty-three-year-old Boston physician was the most popular and influential political figure in the colony.

The youngest of the provincial leaders, Warren had been educated at Harvard in the closing years of Edward Holyoke's incumbency as president, taught at the grammar school in Roxbury, studied medicine, and began his practice at twenty-three. Dr. Warren was an attractive personality, friendly, somewhat elegant in his manners, exceptionally well read, and genuinely democratic. He developed considerable skill and reputation as a physician and rapidly built up one of the largest practices in Boston among both the rich merchants and the poor laborers. He paid little attention to his financial affairs. After the passage of the Stamp Act, in 1765—the year after Warren started his practice—he became intensely interested in the constitutional aspects of the controversy and took to spending all his evenings in study and discussion of political philosophy. He finally concluded that the conduct of England with regard to the American colonies was a rejection of principles as old as British liberty. His contributions to the press on the subject brought him to the attention of both the Samuel Adams factions in Boston and the ministry in London, and he soon became a frequenter of the political clubs. His dedication to the idea of freedom was as passionate as Adams' own, but he saw the job of the patriots to be a restoration of traditional British rights and freedoms and not severance from England. To restore those rights he was willing to fight, if necessary, but he was a powerful believer in the strength of the pen and of the spoken word. He became, while still in his twenties, a gifted and persuasive orator, an effective and indefatigable committee worker, and gradually the second-in-command to Adams. Unlike the latter, he had as much enthusiasm for the physical tasks of the little faction that strove to keep the fires of resistance alive as he did for the intellectual chores.

After his young wife died in 1773 and left four small children, Warren brought their grandmother to his house to care for them, while he stood watch with the mechanics and tradesmen, sometimes patrolling the streets of Boston all night and then going about his medical practice after breakfast in the morning. Although he was urbane and gregarious, he was also fiery on occasion, quick-tempered and impulsive and enormously courageous. Once when he did not like the surly tone of a British sentry in challenging him, he knocked the armed soldier down with his bare fist. Nothing irritated him so much as the repeated British refrain, also taken up in somewhat vociferous echoes by the domestic Tories, that the colonials would run from British regular troops. "These fellows say we won't fight; by heavens, I hope I shall die up to my knees in blood."[4]

By 1775, Dr. Warren had developed a skill in propaganda that was matched only by that of Samuel Adams. He had, as Adams' understudy, gone through the ten-year cold war in Boston among the mobs, the tradesmen and mechanics, the political clubs, the common men of the town; and he had learned a great deal about the sway that emotions could have over their minds. He learned how to fortify reason with appeals to the emotions and also learned Samuel Adams' doctrine that facts were useful only to begin with, that they have to be built upon, exaggerated, sometimes distorted, that a fact in itself was a dead thing, that it came to life only with the uses made of it. In March of 1772, when apathy in the dispute with Britain was at its worst, his fervid oration on the second anniversary of the Boston Massacre had whipped up a new enthusiasm and, aided by an incendiary peroration by Adams, nearly started a riot in the Old South Church against the British soldiers present.

Gradually, Samuel Adams came to trust Warren more than any of the patriot leaders, and Warren became in turn an extension of Adams' own dedicated personality, though with infinitely more grace. As Adams spent more and more time out of Boston after the Port Act went into effect in May 1774, in order to cement provincial feelings against the British and to create a provincial governmental structure, he left the cause in Boston in the hands of Warren.

Adams was always moving on, always widening the arena of colonial resentment. After the Massacre of 1770, it was the town of Boston he wanted to consolidate in a spirit of rebellion. After the closing of the port in 1774, it was the province of Massachusetts Bay. After the punitive Regulating Act, it was all the New England colonies. After Lexington, it was all the American colonies. He had great work to do in Philadelphia, and he left the great work at home to Dr. Warren.

Warren did not fail him. Although he had twice given the Boston Massacre anniversary orations, he knew as well as John Adams did that the event had furnished something less than pure martyrs. The mischievous Boston ropewalkers, taunting and attacking British patrols, had proved an impossibly difficult cluster of sacrificial lambs to sell the other colonies, and in five years the canonization of the victims had not got beyond a local consistory. Now, however, on the morning of April twentieth, there were simple country yeomen, good farmers and craftsmen, physicians and ministers, who were the combatants—men who could never be accused of mobbism and irresponsible agitation. And they had fallen not in the streets of Boston in the shadow of British barracks but on country roads in front of their own houses, some of them on their own doorsteps. Dr. Warren, keenly aware of the value of every thread in the narrative of the day's events, started weaving together a net of evidence, incidents, premises, and testimony that accomplished in a matter of days what debate and oration had failed to bring about in ten years.

On Thursday morning, April twentieth, Warren was in Cambridge with the militia who were encamped there after chasing Percy's brigade back to Boston. The Provincial Congress would not be meeting until Saturday, the twenty-second, and Warren accordingly set up a civil headquarters, run by himself, as the first American generals, headed by Artemas Ward, set up their military headquarters. At noon there came a letter from the Committee of Supplies, meeting at Concord, "expressing their joy at the event of the preceding day."[5] Warren ignored the elation of the official body, knowing full well that the one completely wrong way to handle the event was to be anything but sorely grieved at it and to allow too much or too premature emphasis to be put upon it as a colonial victory. He himself wrote the first circular on Lexington and Concord, and it went out to the towns of the colony, with the authority of the Committee of Safety, of which he was chairman in Hancock's absence, less than twenty-four hours after the battle ended. There was none of the Committee of Supplies' "joy" in it.

"Gentlemen,— The barbarous murders committed on our innocent brethren, on Wednesday, the 19th instant, have made it absolutely necessary that we immediately raise an army to defend

our wives and our children from the butchering hands of an in-
human soldiery, who, incensed at the obstacles they met with in
their bloody progress, and enraged at being repulsed from the field
of slaughter, will, without the least doubt, take the first opportunity
in their power to ravage this devoted country with fire and sword.
We conjure you, therefore, by all that is dear, by all that is sacred,
that you give all assistance possible in forming an army. Our all is
at stake. Death and devastation are the instant consequences of
delay. Every moment is infinitely precious. An hour lost may
deluge your country in blood and entail perpetual slavery upon the
few of your posterity who may survive the carnage. We beg and
entreat, as you will answer to God himself, that you will hasten
and encourage by all possible means the enlistment of men to form
the army, *and send them forward to headquarters, at Cambridge,*
with that expedition which the vast importance and instant ur-
gency of the affair demand."[6]

This is a remarkably skillful document. There is not a single
fact in it. There is not a place named, a detail revealed, a statistic
given. There is not a military objective stated nor a military action
reported. There is not an inkling of what happened, what was involved, what the outcome was—or even where. There is, indeed,
not a single reference, beyond the general language of the opening
phrase, to what had happened. It is concerned with what was
ahead rather than with what had occurred. It had one objective—
the one objective Samuel Adams had worked on assiduously ever
since the First Provincial Congress assembled in October 1774
and the objective that was failing so miserably as the Second
Provincial Congress shrunk to a halfhearted end at Concord not
a week earlier—the raising of a provincial army. Dr. Warren was
going to get the army.

His first move was wisely made. He knew that rumors were
flying all over Massachusetts and that the facts, however awful in
their significance, would be pale beside them. Four thousand

minutemen from forty towns had seen blood and death. Four thousand reports were already getting back to virtually the entire population of eastern Massachusetts. They would vary from slight exaggerations, as oral reports in the first excitement of great events almost always do, to the wildest stories of murder and despoilation. They would be repeated and grow in the repetition. Dr. Warren, in his circular, used language that could confirm any rumor and in so doing put the rumors to work for him in his plea for the army.

Warren had the physician's cold diagnostic approach to all this. No fanatic, he simply, and with the greatest objectivity, chose a means he thought suitable to the end desired. On the very same day that he used such terms as "the butchering hands of an inhuman soldiery" in referring to the British army, he wrote General Gage a gentle and strangely sad letter: ". . . Your Excellency, I believe, knows very well the part I have taken in public affairs: I ever scorned disguise. I think I have done my duty: some may think otherwise; but be assured, sir, as far as my influence goes, every thing that can reasonably be required of us to do shall be done, and every thing promised shall be religiously performed. . . . I have many things that I wish to say to Your Excellency, and most sincerely wish I had broken through the formalities which I thought due to your rank, and freely had told you all I knew or thought of public affairs; and I must ever confess, whatever may be the event, that you generously gave me such opening as I now think I ought to have embraced. . . ."[7] This young physician was a knowing man, sensitive to the unhappy twists of history for all his active partisanship.

And the rumors were all that Dr. Warren had assumed. In the absence of any authoritative news from Warren himself, every man created his own version of the affair in letters, in verbal reports, in abrupt "accounts" passed on to Committees of Correspondence. "Rumor on rumor," an aged deacon of Brighton wrote in his diary; "men and horses driving post up and down the roads . . . people were in great perplexity. Women in distress for their husbands and friends who had marched . . ."8 From a Boston Whig, John Andrews, there went out a story of massacre in Jonas Clarke's meetinghouse on Lexington Common, "when the soldiers shoved up the windows and pointed their guns and killed three there."9

One atrocity story after another spread through the province, then to the other colonies, and finally overseas. "Such is the barbarity of the king's troops that seven of the mercenaries, with their bayonets fixed, entered the house of one Hindman, a husbandman near Concord and inhumanly murdered his wife, who had laid in but a few days, by stabbing her several parts of the body. . . ."10 There was nobody, male or female, named Hindman even wounded that day. There was no woman, in Concord or anywhere else, so much as slapped by a British soldier. And in Concord, of course, the women were treated with such consideration that the munitions raid was reduced almost to an absurdity. From another quarter came a story of the invasion of a house where the British "put the inhabitants, being thirteen in number, to the sword. This gentleman bears ample testimony to the courage of the Americans and observes that, out of the thirteen, one only pleaded for his life, alleging that he could not possibly have annoyed the troops, being confined to his bed with a broken thigh."11 Not even a single town, let alone one house, suffered as many as thirteen deaths—Lexington had the greatest number with nine—and there is no record of deaths by the sword. "They entered one house in Lexington where were two old men, one a deacon of the church, who was bed-ridden, and another not able to walk, who was sitting in his chair; both these they stabbed and killed on the spot, as well as an innocent child running out of the house."12 No one was killed in any house in Lexington, nor were any ancient immobile men or little children; all Lexington fatalities were members of Captain Parker's company.

Eyewitnesses saw things that never happened. "I saw some houses that had been set on fire, and some old men, women and children that had been killed," and "There was a number of women and children burnt in their houses."[13] As the rumors had it, only old men, women, and children were killed, except for a cripple here and there. There were actually, of course, no women or children even wounded, although an adolescent boy, sitting in the window of a Charlestown house from which snipers fired on the British in the last stages of their retreat at dusk, was shot in the neck. Most all the men killed were actively engaged in combat, and the average age was very low. Only two of the men killed on Lexington Common were over thirty-one; and of the seven killed in the Danvers company, all were under twenty-five, except the captain, who was thirty-three. The only really old man who met his death from British action was Sudbury's seventy-nine-year-old Deacon Josiah Haynes. Far from being helpless, he was up at dawn, marched, bearing his heavy musket, eight miles to the bridge at Concord, and there berated his captain, John Nixon, for not starting an attack ("If you don't go and drive them British from that bridge, I shall call you a coward."[14]), and joined enthusiastically in the pursuit of the British in the afternoon, when he was killed while energetically reloading his musket to kill more of them.

The rumors reached an extreme in some towns that led to mass evacuations in the face of the wildest imaginings of insatiable British troops storming across the countryside, burning, robbing, torturing and murdering—all because nobody knew what had happened and that the British army was even then licking its wounds in impotent isolation in a now-besieged Boston, with no intention and little hope of going anywhere. At Ipswich, twenty-five miles northeast of Boston, someone started a rumor that British soldiers were being landed from cutters and were already hacking their way through the village. Within an hour the news that the population of Ipswich was all but wiped out reached Beverly, ten miles to the south. At a town meeting in Newbury, ten miles to the north, a courier unceremoniously interrupted a long prayer of the Reverend Thomas Cary with an alarm: "Turn out, for God's sake, or you will all be killed. The regulars are marching on us; they are at Ipswich now, cutting and slashing all before them."[15] As the alarm spread all through the towns of eastern Essex County, old ladies were bundled in chaises off to the back country, papers and valuables were hidden, men grabbed their muskets to march somewhere—anywhere—and women and children hiked away into the woods, leaving the villages completely deserted. The townspeople of one town rushed to the next, taking up temporary residences in houses vacated by populations who had in turn moved on to the next town and up into the coastal towns of New Hampshire. Oxen were yoked to haul household effects, and the streets of empty villages were strewn with utensils and bedding that fell off the carts and wagons. In Portsmouth the militia were notified by seven different express riders to march in seven different directions, and everyone seemed to think that Portsmouth itself was doomed, due to the absence of its local militia leader, John Sullivan: "Oh! if Major Sullivan was here! I wish to God Major Sullivan was here!"[16] But Major Sullivan was on his way to the Continental Congress in Philadelphia, and they posted a guard around his house to save it from the invisible invader.

But the rumors did the work that Dr. Warren had in mind. A provincial army sprang into being, after all the exhortations of the Provincial Congress had failed, overnight. In a steady stream, from twenty-five, fifty, a hundred miles away, militia set out for the camp in the Harvard Yard at Cambridge, most of them reaching the headquarters during the morning and afternoon of the twentieth. General Artemas Ward left with the Shrewsbury militia and, arriving in Cambridge, took over the command from "our General" Heath. From Connecticut, Israel Putnam, lieutenant colonel of all the Connecticut militia, mounted his plow horse in the field where he was working and, without stopping to change his clothes, rode the hundred miles to Cambridge in eighteen hours. At New Haven, Captain Benedict Arnold of the Governor's Guards threatened to break the lock of the town's ammunition store when the selectmen were slow in delivering powder and balls for his company. Altogether some twenty thousand militia converged on Cambridge and laid siege to Gage's four thousand soldiers in Boston. Part of the provincial force, under the command of Artemas Ward, stayed in Cambridge to stop any British move out from Boston through Charlestown or across the Charles at Cambridge. The remainder of the motley army, under Dr. John Thomas, went to Roxbury to shut off the British from the mainland at Boston Neck.

The directorate, the Committee of Safety with Dr. Warren as its chairman, now had its army. But it had no illusions about it. The twenty thousand men besieging Boston on April twentieth had come in response to the most outrageous accounts of British predacity, and it is of the nature of rumors of wickedness that the wickedness turns out to be something less than fiendish. No one could hope to keep up a sufficient fire of indignation to prevail upon the twenty thousand militia to think of nothing else but evening scores with the British—particularly when in due course it would have to be known that the British had come out at the short end of the score anyhow. And most of the twenty thousand had not marched to Boston to join an army, in any case. They had left their fields and shops and studies to put a stop to a specific act of British arrogance. They had brought no clothes or food with them, had made no arrangements for the discharge of their responsibilities at home, and had conceived of their undertaking as the carrying out of their individual decisions to "go to meet the British." Many of them were magnificently unfit for army campaigns and prolonged service. There were very old men like Deacon Haynes, young men who were little more than boys, married men with large families who must be supported, even clergymen who had to get back to their meetinghouses by the next Sabbath.

Dr. Warren was fully aware that many of this varied throng, whom he was already having trouble feeding, would depart as spontaneously as they had come, most of them without even giving any notice of their intention. Milling around Cambridge, they were almost wholly unorganized. Some, of course, had a company structure, with their elected officers to whom they gave no real binding authority. Others came in little groups of individuals, every man his own general, and they would stay as long as they saw fit and then go home again. Some were unarmed, there to see what all the excitement was about or else to carry voluntary food offerings to fighting men from their home towns. "There were also in the aforesaid Company a number of aged men, and some unable to bear arms, who rode to Cambridge on the day of alarm and the day following to carry provision to those who stood in need. . . ."[17] When Dr. Warren's Committee of Safety concluded that the strategy would be to keep the British locked up in Boston, some militia officers simply refused to go along with the decision, among them Timothy Pickering, who was so reluctant the day before to march his Salem men all the way to the Charles. "To me the idea was new and unexpected," he wrote. "I expressed the opinion which at the moment occurred to me—that the hostilities of the preceding day did not render a civil war inevitable: That a negotiation with General Gage might probably effect a present compromise and therefore that the immediate formation of an army did not appear to me to be necessary."[18] Pickering went home, and so did most of his men.

From all this, Warren saw that he must first get the militia that Benjamin Thompson, one of Gage's informers, called "that mass of confusion"[19] under some sort of authority, then be sure that they could be counted upon to stay in service, and finally eliminate those who should or could not undertake unlimited military duties. He moved swiftly to accomplish all three at a meeting of the Committee of Safety on April twenty-first.

The first two, acknowledgment of authority and duration of service, were taken care of by the adoption of a form of enlistment: "I, *A.B.*, do hereby solemnly engage and enlist myself as a soldier in the *Massachusetts* service, from the day of my enlistment to the last day of December next, unless the service should admit of a discharge of a part or the whole sooner, which shall be at the discretion of the Committee of Safety; and I hereby promise to submit myself to all the orders and regulations of the Army, and faithfully to observe and obey all such orders as I shall receive from any superior officer."[20] The third of Warren's objectives, culling a manageable force from the mass teeming around Cambridge, was dealt with in the Committee's next action. Since Gage's force was only about four thousand and it was virtually immobilized by the geography of Boston, Warren concluded that a provincial force of eight thousand would be adequate for the immediate job of keeping the British isolated on the peninsula. This meant that he needed little more than a third of the men who responded to the Lexington alarm. And he took care that the Committee's resolution creating the army left room for qualitative as well as quantitative criteria: "*Resolved,* that there be immediately enlisted, out of the *Massachusetts* Forces, eight thousand effective men, to be formed into Companies, to consist of a Captain, one Lieutenant, one Ensign, four Sergeants, one Fifer, one Drummer, and seventy rank and file; nine Companies to form a Regiment, to be commanded by a Colonel, Lieutenant Colonel and Major; each Regiment to be composed of men suitable for the service, which shall be determined by a Muster-Master or Muster-Masters, to be appointed for that purpose. Said officers and men to continue in the service of the Province for the space of seven months from the time of enlistment, unless the safety of the Province will admit of their being discharged sooner; the Army to be under proper rules and regulations."[21]

This was a sensible and manageable plan. But as soon as it reached the officers of the old companies milling around outside the Committee doors, there were complaints that the size of the companies proposed was too big, the obvious result being that many present officers would have to be reduced in rank. With quick adaptability, the Committee immediately reduced the size of the new companies to fifty men and avoided squabbling. General Ward created a council of war, doled out assignments to officers, deployed his men; and Samuel Adams, poking along the highways of western Massachusetts toward Philadelphia with John Hancock, at last had a provincial army to break down the decade-old barrier between the idea and the reality of organized forcible resistance to Great Britain.

iii

On Saturday, April twenty-second, the Provincial Congress, parent body and source of authority of the Committee of Safety, met at Concord and then adjourned to Watertown in order to be near the fledgling army. In the absence of Hancock, Dr. Warren was unanimously elected its president, and he proceeded to cope with problems that he had been unable to attend during the short, harried sessions of the Committee of Safety. First among these was the next stage of the propaganda war.

Before the guns of Earl Percy's retreat were silenced, the three uses of the battle of Lexington were joyously apparent to the provincial leadership: as an immediate and unarguable call for a provincial army; as a dramatic event behind which to consolidate a public opinion that had been wavering and indifferent; and, finally, as an act of aggressive violence by British troops that would divide the English in the home country on support of the policies of the Crown and the North ministry. Through the Committee of Safety, within forty-eight hours of the battle, Dr. Warren had promptly and efficiently brought about the provincial army. He moved now, through the Provincial Congress, to make the most of the propaganda uses of the battle.

This involved innovations, in the political history of wars, of which Dr. Warren and his colleagues were fully capable. Never before had wars required a direct verdict of the people for their prosecution. Never had a war been started without even a government to direct it. Never had it been of such urgent importance to get the case before a people. For this the vague communiqué and the wild rumors were totally inadequate—useful as they had proved to be for more immediate purposes. What was needed was foolproof documentation that the colonists were innocent but honorable victims, the King's troops ruthless and unreasoning aggressors. And all this had to be done before the British, saddled with the red tape of formal militarism, could get their version of the affair to the people. Accordingly, at its afternoon session on April twenty-second the Congress appointed a committee of nine to take depositions, "from which a full account of the transactions of the troops under General Gage, in their route to and from Concord, &c., on Wednesday last, may be collected."[22] The next day it appointed a committee to construct an official narrative of the event.

On April twenty-third, the Sunday following Wednesday's battle, the congressional committee went to Lexington and spent three days in taking depositions from the participants in the battle, supplementing them with other accounts from Concord, civilians on the line of retreat, and British captives. In all, the Committee interviewed ninety-seven people in three days and got signed and sworn statements from all of them in twenty-one documents. They took a corps of justices of the peace with them to administer the oaths to the deponents and then got a notary public to certify the good faith of the justices of the peace. The signatories to the individual depositions varied from single deponents, like Captain Parker, to groups of four to over thirty. The gist of all the depositions was that not a provincial at either Lexington or Concord fired until the British had fired first. This point was not omitted from a single deposition, and it was obviously an instruction of the Committee of the Congress to the deponents to be specific on this point, since several of the deponents had not in fact been in a position to know who fired first.

The committee sent to Concord and to Medford to get depositions from three British captives; John Bateman, a private of the Fifty-second Regiment, James Marr, a private of the Fourth (King's Own) Regiment, and Lieutenant Edward Thornton Gould, also of The King's Own. The committee apparently felt that testimony from men of the British army would lend weight and added authority to the provincial depositions. It was, indeed, a good thought and had its effect. Bateman was an eagerly satisfying deponent. His company was not in the van of the march on Lexington Common, and from his position down the road toward Boston not only distance but the great bulk of the meetinghouse would have prevented him from seeing who fired first or, until the gunsmoke rose, if anyone fired at all. Nevertheless, Bateman was the most positive of witnesses: ". . . being nigh the meetinghouse in said Lexington, there was a small party of men gathered together in that place when our troops marched by, and I testify and declare, that I heard the word of command given to the troops to fire, and some of said troops did fire, and I saw one of said small party lay dead on the ground nigh said meetinghouse, and I testify that I never heard any of the inhabitants so much as fire one gun on said troops."[23] James Marr and Lieutenant Gould of The King's Own were also in the rear at Lexington and claimed no knowledge of who fired first, but they both testified that the British fired first as the minutemen approached the North Bridge at Concord.

Except for the uncommonly good eyesight of all ninety-seven deponents in observing, in the pale light of dawn from odd positions and amid the turmoil of dashing horses, rushing soldiers and widely scattered provincial militia and spectators, exactly where the first shot came from, the twenty-one depositions were brief, crisp, economic in detail, and without dramatic accusations. No atrocities were charged to the British; and some were careful to limit the destruction of houses and property by the troops, although others claimed, at the same time, rather vaguely that they "committed damage, more or less, to almost every house from Concord to Charlestown."[24] The depositions were delivered to the Congress by the committee on April twenty-sixth, and the official narrative was meanwhile composed by another committee.

The narrative was far more emotional and accusatory than the depositions, in places somewhat childish in the innocence attributed to the provincials and almost fantastic in its version of the retreat. The chairman of the committee appointed to compose the narrative had reason to show ardor in the patriot's cause. He was Dr. Benjamin Church, the same member of the Congress who had been selling Gage its secrets, including the location of the colonial munitions, right up until the eve of the march to Concord. Church, on the day after the battle, was met in Cambridge by Paul Revere, to whom it seemed that Church was excessively anxious to demonstrate his patriotism. "The day after the Battle of Lexington, I met him in Cambridge, when he showed me some blood on his stocking, which he said spirted on him from a man who was killed near him, as he was urging the Militia on."[25] Then in his fortieth year, Church was dependent upon the moneys paid him by General Gage as an informer. With the outbreak of hostilities he was in all the more advantageous position as a member of both the Congress and war committees to command heavy prices for the information he sold. Dr. Church was appointed to the narrative committee at the session of Congress on Sunday, April twenty-third. On the previous Friday, just two days after the battle, he was sitting with the Committee of Safety at Cambridge, when he startled Dr. Warren by announcing his intention to go into Boston the next day. Dr. Church's declaration "set them all a staring. Dr. Warren replied, 'Are you serious, Dr. Church? They will hang you if they catch you in Boston!' He replied, 'I am serious and determined to go at all adventures.' "[26]

So Dr. Church spent all day Saturday and part of Sunday in Boston, Warren and the Committee of Safety ordering him to bring medicine back for the wounded as long as he was determined to go. Church told the suspicious Revere, when he got back, that he was taken prisoner and sent to Gage's headquarters, but Revere later talked to Deacon Caleb Davis, of Boston, who happened to see Church emerge from Gage's house that morning in amiable and friendly conversation with the General, "like persons who had been long acquainted." Church got back from his traitorous visit in time to accept the appointment to the committee to write the official narrative.

Not even the most fanatical of those who despised the British and advanced the colonial cause were quite capable of Church's condemnation of the British and admiration of the childlike Americans that he invented. Fresh from Gage's headquarters, he presided over the composing of the official American report to the people of the colonies:

"On the nineteenth day of April, one thousand seven hundred and seventy-five, a day to be remembered by all Americans of the present generation, and which ought, and doubtless will be handed down to ages yet unborn, the troops of Britain, unprovoked, shed the blood of sundry of the loyal American subjects of the British king in the field of Lexington. Early in the morning of said day, a detachment of the forces under General Gage, stationed at Boston, attacked a small party of the inhabitants of Lexington and some other towns adjacent, the detachment consisting of about nine hundred men, commanded by Lieutenant Colonel Smith: The inhabitants of Lexington and the other towns were about one hundred, some with and some without firearms, who had collected upon information that the detachment had secretly marched from Boston the preceding night, and landed on Phipps's Farm in Cambridge, and were proceeding on their way with a brisk pace towards Concord, as the inhabitants supposed, to take or destroy a quantity of stores deposited there for the use of the colony; sundry peaceable inhabitants having the same night been taken, held by force, and otherwise abused on the road, by some officers of General

Gage's army, which caused a just alarm and a suspicion that some fatal design was immediately to be put into execution against them. This small party of the inhabitants were so far from being disposed to commit hostilities against the troops of their sovereign, that unless attacked, they were determined to be peaceable spectators of this extraordinary movement; immediately on the approach of Colonel Smith with the detachment under his command, they dispersed; but the detachment, seeming to thirst for blood, wantonly rushed on, and first began the hostile scene by firing on this small party, by which they killed eight men on the spot and wounded several others before any guns were fired upon the troops by our men. Not content with this effusion of blood, as if malice had occupied their whole souls, they continued the fire, until all of this small party who escaped the dismal carnage were out of the reach of their fire. Colonel Smith, with the detachment, then proceeded to Concord, where a part of this detachment again made the first fire upon some of the inhabitants of Concord and the adjacent towns, who were collected upon a bridge at this just alarm, and killed two of them and wounded several others, before any of the provincials there had done one hostile act. Then the provincials, roused with zeal for the liberties of their country, finding life and every thing dear and valuable at stake, assumed their native valor and returned the fire, and the engagement on both sides began. Soon after the British troops returned towards Charlestown, having first committed violence and waste on public and private property, and on their retreat was joined by another detachment of General Gage's troops, consisting of about a thousand men, under the command of Earl Percy, who continued the retreat; the engagement lasted through the day; and many were killed and wounded on each side, though the loss on the part of the British troops far exceeded that of the provincials. The devastation committed by the British troops on their retreat, the whole of the way from Concord to Charlestown, is almost beyond description; such as plundering and burning of dwelling-houses and other buildings, driving into the street women in child-bed, killing old men in their houses unarmed. Such scenes of desolation would be a reproach to the perpetrators, even if committed by the most barbarous nations, how much more when done by Britons famed for humanity and tenderness: And all this because these colonies will not submit to the iron yoke of arbitrary power."[27]

This version of the battle by the Church committee was obviously written while the committee on depositions was still in Lexington, and it was ready for release with the depositions, none of which were quoted in the narrative. Church had the details of the British force very clear—none of the deponents did—and he also knew that Smith was in command and exactly where—Phipps' Farm—his force had debarked at Cambridge. And if he knew too much about the British, he also protested too much on behalf of the Americans.

Nowhere in the narrative is there any reference to militia or minutemen or any military organization or military action at all. The provincials are all "a small party of the inhabitants . . . some with and some without fire-arms," or just "peaceable spectators," or "inhabitants . . . collected at the bridge." There is no mention of Captain Parker's company lined up in ranks on Lexington Common, or the Concord minutemen parading up the Lexington road with drum and fife "to meet the British," or those four hundred militia marching down the hill to force the North Bridge held perilously by Captain Parsons' thirty-five regulars. Not until the provincials "assumed their native valor" on the British retreat is there any suggestion that this was a tough breed of men not much inclined to be peaceable spectators.

But if Church's narrative conceded the provincials some belligerence on the retreat, it had nothing but contempt for the British, who, according to this version, were occupied not in saving their own lives under somewhat difficult circumstances but in "the burning of dwelling-houses and other buildings, driving into the street

women in child-bed, killing old men in their houses unarmed."
Actually, in some fifty miles of marching, half of it a running
battle, the British burned three houses, according to the returns
made to the Provincial Congress [28]—all three at the Lexington
staging area where Lord Percy was reforming the British forces for
the retreat to Charlestown. The houses had been evacuated and
seemed to have been burned reluctantly by Percy after Smith and
Pitcairn had told him how the provincials used the houses as
fortresses all along the route of the march. There was, of course,
some looting by the British flankers who searched the houses for
snipers, but again the damage returns make it very small. The
British troops were near exhaustion by then and under constant
fire, and they had neither the time to do much selective looting
nor the strength to carry unnecessary burdens as they stumbled to
the protection of the Charlestown hills. In any case, the committee of the Provincial Congress "appointed to estimate the dam-
ages done at Cambridge, Lexington and Concord" reported that
the total, including the three houses burned at Lexington,
amounted to a little over £3000, and most of the inhabitants
made very generous estimates of the value of such casualties as
"two large moose skins" and "one lawn apron."[29]

The charge of "driving into the street women in child-bed" was
one of the most popular features of the Church narrative. When
Dr. Warren edited and rewrote it for the consumption of the
English in an open letter "To The Inhabitants of Great Britain"
and when the American newspapers rewrote it, the women's plight
was rendered even more pitiable by describing them as "naked,"
although why good Massachusetts mothers should be lying around
naked on a mid-April afternoon is not apparent. This example
of British inhumanity was not to be found in any of the depositions
secured by the Congress; but after it was reported in the narrative,
a deposition was sought from Hannah Adams, the wife of Joseph
Adams, the Cambridge deacon who had fled from his house and
left his wife and six children unprotected because he was afraid

that he would be killed. The Adams house was in Cambridge in an area where the British retreat underwent the heaviest sniper fire of the entire day. According to Hannah Adams' own account, the British flank infantrymen searching the house said, "We will not hurt the woman if she will go out of the house, but we will surely burn it."[30] The infantrymen were, of course, under orders to burn houses protecting snipers, and they had just seen the deacon—who was a sniper, for all they knew—dart from the house to the Reverend Samuel Cooke's barn. If Mrs. Adams was bedded from childbirth, it was an unusually long accouchement; the Cambridge vital records show that the baby was born nineteen days earlier.[31] And even though it was her tenth child and she was forty-five, Mrs. Adams was apparently a rugged woman, living to the good age of seventy-three. In any case, Mrs. Adams was actually fully dressed when the soldiers came to her house; and she had two daughters, Rebecca, twenty-two, and Susanna, seventeen, helping her and the child, according to her daughter's account in later years.[32] She went to an outer building until the troops left and then went back into the house again. This was the only case in which, according to Dr. Warren's information to the English people, "women in child-bed were driven by the soldiery naked in the streets."[33]

The charge with regard to old men was also unsubstantiated by any of the depositions taken by the committee. Most of the old men of the day showed astonishing agility in chasing the British, were faster at loading and firing than their younger fellows, and, like old Samuel Whittemore of Cambridge, displayed admirable surviving powers even after being left for dead. So once more the provincials sought substantiation of the charges after they were made. The "old men" turned out not to have been very old and not to have been "in their houses unarmed." They were Jason Winship, forty-three, and Jabez Wyman, thirty-nine, the jovial brothers-in-law, who sat drinking in Benjamin Cooper's tavern, insisting that there was time for just one more. There had been intense provincial firing from the environs of the Cooper Tavern, when the British, according to the delayed deposition of the Coopers, "entered the house, where we and two aged gentlemen were all unarmed. We escaped for our lives into the cellar. The two aged gentlemen were immediately, most barbarously and inhumanly murdered by them." A local clergyman, appraising this atrocity, said that "both died like fools."[34] But they were the only "aged" unarmed men slain.

Thus, the official narrative went out to the province, the colonies, Great Britain, and the world. Couriers, in a chain operation with fresh men and horses ready at key points, carried the news down the Atlantic coast to Georgia. The newspapers, all of them weeklies, published their stories, borrowing liberally from each other and embroidering the apocryphal details of atrocities. On the Monday after the battle, accounts were in the Connecticut and New York papers; on Wednesday, in the Pennsylvania papers; on Thursday, in those of Maryland; on Saturday, in Dixon and Hunter's *Virginia Gazette;* and on through the Carolinas, until the news reached the *Georgia Gazette* in Savannah. Many of the papers, unwilling to wait for their weekly publication date, got out handbills as soon as the news was received. Using inverted rules to make heavy black borders, decorated with rows of black coffins to represent the dead and bearing such headlines as "Bloody Butchery by the British Troops,"[35] the press accounts, based upon the official narrative, wiped out overnight all the issues of the long debate on taxation and representation. The voices of the orators were drowned out by the outraged cries of the propagandists repeated from the press in appeals to the emotions. Vast indignation over a professional soldiery turned loose to murder and ravage was fed by the quick, inevitable multiplication of the charges of British wickedness. Massachusetts, with its population exclusively made up of unarmed old men and of women in the midst of childbirth, became the rallying cry of a "There but for the grace of God go you" sort of barrage from the whole Whig press. Isaiah Thomas, who had moved his *Massachusetts Spy* press out of Boston across the Charles on the Sunday night before the battle, set up shop in Worcester and fired a broadside that was reprinted in a score of papers thoughout the colonies: "AMERICANS! forever bear in mind the BATTLE OF LEXINGTON! —where British Troops, unmolested and unprovoked, wantonly and in a most inhuman manner fired upon and killed a number of our countrymen, then robbed them of their provisions, ransacked, plundered and burned their houses! Nor could the tears of defenceless women, some of whom were in the pains of childbirth, and cries of helpless babes, nor the prayers of old age, confined to beds of sickness, appease their thirst for blood!—or divert them from their DESIGN of MURDER and ROBBERY!"[36] And in New York, where a throng marched on the City Hall to demand the keys to the armory when they heard the news, the exhortation went out to "Let every inhabitant consider what he is likely to suffer if he falls into the hands of such cruel and merciless wretches."[37]

Here was the real victory of Lexington. The little town, somewhat removed from affairs, that had gone about its quiet business for a century and a half, was suddenly a symbol that united an irresolute people in a spirit of revolt that was to end only with independence. For the propaganda uses made of Lexington were carried out with such skill that in the wars of the future, which were impossible to carry on without the consent and support of the people, the same essential pattern was followed.

iv

Even as he was presiding over this war of propaganda, Dr. Joseph Warren held a contained view of the outbreak of hostilities, and he saw it still as a civil war—loyal citizens' fighting an usurpatory government. In his mind, it was of paramount importance that his fellow subjects in Great Britain have the provincial version of the beginning of hostilities before the routine, military man's report of Gage got there. On April twenty-sixth, one week after the battle, after he had all the depositions at hand, he himself wrote the account that went to the British people, together with copies of the depositions. In it he made an outright appeal to His Majesty's subjects in England to make common cause with their brothers in the colonies. He followed a brief account of the nineteenth and its events with a quiet overture to the bonds that still united them:

"We cannot think that the honour, wisdom and valour of Britons will suffer them longer to be inactive spectators of measures in which they themselves are so deeply interested; measures pursued in opposition to the solemn protests of many noble Lords, and expressed sense of conspicuous Commoners, whose knowledge and virtue have long characterized them as some of the greatest men in the Nation; measures executing contrary to the interest, Petitions and Resolves of many large, respectable and opulent Counties, Cities and Boroughs, in Great Britain; measures highly incompatible with justice, but still pursued with a specious pretence of easing the nation of its burden; measures which, if successful, must end in the ruin and slavery of Britain, as well as the persecuted American colonies.

"We sincerely hope that the great Sovereign of the Universe, who hath so often appeared for the English nation, will support you in very rational and manly exertion with these Colonies, for saving it from ruin; and that in a constitutional connection with the Mother Country, we shall soon be altogether a free and happy people."[38]

It was, of course, Warren's purpose to hinder the North ministry in its conduct of a war three thousand miles from home, particularly in the pressing problems of raising moneys from domestic revenues to pay for it and men to cross the seas to fight it. This could be, in his judgment, a most unpopular war among Britons, the more so if they thought it unjust.

In its determination to get the provincial version of the affair to England first, the Provincial Congress commissioned a schooner belonging to a Salem merchant, Richard Derby, and commanded by his son, John, to take copies of the Salem *Gazette,* the official narrative letter, the depositions, and letters of instructions to the American agents, Arthur Lee and Benjamin Franklin. On April twenty-seventh, Dr. Warren gave Captain John Derby his orders from the Committee of Safety:

Resolved: *that Captain Derby be directed and he hereby is directed to make for Dublin or any other good port in Ireland, and from thence to cross to Scotland or England and hasten to London. This direction is given that so he may escape all enemies that may be in the chops of the channel to stop the communication of the Provincial intelligence to the agent. He will forthwith deliver his papers to the agent on reaching London.*

J. Warren, CHAIRMAN

P.S. You are to keep this order a profound secret from every person on earth.[39]

Captain Derby sailed from Salem in his little schooner in the darkness of the night of April twenty-eighth. Four days earlier Gage had written sparse reports to the Viscount Barrington, the Secretary at War, and to Earl Dartmouth, the Secretary of State for the Colonies (he began the former with the fine understatement, "I have now nothing to trouble your lordship with, but of an affair that happened here on the 19th instant . . ."[40]). On the twenty-fourth Gage dispatched his reports on the cargo-laden, two hundred ton packet, *Sukey.* John Derby's assignment was to beat the packet to the British Isles.

The Derby schooner, *Quero,* was a light, fast ship of sixty-two tons' burden, carrying a small crew and no cargo. The Derby family had been Salem shipmasters for over a century, and Captain John Derby, then thirty-four, was an outstandingly brilliant mariner. He made the westward crossing in four weeks, sailed *Quero* up a stream at the Isle of Wight, where she would be unnoticed, and then took a public transport to Southampton whence he made his way to London. Derby's boldness in ignoring Warren's directions to land in Ireland and in sailing under the noses of the British navy station at Portsmouth was almost arrogant, but by doing so he got to London on May twenty-eighth. He took his papers, with letters from Dr. Warren, to Arthur Lee. Copies of the narrative and depositions were made quickly and the originals placed in the custody of the Lord Mayor of London, the notorious radical, John Wilkes. Dr. Franklin, his mighty and persistent efforts at conciliation having come to nothing after ten years in London as the ambassador extraordinary of the colonies, had already sailed for home.

On the day after Derby's arrival, the news of Lexington—colonial version—was all over England, where support of the North ministry and its colonial policy was far from unanimous. The American colonies were the richest possessions of the British, and the merchants of England viewed the drift toward war as suicidal. Political liberals were openly sympathetic with the colonial point of view on basic freedoms common to all Englishmen. The Quakers and other religious groups were opposed to war on any account. Moreover, England was badly prepared for any war. There was a heavy debt still from the war with France. Domestic taxes in Britain were already high. Recruitment for army service was sagging dangerously, particularly for overseas duty in the colonies. To this England the news of Lexington was of tremendous impact. The London *Evening Post* published an extra, reprinting the Salem *Gazette's* account and some of the depositions. The combined efforts of the American agent and the Lord Mayor resulted in an incredibly swift spreading of the news by bulletins and word of mouth. The former colonial governor, Thomas Hutchinson, went to Lord Dartmouth with the news. On the next day Dartmouth issued a government bulletin saying that the news was unofficial and the government had had no information from Gage. The following day Lee published a notice that if anyone doubted the accounts, original affidavits confirming the news could be seen at the Lord Mayor's mansion. The historian, Edward Gibbon, independent member of Parliament, wrote, "This looks serious and is indeed so," but he saw hope in the fact that "the month of May is the time for sowing Indian corn" and the Americans would face famine if they interrupted the planting to fight a war.[41] The Reverend John Horne, former vicar of New Brentford and founder of the Society for Supporting the Bill of Rights, issued an appeal for funds in which he repeated literally the claims of "our beloved American fellow-subjects, who, faithful to the character of Englishmen, preferring death to slavery, were, for that reason only, inhumanly murdered by the King's Troops at or near Lexington and Concord." He sent the money that he raised to Franklin and then was himself sent off to King's Bench Prison for his pains.

The British Government, for two weeks, did nothing in the absence of any information from Gage. Efforts were made to find Derby and his ship. Derby flashed in and out of London as he pleased but disappeared completely when his presence was desired by Dartmouth. Agents were sent by the government to find his ship, and Southampton was searched thoroughly without result. Meanwhile, the Salem *Gazette* story was gaining wider and wider circulation, the *Gentleman's Magazine* even crediting the elusive Captain Derby with bringing government dispatches. Dartmouth's undersecretary, John Pownall, took the story directly to the King at Kew, telling the monarch that he bore "bad news." The King spent his temper on Pownall, telling Dartmouth that the expression "bad news" left a lot to be desired and that all Pownall would ever be fit for was to carry out the orders of others. But the King's real frustration was better reflected in a rather pointless letter that Dartmouth at last dispatched to Gage—pointless because Gage could not possibly get it for four or five weeks: ". . . It appears, upon the fullest inquiry, that this account, which is chiefly taken from a Salem newspaper, has been published by a Captain Derby, who arrived on Friday or Saturday at Southampton, in a small vessel in ballast, directly from Salem; and from every circumstance relating to this person and the vessel, it is evident he was employed by the Provincial Congress to bring this account, which is plainly made up for the purpose of conveying every possible prejudice and misrepresentation of the truth . . .

"At the same time it is very much to be lamented that we have not some account from you of this transaction, which I do not mention from any supposition that you did not send the earliest intelligence of it, for we know from Derby that a vessel with dispatches from you sailed four days before him. We expect the arrival of that vessel with great impatience. . . ."[42]

During the first weeks of June, as other ships from America brought oral confirmation, the ministry was shaken in its official view that maybe the whole story was fictitious. Yet it persisted in refusing to recognize the existence of the event and left the English people more and more convinced that their American fellow subjects had been done a great wrong—an impression that the ministry was never able to alter.

Finally, two weeks after Derby's *Quero* shipped up the Isle of Wight inlet, the heavily loaded *Sukey,* bearing General Gage's dispatches, got to Southampton. With regard to the security of his all but useless communications, Gage had gone to great pains. He had, of course, foreseen the probability that the provincials would want to get their own account of April nineteenth to London, but he credited them with little imagination or even, despite his experience of the night of the eighteenth, with much skill at espionage. Actually, the provincials knew that his dispatches were aboard *Sukey* when they commissioned Derby's schooner. Gage, however, assumed that they would attempt to communicate with the colony's agents in London by the same ship that he used. Accordingly, he sent orders to the captain to intercept all mail addressed to Franklin and Lee and send it back to Boston and to seize all "other suspicious letters, to be put under cover to the Secretary of State."[43]

After all the excitement aroused in England by the spirited account brought by Captain Derby, General Gage's account fell as a dull anticlimax that served only to confirm the former. The official dispatches consisted of Gage's account, which was an abrupt minimizing of the entire episode, the reports that he had from Earl Percy and Lieutenant Colonel Smith, and an account of the British losses. The press leaped with delight and disdain on some of the general's locutions, which sought to convey the impression that it was no defeat. The American accounts had given a vivid picture of the inglorious British retreat that had become familiar to every English newspaper reader. Of this, Gage said only that Lord Percy "brought the troops to Charlestown."[44] Commented the London *Press:* "Whether they marched like mutes at a funeral, or whether they fled like the relations and friends of the present ministry . . . is left entirely to the conjecture of the reader: though it should seem that a scattering fire, poured in upon a retreating enemy for fifteen miles together, would naturally, like goads applied to the sides of oxen, make them march off as fast as they could."[45]

The British Government did nothing to improve the ridiculous situation in which it found itself so far as public opinion went. Dr. Warren's skilled handling of the news for British consumption had tended to unite the American people with the people of England. Not only in his letter to the inhabitants of Great Britain but in his covering letters to Lee and Franklin, he used such terms as "fellow subjects," "*our* royal Sovereign," and "the united efforts of both Englands." He carefully separated the English people from the troops and, with infinitely less justification, the King from his ministers. He credited the English with the character that would lead them to resist the same kind of military force in England that the farmers did in Massachusetts. But the North ministry, in re-

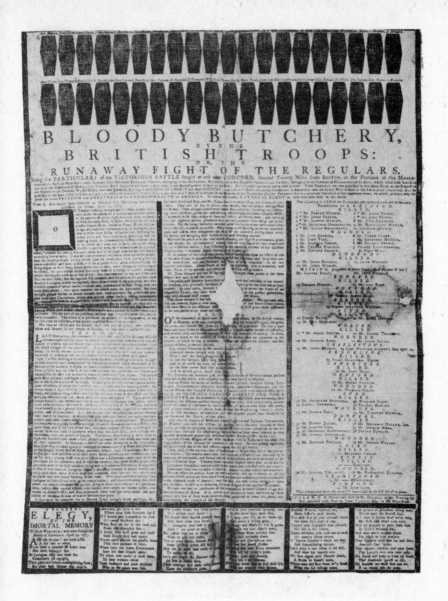

Newspaper broadsides, such as this from the Salem Gazette, dramatized the Lexington battle and were effectively distributed as propaganda both in the colonies and in Great Britain.
ESSEX INSTITUTE, SALEM, MASS.

John Adams (1735–1826), a thirty-nine-year-old Braintree lawyer when the Revolution broke out, was the leading force in the Second Continental Congress and brought about the appointment of Washington as commander in chief. MUSEUM OF FINE ARTS, BOSTON

The Retreat

From Concord to Lexington of the Army of Wild Irish Asses Defeated by the Brave American Militia

Mr Deacon. Mr Lorings. Mr Mulikens. Mr Bonds Mr Bruts Forgios and Barn all Plunderd and Burnt m April 9th

The Whig press in England, which credited the Provincials' version of the battles over that of Gage, became valuable partisans of the colonial cause. This cartoon was published as a broadside in London where it was very widely circulated. There are errors in the captions "Loeing" for "Loring," "Muliken" for "Mulliken." The cartoonist assumed four houses were destroyed, because he thought the "Deacon" of Deacon Lorings' name referred to another man whom he called Mr. Deacon. JOHN CARTER BROWN LIBRARY, PROVIDENCE

Boston Common, from the Tremont Street Mall, while the British troops were encamped there. The townspeople customarily watched the soldiers drill. John Hancock's luxurious house (upper right) dominated the Common from the site of the present State House. The beacon, from which Beacon Hill got its name, is behind Hancock's orchard. PHELPS STOKES COLLECTION, NEW YORK PUBLIC LIBRARY leasing Gage's version of the affair, fell to the use of such terms as "rebels" and "villians," and the British press laughed them out of a hearing. And so Great Britain moved into one of the most fateful wars in history with the enemy's achieving a triumphant public-opinion success right in the home realm. A month later the Secretary of State for the Colonies, writing rebukingly to Gage, was still hurt by it: "On the tenth of last month in the morning, Lieutenant Nunn arrived at my office with your dispatch containing an account of the transactions on the 19th of April, of which the public had before received intelligence by a schooner, to all appearance sent by the enemies of Government on purpose to make an impression here, by representing the affair between the King's troops and the rebel provincials in a light the most favorable to their own views. Their industry on this occasion had its effect. . . ."[46]

During that spring of 1775 the minds of the King's ministers might well have been haunted by some words uttered in Commons, four weeks to the day before Lexington, by Edmund Burke, who loved justice but despised radicalism. In his last and most magnificent plea for conciliation between England and her colonies, he said:

"Three thousand miles of ocean lie between you and them. No contrivance can prevent the effect of this distance in weakening government. Seas roll, and months pass, between the order and the execution; and the want of a speedy explanation of a single point is enough to defeat a whole system. You have, indeed, winged ministers of vengeance, who carry their bolts in their pounces to the remotest verge of the sea; but there a power steps in that limits the arrogance of raging passions and furious elements, and says, 'So far shalt thou go, and no farther.' "[47]

8

BIRTH OF AN ARMY

"I am imbarked on a wide ocean, boundless in its prospect and from whence, perhaps, no safe harbour is to be found."

GEORGE WASHINGTON[1]

The battle of Concord and Lexington was still a provincial affair—a matter between the people of the Massachusetts Bay province and the occupation troops of General Gage in Boston. There was no united authority on behalf of all the American colonies behind the variously assembling and departing companies of militia arriving at Cambridge to besiege Boston. The generals there were all creations of the Massachusetts Provincial Congress; if the men were to be housed, fed and supplied, they could turn only to the Massachusetts leaders; the entire diplomatic and military correspondence both with Gage in Boston and the ministry in London represented only the province of Massachusetts. It was the purpose of the Massachusetts delegation to the Second Continental Congress to change all this—to get the united Congress to adopt the provincial army, to stop any conciliation efforts by the other colonies, to make the cause of Massachusetts the cause of all the colonies, and to make this clear to the whole civilized world.

This was an ambitious set of objectives, and without Lexington it would have been utterly impossible. In the martyrs of Lexington, however, the Massachusetts delegation had a force behind them stronger than oratory or prophecies, and one that so stirred the people of the other colonies that their delegates would have no alternative to supporting Massachusetts. But it would not come without further internal struggle within the Congress. "America is a great unwieldy body," John Adams said. "Its progress must be slow. It is like a large fleet sailing under convoy. The fleetest sailors must wait for the dullest and slowest. Like a coach and six, the swiftest horses must be slackened, and the slowest quickened, that all may keep an even pace."[2]

The Second Continental Congress was to meet in Philadelphia on May tenth. John Adams, before leaving for the sessions, went to Cambridge to visit the New England militia. "There was great confusion and much distress," he wrote in his diary. "Artillery, arms, clothing were wanting, and a sufficient supply of provisions not easily obtained. Neither the officers nor men, however, wanted spirits or resolution."[3] From Cambridge, Adams followed the route of the British expedition to Lexington, stopping to talk to the inhabitants along the way about the details of the action of April nineteenth. "These were not calculated to diminish my ardor in the cause; they, on the contrary, convinced me that the die was cast, the Rubicon passed. . . ."[4] The next day, beset with a fever, he set out for Philadelphia, somewhat disgusted with himself because he had to ride in a sulky, attended by a servant, instead of riding the three hundred miles on horseback as he had intended.

Two of the remaining four Massachusetts delegates had already left for Philadelphia: Thomas Cushing, of Boston, and Robert Treat Paine, of Taunton. The other two, Samuel Adams and John Hancock, were still traveling around central Massachusetts in tandem. They had spent the night of April twentieth, the day after the battle, in the Wyman house at Billerica, and went back to Woburn the next day to get Dorothy Quincy and Aunt Lydia

Hancock, who had been left there overnight. Their movements for the next three days are lost to history. Apparently, they dodged around Middlesex and Worcester counties and finally turned up in the town of Worcester on Monday, April twenty-fourth.

Hancock was infuriated because there was no committee to welcome them there, no escort to accompany them on the first stage of their journey, and no sign of the other three delegates to the Continental Congress. He accordingly sat down and wrote a blistering letter "to the Gentlemen Committee of Safety" meeting with the Provincial Congress at Watertown and occupied with far more urgent problems than Hancock's pride. "Where is Mr. Cushing? Are Mr. Paine and Mr. John Adams to be with us? What are we to depend upon? We travel rather as deserters, which I will not submit to. . . ."[5] For three days they waited in Worcester for an escort for Hancock, while Adams pondered his beloved projects of moving the Continental Congress down the road toward independence and getting the other colonies to join the rebellion. Meanwhile, Dorothy Quincy and Aunt Lydia turned up again, much to Samuel Adams' distress, and all four left for New York and Philadelphia, by way of Hartford, on April twenty-seventh, a week and a day after the battle of Lexington.

At Hartford, Hancock and Adams stopped to confer with Governor Trumbull of Connecticut. Samuel Adams was convinced that the first strategy of the British would be to split the colonies by sending an army down through Lake Champlain, Lake George, and the Hudson River to New York City, isolating New England from the West and the South. Accordingly, long before Lexington he had dispatched a member of the Provincial Congress, John Brown, a Pittsfield lawyer, to Canada to get information on Canadian public opinion and the state of the old forts garrisoned since the end of the French War. Three weeks before Lexington, Brown reported that, in his judgment, the fort at Ticonderoga "must be seized as soon as possible, should hostilities be committed by the king's troops."[6] (On the day of Lexington, Gage wrote to

Guy Carleton, the British commander in Canada, directing him to dispatch the Seventh Regiment to protect Ticonderoga; this letter, of course, reached Carleton too late.) Adams now consulted with Trumbull, for the Massachusetts Committee of Safety had appointed Benedict Arnold of Connecticut to go and seize Fort Ticonderoga—a chore which Adams' agent, Brown, had already entrusted to a local group from the New Hampshire Grants who called themselves the Green Mountain Boys. This semi-outlaw band had been organized under Ethan Allen to harass the New York colony in its controversy with New Hampshire over the territory that is now Vermont. The Hartford Committee of Safety had added to the confusion by commissioning the taking of Ticonderoga to yet a third man, Colonel Samuel Parsons. There was nothing at this late date that Trumbull, Adams, and Hancock could do to straighten out all this complexity, but they talked eagerly of the forty-three cannon, fourteen mortars, and two howitzers at Ticonderoga and how precious their capture would be to the patriot cause.

Even as they talked, Arnold was on his way to Vermont with his commission as colonel and his authorization to enlist four hundred men for his expedition. Without stopping to enlist, he went with a servant directly to Castleton, where Ethan Allen and his Green Mountain Boys were gathered. There followed a dispute between Arnold and Allen on the command of the expedition, Arnold having his papers and Allen having the men. They settled the dispute by agreeing to storm Ticonderoga side by side at the head of their columns. This they did, with two boatloads of eighty-three men altogether, on May ninth. The British had let the fort fall apart after the French War, with great breaches in its walls; and it was garrisoned by only forty-two men, twenty of whom were unfit for unlimited duty. When Allen and Arnold arrived, carefully in step side by side, they were all asleep except the sentry, who simply ran away. Arnold tried to act with military dignity once inside the fort, but Allen was having none of that; he brandished his sword over his head and kept shouting at the door of the commanding officer's quarters: "Come out, you old rat."[7] Thus, on the day before the Second Continental Congress met, the first offensive American action succeeded at a remote spot in the wilderness on Lake George.

Meanwhile, after leaving Hartford, the Hancock party proceeded to Fairfield, where Dorothy Quincy and Aunt Lydia were installed in the mansion of Hancock's friend, Thaddeus Burr, high sheriff of Fairfield County. Hancock and Adams continued on to New York, where they met their fellow delegates, John Adams, Cushing, and Paine, at King's Bridge, just north of the city. Hancock's spirits soared at their triumphant entry into New York.

It was midafternoon of Saturday, May sixth. Hancock and Adams—the former slender and elegant and somewhat delicate for his thirty-eight years and the latter shaking with his palsy and seedy and old beyond his fifty-two years—rode ahead in Hancock's fine phaeton. Behind them was John Adams, the intellectual young lawyer, thirty-nine and serious, sober, and responsible, sharing his chaise with his fellow delegate, the Boston merchant, Thomas Cushing, a mild man who still hoped that strong economic action by the colonies could prevent severance from England. The fifth Massachusetts delegate, Robert Treat Paine, the small-town lawyer from Taunton, who had appeared for the prosecution against John Adams at the trial of the Boston Massacre soldiers, rode alone behind. Word of Lexington had, of course, preceded the delegates to New York, and the latter colony, which previously had not even chosen delegates to the Continental Congress, was ready with a spectacular reception for the heroic delegation from Massachusetts.

As soon as word of the approach of the delegates reached New York, thousands of people rode out of the town in their carriages and on horseback to meet them. Three miles from the town boundary a battalion of eight hundred uniformed militia arrived to escort them with bayonets fixed and a great band of musicians blaring forth. Thousands of spectators tramped through the dirt roads to see the great men, and hundreds of church bells in New York rang joyously. "You can easier fancy than I describe the amazing concourse of people," a Connecticut delegate wrote to his wife: "I believe well nigh every open carriage in the city, and thousands on foot trudging and sweating through the dirt. At the Fresh Water, the battalion halted, and we again passed their front and received a second salute from the left, and were received by our friends, the delegates of the city."[8]

As the procession reached the city proper, the crowds mounted in size and noisy enthusiasm. "The doors, the windows, the stoops, the roofs of the piazzas, were loaded with all ranks, ages and sexes; in short, I feared every moment lest someone would be crushed to death; but no accident. A little dispute arose as we came near the town—the populace insisting on taking out our horses and drawing the carriages by hand."[9]

In his diary John Adams, deeply concerned with the problems that faced Massachusetts in the new session of the Continental Congress, dismissed this turbulent reception in a sentence: "At Kings Bridge we were met by a great number of gentlemen in carriages and on horseback, and all the way their numbers increased, till I thought the whole city was come out to meet us."[10] And that was all on the subject from John Adams. Hancock, however, was beside himself with vanity and excitement, and wrote an astonishing letter to Dorothy Quincy in Fairfield, in which he took the view that the reception was meant solely for him and that it was only his carriage that the populace sought to pull by hand. He even ignored the fact that the father of the Revolution, Samuel Adams, sat dourly beside him in the phaeton. "I dined and then set out in the procession for New York," Hancock wrote. "The carriage of your humble servant of course being first in the procession. When we arrived within three miles of the City, we were met by the grenadier company and regiment of the city militia under arms, gentlemen in carriages and on horseback and many thousands of persons on foot, the roads filled with people, and the greatest cloud of dust I ever saw. In this situation, we entered the city, and passing through the principal streets of New York amidst the acclamations of thousands were set down at Mr. Fraunces's. After entering the house, three huzzas were given, and the people by degrees dispersed.

"When I got within a mile of the city my carriage was stopped, and persons appearing with proper harnesses insisted upon taking out my horses and dragging me into and through the city, a circumstance I would not have had taken place upon any consideration, not being fond of such parade.

"I begged and entreated that they would suspend the design and asked it as a favor, and the matter subsided, but when I got to the entrance of the city and the numbers of spectators increased to perhaps seven thousand or more, they declared they would have the horses out and drag me through the city. I repeated my request, and I was obliged to apply to the leading gentleman in the procession to intercede with them not to carry their designs into execution, as it was very disagreeable to me. They were at last prevailed upon, and I proceeded. I was much obliged to them for their good wishes and opinion, in short no person could possibly be more noticed than myself."[11]

In the self-adulating letter, which continues for six more paragraphs, there is not a word of the significance of the reception: the effect of the news of Lexington on the colony most loyal to the Crown and its wholly new embracement of the patriot cause. It is impossible to escape the impression that not Hancock but his austere carriage mate, Samuel Adams, prevented the hauling of the carriage by the citizens of New York. "If you wish to be gratified with so humiliating a spectacle, I will get out and walk, for I will not countenance an act by which my fellow citizens will degrade themselves into beasts,"[12] was Samuel Adams' known comment to a companion under similar circumstances later that year.

ii

Samuel Adams had his own brooding thoughts to occupy him. He was beginning to see the limits of his own genius. As an agitator, as a mob manipulator, as a town politician, he was extraordinarily competent. As a statesman, he had infinitely less confidence in himself. And the management of the program for the Continental Congress would call for statesmanship, and Samuel Adams knew it. For the suspicions, fears, and downright dislike of Massachusetts ran deep in the other colonies, and Samuel Adams knew that it would take more than a Lexington wholly to dissipate them. A pessimism seemed to settle over him as he neared Philadelphia—a pessimism undoubtedly springing from both his reservations about coping with fifty men from all the colonies with little in common and the historic tendencies of the other colonies to look with misgivings upon Massachusetts. Samuel Adams was much too stern a Puritan to recognize either the necessary role of compromise in democratic action or the possibility that Massachusetts might not always be right.

The narrowness of Puritan doctrine was offensive to both the Middle Atlantic and the Southern states, and the equalitarian practices of the New England militia were also repugnant to the aristocrats of the South, who loved their romantic illusions about an officer-gentleman class. General Ward and General Putnam were a storekeeper and a working farmer, respectively, and the colonial officers of the South liked to think themselves above such pursuits. There were also very serious doubts in the other colonies about independence—a doctrine that both the Adamses were beginning to preach openly. Traditional ties of Virginia, for example, with England were strongly emotional—the Church of England, the efforts to create a landed aristocracy, the attachment to ceremony and formality. In New York the Church of England was immensely strong, particularly in New York City, where it was the established church. In Pennsylvania the Quakers had grave religious misgivings about Massachusetts' militancy. Many of the colonies were unsympathetic with the trade problems of Massachusetts, some of them being themselves primarily agrarian societies. Almost all of them feared—as they had in the First Continental Congress of the previous autumn—a new and struggling nation run by the zealots of Boston, whose moral principles they believed to be tempered with shrewd concern for their own economic interests. Finally, more than one serious observer was certain that if it were not for the union imposed by the British crown, the colonies would be involved in a whole series of intracolonial disputes and wars.

To one so consistently and so early dedicated to independence as Samuel Adams, all these factors conditioning the opening of the new session of the Continental Congress were dispiriting. Adams, moreover, was tired and depressed. He had not been home since the opening of the Provincial Congress in Concord two months earlier. In his hasty and circuitous departure from Clarke's house in Lexington, he had been unable to return to Boston to get the suit that his friends had bought for him to wear at such important occasions as the Continental Congress meetings. He spent his first days in Philadelphia struggling with the problem of whether he could properly buy himself a new suit with public moneys advanced to him for expenses, for he had no funds of his own; he decided finally to get the suit. Then word came to him of the death, of consumption on board ship from England, of Josiah Quincy, Junior, at the age of thirty-one. Quincy, a brilliant lawyer, was one of the great theoreticians of the American case against England and had been in London as an American agent. To Samuel Adams he had been like a son, and his admiration for Adams was unlimited. His death added to the heaviness with which Samuel Adams faced the tasks that lay before the Massachusetts delegation at Philadelphia.

His cousin, John Adams, felt no such melancholy. Thirteen

years younger than Samuel, far more intellectual and far less emotional, John Adams had not just the competences of the statesman but also the statesman's values and insights. Moreover, John Adams believed thoroughly in the strength of law rather than that of great men as the foundation of the really good society. Where Samuel Adams was a great Puritan, John was a great moralist. While Samuel had to manipulate events to bring about an end he sought, John Adams could conceive of no path to an end he sought except through reason. With Samuel Adams, the Revolution was almost a religious matter; with John, it belonged, as one more episode, to the long struggle of man to improve himself through the use of reason and the establishment of rational institutions. And John Adams came to Philadelphia with as much zest for the intellectual exercise in the sessions of Congress as his older cousin did with reluctance.

John Adams wrote in his diary an entire program for the Second Continental Congress: "I thought the first step ought to be to recommend to the people . . . to seize on all the Crown officers, and hold them with civility, humanity, and generosity, as hostages for the security of the people of Boston and to be exchanged for them as soon as the British army would release them [this was unnecessary, because—then unknown to Adams—Gage permitted inhabitants who wished to do so to leave Boston]; that we ought to recommend to people of all the States to institute governments for themselves, under their own authority, and that without loss of time; that we ought to declare the Colonies free, sovereign and independent states, and then to inform Great Britain we were willing to enter into negotiations with them for the redress of all grievances, and a restoration of harmony between the two countries, upon permanent principles. All this I thought might be done before we entered into any connections, alliances or negotiations with foreign powers. I was also for informing Great Britain very frankly that hitherto we were free; but, if the war should be continued, we were determined to seek alliances with France, Spain and any other power of Europe that would contract with us. That we ought immediately to adopt the army in Cambridge as a continental army, to appoint a General and all other officers, take upon ourselves the pay, subsistence, clothing, armor and munitions of the troops."[13]

On Wednesday, May tenth, the forty-eight delegates present convened in Pennsylvania's State House on Chestnut Street in Philadelphia. If the Provincial Congress of Massachusetts was an illegal body, the Continental Congress was a step further from legality. As an institution it was nothing more than an assemblage of four dozen men from the various colonies, met together to discuss the difficulties that they were variously facing with England. The delegates had no uniform authority whatever, some being authorized by their colonial legislatures merely to attend the Congress. Only two colonies, Maryland and North Carolina, were committed to supporting whatever acts the Congress might pass. Yet resistance to the British rule was in the air, and there is no doubt that the differences that occurred were due to varying judgment on the pacing and degree of the resistance.

The first three days were spent in reading the Lexington depositions, fixing the blame for the first bloodshed upon the British and so memorializing the ministry in London. An official request from the Provincial Congress in Massachusetts that the Continental Congress take over the army "by appointing a generalissimo,"[14] was read, but then the news of Ticonderoga arrived. Attention was diverted to the problem of what to do with the captured fort and with nearby Crown Point, also captured. Samuel Adams wanted to use them as a point of departure for a march on Canada and was voted down in a resolution that provided merely for the occupation of the captured forts. The Congress then considered two requests for advice from New York on what course it should take if, as was expected, British troops were landed. The answer: a peaceable landing was all right, but force should be met with force.

The hot Philadelphia May droned on, and as Samuel Adams seemed to withdraw more and more into himself, John Adams began to fume at the reluctance of the Congress to take any bold or even significant action. He blew up in anger when the conservative faction, led by John Dickinson of Pennsylvania, introduced a resolution petitioning the King for negotiations leading to reconciliation. John Adams gave a long speech in opposition, after which Dickinson followed him into the courtyard and told him that if the New Englanders "don't concur with us in our pacific system, I and a number of us will break off from you in New England, and we will carry on the opposition ourselves in our own way."[15] Furious as he was at this threat, Adams was determined not to walk into any trap that would divide the Congress before it had achieved what he had thought to be its proper objectives. He voted for the resolution and bided his time.

Most of the debating soared far over the head of John Hancock, who was having his troubles, even at a distance, with his fiancée, Dorothy Quincy. She refused to answer any of his letters and even to acknowledge pretty gifts he kept sending her by messenger to Fairfield. He was, moreover, getting word that Dorothy's host's nephew, Aaron Burr, was in Fairfield and paying too much attention to her and that she was gleefully accepting it. Hancock's papers, during these epochal birth pains of the American nation that he witnessed, consist of scolding letters to Dorothy Quincy. Meanwhile, his great vanity was indulged by his election as president of the Congress. Actually, the presidency had no more authority than a clerkship, and Peyton Randolph of Virginia had resigned it because he felt that the speakership of the Virginia Assembly was more important. There is no record that, as president, Hancock showed either organizational or intellectual leadership. He simply presided as a chairman and functioned largely as a correspondence clerk. If history were beckoning John Hancock, it would have to be more obvious. He made nothing of the opportunity for leadership that, however vague its capacity, the post represented. Instead, he waited for a place of greater glory commensurate with what he thought to be his ability.

iii

Probably the most tenacious political entity of the time was the Provincial Congress sitting under Dr. Warren at Watertown, Massachusetts. Its communication to the Continental Congress having gone unanswered, it sent another on May sixteenth and had it delivered personally by one of its own members, Dr. Benjamin Church, who wrote a very polite note to Gage, saying that he would not be able to do any spying for a while because of the journey to Philadelphia. It was Thursday, June first—the Continental Congress had been in session for three weeks—when Dr. Church arrived in Philadelphia. He delivered the Provincial Congress letter to the State House, stayed around for a week, possibly to gather what information he could get to sell to Gage, prescribed a lotion for John Adams' eyes, which had been smarting badly ever since his long, feverish ride from Massachusetts, and then returned home, carrying with him letters from the delegates to their families and friends.

The effects of the carefully prepared document from Massachusetts, bearing the stamp of Dr. Joseph Warren in its style, was to force the Continental Congress to action. It shrewdly associated the problems of local self-government for the colonies—thereby declaring a *de facto* interruption if not an end to British rule—and of the creation of a continental army. Formally it petitioned the Continental Congress for advice in setting up a civil government to replace that of the Crown. The petition was in itself less important than its implication, for the Provincial Congress had for six months been functioning as the only civil government of Massachusetts in any case. But the implication that Massachusetts could not and would not set up a permanent civil government without the consent of the Continental Congress forced upon the latter body the role of central authority over all the colonies. Similarly, the petition gave a civil authority power over the military by urging and pleading that the Continental Congress take over the army assembling at Cambridge. The formal acts that Massachusetts would require of the Congress were, of course, advice to go ahead and set up a civil government and the appointment of a continental commander in chief of the army. All this obviously was forcing the hand of a body which had no power to set up governments and wage wars unless it assumed such powers. Its only present purpose was as a forum for its members to advise and consult with one another as representatives of wholly separate chartered colonies. Massachusetts would have the Continental Congress become a governing legislature.

John Adams thought that the Continental Congress avoided facing this essential metamorphosis by occupying itself with more conciliatory proposals. "This measure of imbecility, the second petition to the King," he grumbled in his diary, "embarrassed every exertion of Congress; it occasioned motions and debates without end for appointing committees to draw up a declaration of the causes, motives, and objects of taking arms with a view to obtain decisive declarations against independence, etc. In the mean time the New England army investing Boston, the New England legislatures, congresses and conventions, and the whole body of the people were left without munitions of war, without arms, clothing, pay, or even countenance and encouragement. Every post brought me letters from my friends . . . urging in pathetic terms the impossibility of keeping their men together without the assistance of Congress."[16]

Many delegates, however, hoped for some peaceable word from England, and the petition from Massachusetts was handled slowly. Hancock read it to the Congress on Friday, June second. John Adams immediately rose to entreat the delegates to give an early and affirmative reply. He saw the first part of the petition, "requesting the Congress to favor them with explicit advice respecting the taking up and exercising the powers of civil government,"[17] as an occasion for the Continental Congress to urge all the colonies to institute new governments. In his diary he observed that he supposed America should probably follow the example of the Greeks and form a confederacy of states. He believed "that the case of Massachusetts was the most urgent, but that it could not be long before every other colony must follow her example. That with a view to this subject, I had looked into the ancient and modern confederacies for example, but they all appeared to me to have been huddled up in a hurry by a few chiefs. But we had a people of more intelligence, curiosity and enterprise, who must be all consulted, and we must realize the theories of the wisest writers, and invite the people to erect the whole building with their own hands, upon the broadest foundation. That this could be done only by conventions of representatives chosen by the people in the several colonies, in the most exact proportions. That it was my opinion that Congress ought now to recommend to the people of every colony to call such conventions immediately, and set up governments of their own, under their own authority; for the people were the source of all authority and original of all power. These were new, strange and terrible doctrines to the greatest part of the members. . . ."[18]

Adams, in this wise and ultimately heeded speech, seemed, as he noted, to be some light years ahead of most of his brothers of the Congress, who still saw the problem as solely one of finding an harmonious way of living under the British. They were still on the whole, more fearful of independence and instability than of occasional British arrogance and enforced stability. So—as though its pestiferous pleas might vanish in the night—they lay the Massachusetts petition on the table. The next morning, of course, they had to face it all over again. This they did by appointing a committee of five—not one of them from New England—to consider the petition. John Adams continued to fume at the inaction. In

Watertown, Dr. Joseph Warren, still presiding over daily sessions of a Provincial Congress trying to hold together an army of several thousands that was no longer just a Massachusetts army, brought up the bugaboo of military rule: "The matter of taking up government, I think, cannot occasion much debate. If the southern colonies have any apprehensions from the northern colonies, they surely must now be for an establishment of civil government here; for, as an army is now necessary or is taking the field, it is obvious to everyone, if they are without control, a military government must certainly take place. . . ."[19]

Oddly enough, it was Samuel Adams who was most relaxed over the slowness with which the Massachusetts petition was dealt: "The spirit of patriotism prevails among the members of this Congress, but from the necessity of things business must go slower than one could wish. It is difficult to possess upwards of sixty gentlemen at once with the same feelings upon questions of importance that are continually arising."[20]

Finally, on June seventh, the Congress responded to the civil government part of the Massachusetts petition. It not only did not go as far as John Adams would wish but it avoided accommodating Massachusetts with any advice or consent to the establishment of a "permanent" government. Nevertheless, it recognized the right of a people to set up their own government and to ignore a tyrannical government. In the specific case of Massachusetts, it ruled "that no obedience being due to the Act of Parliament for altering the charter of the Colony of Massachusetts Bay, nor to a Governor or Lieutenant-Governor who will not observe the directions of, but endeavor to subvert, that charter. The Governor and Lieutenant-Governor of that colony are to be considered as absent, and their offices vacant; and as there is no Council there, and the inconveniences arising from the suspension of the powers of government are intolerable, especially at a time when General Gage hath actually levied war and is carrying on hostilities against his Majesty's peaceable and loyal subjects of that Colony; that, in

order to conform as near as may be to the spirit and substance of
the charter, it be recommended to the Provincial Convention to
write letters to the inhabitants of the several places, which are entitled to representation in Assembly, requesting them to choose
such representatives, and that the Assembly when chosen do elect
Counsellors; and that such assembly or Council exercise the powers
of government, until a Governor of His Majesty's appointment
will consent to govern the Colony according to its charter."[21]

Although it both expressed loyalty to the King and went no
further in the assertion of rights than those granted in the old
charters, this resolution represented a tremendous commitment
to the Congress. Not only did it advise a colony to institute its
own government, albeit temporary, but it, *ipso facto,* set itself
up as a central authority within the colonies. The resolution went
off to Massachusetts. The Congress in Philadelphia now faced the
thorny question of adopting the New England army. In doing so,
it would be committing all the colonies to a war with Britain that
before Lexington was utterly inconceivable to any delegate there—
with the possible exception of the radical and rhetorical Patrick
Henry, Samuel Adams' Virginia counterpart, who could hardly
wait for hostilities to resume.

iv

The key to the adoption of the New England army at Cambridge
by the Continental Congress was the appointment of a commander
in chief. Yet John Adams was the only delegate ready to press the
matter. Samuel Adams, who distrusted generals, was in favor of
soldiers' electing their own officers and was not anxious to see any
general appointed. Whenever his cousin tried to consult with him
on the subject, he withdrew into silence and said nothing.

Nor were John Adams' other colleagues from Massachusetts
much help to him. "Mr. Hancock himself had an ambition to be
appointed commander in chief. Whether he thought an election

a compliment due to him, and intended to have the honor of declining it, or whether he would have accepted, I know not."[22] Cushing wanted a New Englander, because the army was from New England. Paine insisted that the post should go to his old college mate, Artemas Ward. But John Adams had made up his mind that it had to be a Southerner. Fear of New England he recognized as far too powerful to permit a New England commander in chief. His alert eye fixed upon the only man attending the Congress in uniform, Colonel George Washington of Virginia. Adams was impressed by Washington's quiet patriotism (Washington's resolution to raise and personally pay for a force of a thousand men and march at their head to the relief of Boston had become widely known), by his sense of economy in speaking, and by the extraordinary strength of his character. By the middle of June he was determined to start the machinery to elect Washington as commander in chief.

John Adams began his tactics with some electioneering outside the State House. With Cushing and Paine he got nowhere, and he would not, of course, even mention Washington's name to Hancock. Even more surprising were objections from other colonies to Washington's lack of proved ability. Whenever Adams brought up the Virginia colonel's record in the French war, he was reminded that every major engagement that Washington participated in was lost. Adams, however, remained convinced that Washington was the only man for the job. Not even the views of some of Washington's fellow delegates from Virginia could change his mind. "In canvassing this subject, out of doors, I found too that even among the delegates of Virginia there were difficulties. The apostolical reasonings among themselves, which should be greatest, were not less energetic among the saints of the ancient dominion than they were among us of New England. In several conversations, I found more than one very cool about the appointment of Washington, and particularly Mr. Pendleton was very clear and full against it."[23] As president of the Virginia Committee of Safety,

Edmund Pendleton had a particularly strong influence. But Adams, contemplating the need and dangers of the weak, quarrelsome cluster of colonies and the shaggy, unorganized army that he had seen at Cambridge, saw Washington's gifts of character and his respect-commanding bearing as necessary to the building of any effective army and to any enlistments or support outside of New England.

On Wednesday, June fourteenth—eight weeks, to the day, after Lexington—John Adams determined that he would that day nominate George Washington as commander in chief of an American army. That morning he took only his cousin, Samuel Adams, into his confidence. John Adams was still troubled by the looseness of the organization of the New England army (of the twenty thousand who besieged Boston right after Lexington, four thousand had gone home), by the irresolute attitude of some of the other colonies, by the doubts expressed during his canvassing of his colleagues on Washington. "Full of anxieties concerning these confusions," he wrote in his diary, "and apprehending daily that we should hear very distressing news from Boston, I walked with Mr. Samuel Adams in the State House yard, for a little exercise and fresh air, before the hour of Congress, and there represented to him the various dangers that surrounded us. He agreed to them all, but said, 'What shall we do?' I answered him, that he knew I had taken great pains to get our colleagues to agree upon some plan, that we might be unanimous; but he knew that they would pledge themselves to nothing; but I was determined to take a step which should compel them and all the other members of Congress to declare themselves for or against something. 'I am determined this morning to make a direct motion that Congress should adopt the army before Boston, and appoint Colonel Washington commander of it.' Mr. Adams seemed to think very seriously of it, but said nothing."[24]

John Adams entered the State House and, as soon as the session was convened, arose to make his speech. He had no idea of how much support he would get from his cousin, but he knew from whom he would get opposition. He pressed the need for the immediate adoption of the army at Cambridge and appointing a commanding general. He then proceeded to describe the ideal man, "who was among us and very well known to all of us, a gentleman whose skill and experience as an officer, whose independent fortune, great talents and excellent universal character would command the approbation of all America and unite the cordial exertions of all the colonies better than any other person. . . ."[25]

At this great speech of John Adams, Hancock, sitting in the president's chair, beamed on the assembled delegates as he imagined his colleague to be leading up to his, Hancock's, nomination as commander in chief. But when Adams came to Washington's name, and as the Virginian left the room to permit the nomination to be debated, Hancock's face fell noticeably. "I never remarked a more sudden and striking change of countenance," Adams said. "Mortification and resentment were expressed as forcibly as his face could exhibit them. Mr. Samuel Adams seconded the motion, and that did not soften the President's physiognomy at all."[26]

John Adams was both surprised and gratified that his nomination of Washington was seconded by Samuel Adams, who "very rarely spoke much in Congress,"[27] though Hancock felt more bitterly about the seconding speech than he did about the nomination. But as soon as Samuel Adams was finished, several delegates leaped to their feet to oppose the nomination. Edmund Pendleton of Virginia and Roger Sherman took the lead in an argument based on the fact that the army was from New England and already had a general with whom they were apparently satisfied in Artemas Ward and who was able to keep the British bottled up in Boston—which was all that anybody wanted them to do at the time. Both the remaining Massachusetts delegates, Cushing and Paine, failed to support the nomination. Cushing was afraid that a Virginia commander would lead to dissent in the ranks, particularly since New England militia were not accustomed to taking orders from their officers even when they chose their own. Paine said that Artemas Ward was at Harvard with him and was a great and competent man. The session ended with no action being taken at all.

John Adams refused to give up. He spent the evening conducting a campaign among the delegates. He was relatively certain that most of the delegates who had made no comment during the debate were for Washington. Consequently, he spent his time with those who opposed the nomination, finally persuading them to withdraw their opposition. He talked with his own delegates from Massachusetts and made them see that their attitude risked all that they had come to Philadelphia to achieve. By the time Adams retired that night, he was no longer doubtful about the outcome. The next morning Thomas Johnson of Maryland formally nominated Washington again. He was unanimously elected. The army had a general. And the Continental Congress had an army.

v

Eight weeks had passed since William Diamond beat his drum on the Common at Lexington and some forty men lined up to face the British regulars. Now, as the hot Philadelphia summer wore on, it began to dawn upon the delegates to the Congress that they were no longer concerned with launching a revolution but merely with the conduct of a war to seal it, "for the revolution was complete in the minds of the people and the union of the colonies, before the war commenced in the skirmishes of Concord and Lexington on the 19th of April, 1775."[28]

Back in Lexington the townspeople followed through, without reservations, without holding back, on what they had started on that April dawn. Captain Parker mustered forty-five men of his company on May sixth and again marched them to Cambridge to help sustain the siege of Boston. In June he marched sixty-four of them to aid in the battle of Bunker's Hill. Three months later, however, Captain Parker was dead at forty-six, having been in an advanced state of tuberculosis all through his fighting days that eventful spring.

After the provincial militia was incorporated into the Continental Army, a hundred and six men of Lexington, out of a total population of seven hundred and fifty, enlisted. From the farms of Lexington they followed the British, for six years, all the way down the coast to Yorktown. Men whose families for four and five generations had not been twelve miles from the Common turned up on the battlefields and camp grounds of New York, New Jersey, Pennsylvania, and Virginia. Some of them, like Edmund Munroe, the veteran of Rogers' Rangers, were killed in those distant places. All the male members of the family of Samuel Hadley, who was killed on the Common—his father and three brothers—followed the British to New York and on to Virginia. Prince Estabrook, the slave, fought throughout the war and came back to his freedom.

William Diamond, the drummer, also went away to the war, grew up in the army, and returned to Lexington. There he married Rebecca Simonds, who had been only eleven when her father marched off with Captain Parker to Cambridge. They had six children and in later years moved to New Hampshire, where William Diamond died during the presidency of John Adams' son. The young fifer, Jonathan Harrington, also returned to Lexington, married, and—surviving five of his seven children—died at ninety-six in 1854, the year that Lincoln and Douglas debated the Kansas-Nebraska Bill. But the family of the other Jonathan Harrington, the young father who had crawled across the Common to die on his own doorstep, disappeared from Lexington. His son died the year after the battle just before his tenth birthday, and his young widow went to Boston to start a new life.

Young Dr. Prescott, of Concord, and Lydia Mulliken, whom he was courting in Lexington the night that he joined Revere in rousing the minutemen of Lincoln and Concord, were never married. The Mulliken house, standing in the staging area for Percy's retreat, had been burned to the ground; and Lydia, her mother, and four younger children all moved into the house of a neighbor. Prescott became a surgeon with the Continental Army, was captured, and died in a British prison at Halifax in 1777. Lydia's two older brothers enlisted in the Continental Army; one of them, the minuteman, Nathaniel, was dead within ten months. Lydia waited until eight years had dimmed the memory of the young doctor, and then she married and moved away. And so the war did not deal easily with the people of Lexington, but they responded with gallantry and dignity and acceptance.

The other hero-physician of the day, Dr. Joseph Warren, who had taken such brilliant command of the province's affairs after the battle, was made a major general by the Continental Congress. He fought as a volunteer at the battle of Bunker's Hill, however, refusing a command because his commission had not yet arrived. He was killed, as he had wished, in active combat, as the British stormed a redoubt whose defenders had run out of ammunition. A few yards away the Royal Marine Major Pitcairn, who had commanded on Lexington Common, fell mortally wounded and died in the arms of his soldier son.

In Lexington the Reverend Jonas Clarke remained a great and dominant influence. On behalf of the town he wrote a thundering disapproval of Jay's Treaty, terminating the war with Britain, in 1795. Three years later he wrote a masterpiece of statesmanship, a persuasive and closely reasoned petition from the town to Congress against the arming of merchant vessels during the quasi-war with France. His twelve children scattered all over the world, some becoming diplomats, some merchant-adventurers, some politicians and judges. None of his sons entered the ministry, but all his daughters who married became the wives of clergymen, including an Anglican who was president of Columbia College in New York.

Half a century after his ministry in Lexington began, Jonas Clarke died, just a month before his seventy-fifth birthday. His people carried him from the old house where the Hancocks and Clarkes had lived for over a hundred years and interred him in the tomb their grandfathers had built for old "Bishop" Hancock. So the great day of Lexington slipped into history, having "given us a name among the nations of the earth."[29]

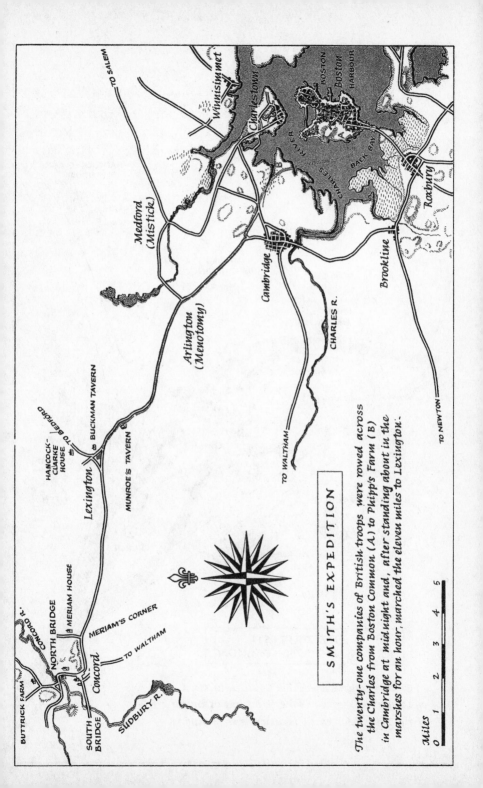

SMITH'S EXPEDITION

The twenty-one companies of British troops were rowed across the Charles from Boston Common (A) to Phipp's Farm (B) in Cambridge at midnight and, after standing about in the marshes for an hour, marched the eleven miles to Lexington.

Miles

0   1   2   3   4   5

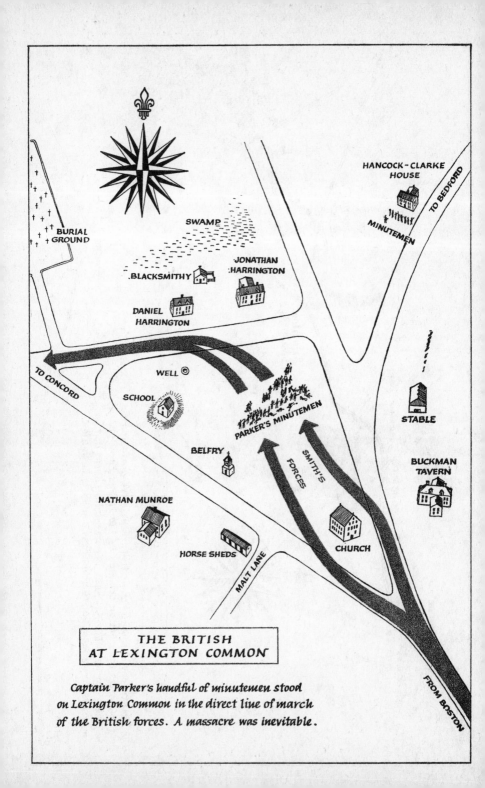

THE BRITISH
AT LEXINGTON COMMON

Captain Parker's handful of minutemen stood
on Lexington Common in the direct line of march
of the British forces. A massacre was inevitable.

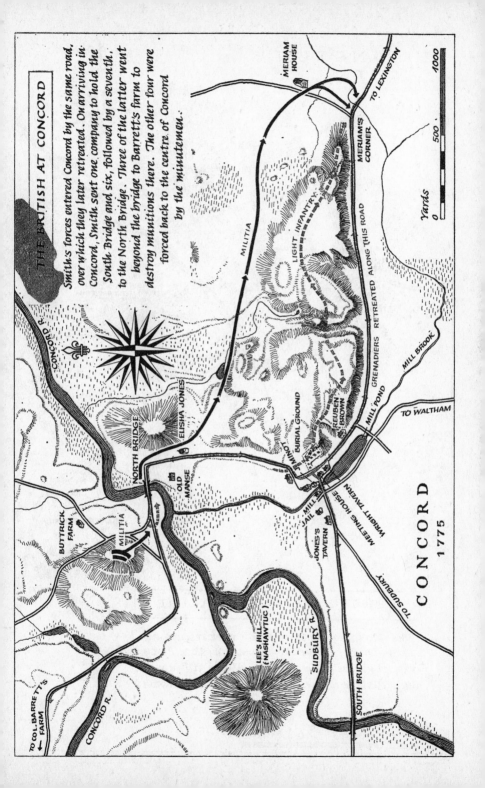

THE BRITISH AT CONCORD

Smith's forces entered Concord by the same road, over which they later retreated. On arriving in Concord, Smith sent one company to hold the South Bridge and six, followed by a seventh, to the North Bridge. Three of the latter went beyond the bridge to Barrett's farm to destroy munitions there. The other four were forced back to the centre of Concord by the minutemen.

CONCORD R.

TO COL. BARRETT'S FARM

BUTTRICK FARM

CONCORD R.

MILITIA

NORTH BRIDGE

ELISHA JONES

OLD MANSE

LEE'S HILL (NASHAWTUC)

SUDBURY R.

SOUTH BRIDGE

CONCORD 1775

JAIL

JONES'S TAVERN

MEETING HOUSE

WRIGHT TAVERN

MILL

MINOT

BURIAL GROUND

REUBEN BROWN

MILL POND

MILL BROOK

GRENADIERS RETREATED ALONG THIS ROAD

TO WALTHAM

TO SUDBURY

LIGHT INFANTRY

MILITIA

MERIAM'S CORNER

MERIAM HOUSE

TO LEXINGTON

Yards

0   500   1000

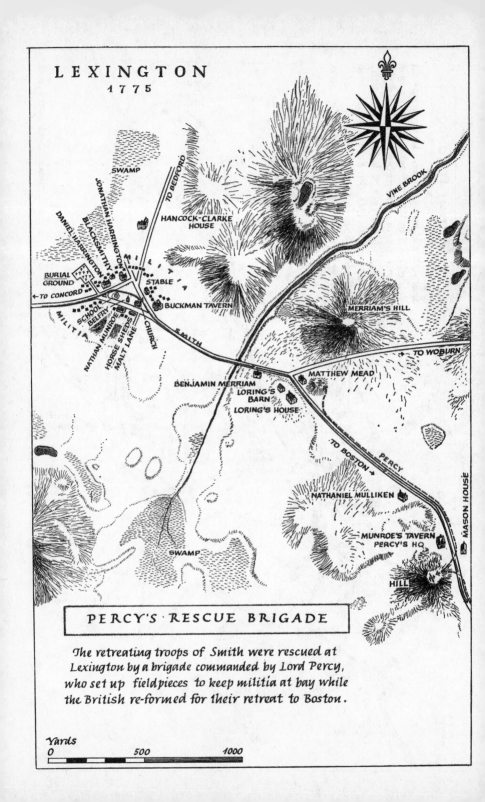

LEXINGTON
1775

SWAMP

TO BEDFORD

HANCOCK-CLARKE HOUSE

VINE BROOK

JONATHAN HARRINGTON

BLACKSMITHY

DANIEL HARRINGTON

BURIAL GROUND

←TO CONCORD

STABLE

BUCKMAN TAVERN

MERRIAM'S HILL

SCHOOL

BELFRY

MILITIA

NATHAN MUNROE

HORSE SHEDS

MALT LANE

CHURCH

SMITH

TO WOBURN

BENJAMIN MERRIAM

LORING'S BARN

LORING'S HOUSE

MATTHEW MEAD

TO BOSTON →

PERCY

NATHANIEL MULLIKEN

MASON HOUSE

SWAMP

MUNROE'S TAVERN

PERCY'S HQ

HILL

PERCY'S RESCUE BRIGADE

The retreating troops of Smith were rescued at
Lexington by a brigade commanded by Lord Percy,
who set up field pieces to keep militia at bay while
the British re-formed for their retreat to Boston.

Yards

0   500   1000

NOTES

(NOTE: *Unorthodox orthography, capitalization, and punctuation have been changed in quotations, except when otherwise noted, to avoid unnecessary distractions. Today such variations as appeared in the originals would misleadingly suggest illiteracy. Actually, of course, in the eighteenth century uniform spellings and punctuation were not common even among the educated.*)

NOTES TO PROLOGUE

[1]Peter Force, *American Archives*, 4th Series, II, 492–93.
[2]Elias Phinney, *History of the Battle at Lexington*, 33.
[3]Ezra Ripley, *A History of the Fight at Concord*, 35.
[4]Major General William Heath, *Memoirs*, 12.
[5]Charles Hudson, *History of Lexington*, II, 527.
[6]Force, *op. cit.*, 4, II, 491. Italics added.

NOTES TO PART 1

[1]*Proceedings of the Centennial of the Battle of Lexington*, 10.

[2]Josiah Quincy, *The History of Harvard University*, II, 120.

[3]*N.Y. Gazette*, April 18, 1768, reprinted in *Boston Gazette*.

[4]*Sermon Preached on the Ordination of Mr. John Hancock* [Jr.]

[5]Diary of Jonas Clarke, October 19, 1766.

[6]Edward Holyoke, *Obedience and Submission*, 7 f.

[7]Edward Holyoke, *Integrity and Religion*, 12 f.

[8]Jonathan Mayhew, *The Snare Broken*, 9.

[9]Instructions "To William Reed, Esq., the present Representative of Lexington," October 21, 1765.

[10]Cited in Carl Becker, *The Eve of the Revolution*, 42.

[11]Instructions, *loc. cit.* Cf. John Stuart Mill: "Thus a people may prefer a free government, but if, from indolence, or carelessness, or cowardice, or want of public spirit, they are unequal to the exertions necessary for preserving it . . . they are unlikely long to enjoy it." (*Representative Government*)

[12]Declarations and Resolves, Town of Lexington, September 21, 1768.

[13]Report of the Committee of Correspondence adopted by the Town of Lexington, December 1773.

[14]*Ibid.*

[15]Resolves, Town of Lexington, September 26, 1774.

[16]Jonas Clarke, *The Importance of Military Skill, Measures for Defense, and a Martial Spirit in a Time of Peace*, 11.

[17]Carleton A. Staples, *Proceedings of the Lexington Historical Society*, IV, 48 ff.

[18]Heath Papers, Massachusetts Historical Society, I, 19, 6.

NOTES TO PART 2

[1]*The Writings of Samuel Adams*, II, 25.
[2]Francis H. Brown, Lexington Historical Society, *A Copy of Epitaphs in the Old Burying-Grounds*, 26.
[3]*Proceedings of the Lexington Historical Society*, II, 158 ff.
[4]*The Writings of Samuel Adams*, II, 115.
[5]W. V. Wells, *The Life and Public Services of Samuel Adams*, I, 196.
[6]From the Salem *Gazette*, cited in Richard Frothingham, *Life and Times of Joseph Warren*, 445. It is not in the journals of the Provincial Congress.
[7]"Intelligence received April 15th, 1775" in Gage Papers, Clements Library, the University of Michigan.
[8]*Warren-Adams Letters*. First Series, Massachusetts Historical Society *Collections*, LXXII, 45.
[9]"Colonial Correspondence on the Boston Port Bill," Fourth Series, Massachusetts Historical Society *Collections*, IV.
[10]Paul Revere to Dr. Jeremy Belknap, First Series, Massachusetts Historical Society, *Collections*, I, 105 ff.

NOTES TO PART 3

[1]Deposition of Paul Revere, undated. In Massachusetts Historical Society.
[2]Lieutenant John Barker, King's Own Regiment, "A British Officer in Boston," in *Atlantic Monthly*, XXXIX, 389 ff.
[3]Gage to the Earl of Dartmouth, March 28, 1775, in *The Correspondence of General Thomas Gage with the Secretaries of State, 1763–1775*, I, 395.

[4]Gage to Dartmouth, October 30, 1774, *loc. cit.*, I, 389.

[5]Dartmouth to Gage, January 27, 1775, *loc. cit.*, II, 183.

[6]Ensign Henry de Berniere, in Second Series, Massachusetts Historical Society *Collections*, IV, 214–15.

[7]Barker, *loc. cit.*, 398.

[8]Bancroft Transcripts, Manuscripts Division, New York Public Library.

[9]Lieutenant Frederick Mackenzie, Royal Welch Fusiliers, *Diary*, I, 18.

[10]First Series, Massachusetts Historical Society *Proceedings*, IV, 85.

[11]Henry W. Holland, *William Dawes,* read before the New England Historic Genealogical Society, June 7, 1876, 9.

[12]Revere to Belknap, *loc. cit.*

[13]Mehitable May (Dawes) Goddard in Holland, *op. cit.*, 35.

[14]Revere to Belknap, *loc. cit.*

[15]*Ibid.*

[16]In the Devens papers, cited by Richard Frothingham, *The Siege of Boston,* 57 n.

[17]G. W. Brown, "Sketch of the Life of Solomon Brown," in *Proceedings of the Lexington Historical Society,* II, 124.

[18]Deposition of Elijah Sanderson.

[19]Elbridge H. Goss, *The Life of Colonel Paul Revere,* I, 199 n.

[20]Reverend Jonas Clarke, *Opening of the War of the Revolution, 19th of April, 1775. A Brief Narrative of the Principal Transactions of that Day.* Appended to a Sermon Preached by Him in Lexington, April 19, 1776. Lexington Historical Society.

[21]Revere to Belknap, *loc. cit.*

[22]Deposition of Paul Revere, *loc. cit.*

[23]*Ibid.*

[24]*Ibid.*

[25]*Ibid.*

[26]Deposition of Elijah Sanderson.

[27]In the Gage Papers, William L. Clements Library, University of Michigan.

[28]Mackenzie, *op. cit.* I, 18.

[29]Cited in Allen French, *General Gage's Informers,* 39. Ensign Lister's narrative account was written in 1782.

[30]*Ibid.,* 40.

[31]Barker, *loc. cit.,* 398.

[32]Lieutenant William Sutherland, in *Late News of the Excursion and Ravages of the King's Troops,* 13.

[33]S. A. Smith, *West Cambridge on the Nineteenth of April, 1775,* 17.

[34]*New England Historical and Genealogical Register,* VIII, 187.

[35]*Ibid.*

[36]*Ibid.*

[37]Munroe deposition.

[38]Sutherland, *op. cit.,* 14.

[39]*Ibid.*

[40]*Ibid.*

[41]Revere to Belknap, *loc. cit.*

NOTES TO PART 4

[1]Resolves of the Town of Lexington, December 1773.

[2]Force, *op. cit.,* 491.

[3]*Journals* of the Second Provincial Congress, 112.

[4]Letter report of Major Pitcairn to General Gage, April 26, 1775, in Gage Papers at William L. Clements Library.

[5]Henry de Berniere, Second Series, Massachusetts Historical Society *Collections,* IV, 216.

[6]Barker, *loc. cit.,* 398.

[7]"Circumstantial Account," by General Gage, Second Series, Massachusetts Historical Society *Collections,* II, 225.

[8]Force, *op. cit.,* 496.

[9]*Ibid.,* 500–1.

[10]Report to Gage, *loc. cit.*

[11]Force, *op. cit.,* 491, emphasis added.

[12]Sutherland, *op. cit.,* 17.

[13]De Berniere, *loc. cit.,* 216.

[14]Jonas Clarke, Appendix to "The Fate of Blood-thirsty Oppressors."

[15]Report to Gage, *loc. cit.*

[16]Barker, *loc. cit.,* 398–99.

[17]Lister's narrative, *loc. cit.,* 55.

[18]De Berniere, *loc. cit.,* 216.

[19]Smith to R. Donkin, October 8, 1775, in Gage Papers.

[20]Sutherland, *op. cit.,* 18.

[21]Smith to Donkin, *loc. cit.*

[22]*Ibid.*

[23]Barker, *loc. cit.,* 398–99.

[24]Sutherland to Gage, April 27, 1775, in Gage Papers.

[25]Clarke, *loc. cit.*

[26]Dorothy Quincy to Sumner, *New England Historical and Genealogical Register,* VIII, 1881.

[27]*Ibid.*

[28]*Proceedings of the Lexington Historical Society,* III, 91–93, original orthography, capitalizing, punctuation, and emphasis preserved.

NOTES TO PART 5

[1]*Proceedings of the Centennial of Concord Fight,* 81.

[2]John Winthrop, *The History of New England,* ed. James Savage, I, 289.

[3]Amos Barrett letters in Henry True, *Journals and Letters,* 31.

[4]*Ibid.*

[5]William Emerson, "Diary," facsimile in "The Literature of the Nineteenth of April," appended to *Proceedings at the Centennial Celebration of Concord Fight,* 163 ff.

[6]Barrett, *loc. cit.,* 31.

[7]Abiel Holmes, *American Annals,* II, 326.

[8]Lemuel Shattuck, *A History of the Town of Concord,* 109.

[9]Affidavit of Amos Baker, of Lincoln, appended to Robert Rantoul, *An Oration Delivered at Concord on the Celebration of the Seventy-fifth Anniversary of the Events of April 19, 1775.*

[10]Barker, *loc. cit.,* 399.

[11]Shattuck, *op. cit.,* 111.

[12]Barrett, *loc. cit.,* 33.

[13]Jeremy Lister, cited in Allen French, *General Gage's Informers,* 79.

[14]Sutherland, *op. cit.,* 20.

[15]*Ibid.*

[16]Barker, *loc. cit.,* 399.

[17]Laurie, Report to Gage, in Gage Papers, William L. Clements Library.

[18]Barrett, *loc. cit.,* 33.

[19]Shattuck, *op. cit.,* 112.

[20]Barrett, *loc. cit.,* 33.

[21]Reverend William Gordon, Letter dated May 17, 1775, in Force, 4th Series, II, 630.

NOTES TO PART 6

[1]Barker, *loc. cit.,* 400.

[2]Dr. William Aspinwall, in Hudson, *op. cit.,* I, 182 n.

[3]Emerson, *loc. cit.,* 164 f.

[4]Barrett, *loc. cit.,* 33.

[5]De Berniere, *loc. cit.,* 217.

[6]Sutherland, *op. cit.,* 20, 22.

[7]The Reverend Edmund Foster to Colonel Daniel Shattuck, cited in Ezra Ripley, *History of the Fight at Concord*, 23.

[8]Mackenzie, *op. cit.*, I, 26.

[9]Foster, *loc. cit.*, 23.

[10]*The Essex Gazette*, April 25, 1775.

[11]Lister, *loc. cit.*, 112.

[12]De Berniere, *loc. cit.*, 217.

[13]Barker, *loc. cit.*, 400.

[14]*Letters of Hugh, Earl Percy*, 54.

[15]Mackenzie, *op. cit.*, I, 29.

[16]*Ibid.*, I, 19.

[17]*Detail and Conduct of the American War*, 10.

[18]Mackenzie, *op. cit.*, I, 19.

[19]Samuel Eliot Morison, *Three Centuries of Harvard*, 147.

[20]Report to Gage, in Percy *Letters*, 50.

[21]Dr. David McLure, "Diary," in First Series, Massachusetts Historical Society *Proceedings*, XVI, 158.

[22]Mackenzie, *op. cit.*, I, 19–20.

[23]Heath, *op. cit.*, 20.

[24]*Ibid.*

[25]Mackenzie, *op. cit.*, 20–21.

[26]The Reverend John Marrett to the Reverend Isaiah Dunster, July 28,1775, in S. Dunster, *Henry Dunster and His Descendants*, 88–89.

[27]*Columbia Centinel*, February 6, 1793.

[28]L. R. Paige, *History of Cambridge, 1630–1877*, 413 n.

[29]Cutler, *History of Arlington*, 69.

[30]S. A. Smith, *West Cambridge on the Nineteenth of April, 1775*, 34.

[31]Anna Adams, in *Christian Register*, XXXIX,169.

[32]Mackenzie, *op. cit.*, 21–22.

[33]Rough draft copy of Percy's report to Gage in Percy *Letters*, 51.

[34]Letter of Pickering to Governor Sullivan, Massachusetts Historical Society.

[85] Jared Sparks, *The Writings of George Washington,* II, 407.
[86] Heath, *op. cit.,* 33.
[87] Barker, *loc. cit.,* 401.
[88] *Ibid.*
[89] Percy to General Harvey, in Percy *Letters,* 52–53.

NOTES TO PART 7

[1] Samuel Adams to Charles Thomson, June 17, 1774.
[2] Lieutenant Colonel Smith's report to Gage, in First Series, Massachusetts Historical Society *Proceedings,* XIV, 350.
[3] Cited in S. A. Drake, *Historic Fields and Mansions of Middlesex,* 356.
[4] To William Eustis, later Governor of Massachusetts, in Richard Frothingham, *Life and Times of Joseph Warren,* 168.
[5] Heath, *op. cit.,* 24.
[6] Original in Dr. Warren's handwriting in Massachusetts Archives. Emphasis added.
[7] Dr. Warren to General Gage, April 20, 1775, Force, *Archives,* 4th Series, II, 370.
[8] Force, *Archives,* 4th Series, II, 360.
[9] First Series, Massachusetts Historical Society *Proceedings,* VIII, 405.
[10] Letter cited in the *Morning Chronicle and London Advertiser,* June 14, 1775.
[11] *Lloyds,* June 19–21, 1775.
[12] Letter cited in *Pennsylvania Journal,* August 2, 1775.
[13] *Essex Gazette,* May 12, 1775.
[14] *Harper's Magazine,* May 1875, cited in E. Chase, *The Beginnings of the American Revolution,* III, 30.
[15] Joshua Coffin, *History of Newbury,* 245.
[16] Alexander Scannell to John Sullivan in Force, *Archives,* 4th Series, II, 501.

[17]Andover Muster Rolls, in *Massachusetts Archives*, XII, 136.

[18]Letter of June 26, 1807, in Massachusetts Historical Society.

[19]Thompson to Gage, May 6, 1775, in Gage Papers.

[20]Proceedings of the Massachusetts Committee of Safety in Force, *Archives*, 4th Series, II, 744.

[21]*Ibid.*

[22]*Journal of the Provincial Congress of Massachusetts,* 671.

[23]Bateman Deposition, Force, *op. cit.,* 501.

[24]*Journal of the Provincial Congress of Massachusetts,* 673.

[25]Revere to Dr. Jeremy Belknap, January 1, 1798, in E. H. Goss, *The Life of Colonel Paul Revere,* I, 208.

[26]*Ibid.,* 209.

[27]*A Narrative of the Excursion and Ravages of the King's Troops, under the Command of General Gage, on the Nineteenth of April, 1775: Together with the Depositions Taken by Order of Congress to Support the Truth of It.* Printed by Isaiah Thomas, at Worcester, May, 1775. It is in *Journal of the Provincial Congress of Massachusetts,* 661.

[28]*Journal of Provincial Congress of Massachusetts,* 684 ff.

[29]*Ibid.*

[30]*Ibid.,* 677.

[31]Cambridge Vital Records, II, 10, also in Lucius R. Paige, Genealogical Register appended to *History of Cambridge.*

[32]In *Christian Register,* XXXIX, 169.

[33]In Force, *Archives,* 4th Series, II, 488.

[34]The Reverend John Marrett to the Reverend Isaiah Dunster, July 28, 1775, in S. Dunster, *Henry Dunster and his Descendants,* 88.

[35]Handbill of the Salem *Gazette.*

[36]*Massachusetts Spy,* May 3, 1775.

[37]Address to the Inhabitants in Force, *Archives,* 4th Series, II, 428.

[38]Proceedings of the Provincial Congress in Force, *Archives,* 4th Series, II, 488.

[39]*Historical Collections of the Essex Institute,* XXXVI, 19.

[40]*Correspondence of Thomas Gage,* II, 673.

[41]Gibbon to Hobroyd (Lord Sheffield), May 30, 1775.

[42]Dartmouth to Gage, June 1, 1775.

[43]Gage memorandum to Admiral Graves, April 23, 1775.

[44]Gage to Dartmouth, April 22, 1775.

[45]The London *Press,* June 12, 1775.

[46]Dartmouth to Gage, July 1, 1775.

[47]*Speech on Moving Resolutions for Conciliation with the Colonies,* March 22, 1775, in *Works,* II, 101–82.

NOTES TO PART 8

[1]Washington to John Augustine Washington, June 20, 1775, in E. C. Burnett, ed., *Letters of Members of Continental Congress,* I, 138.

[2]John Adams to Abigail Adams, June 17, 1775, in *Letters of John Adams, Addressed to his Wife,* I, 45–46.

[3]*The Works of John Adams,* II, 406.

[4]*Ibid.*

[5]Hancock to the Committee of Safety, April 24, 1775, in William V. Wells, *The Life and Public Services of Samuel Adams,* II, 296–97.

[6]Letter from Brown to Samuel Adams and Dr. Warren, March 29, 1775, appended to L. E. Chittendon, *The Capture of Ticonderoga.*

[7]Gordon, *History of the Rise, Progress and Establishment of the Independence of the United States,* I, 332 ff.

[8]Silas Deane to Elizabeth Saltonstall Deane, May 7, 1775, in Connecticut Historical Society *Collections,* II, 222.

[9]*Ibid.,* 223.

[10]*The Works of John Adams,* II, 406.

[11]Hancock to Dorothy Quincy, May 7, 1775, in *New England Historical and Genealogical Register,* XIX, 135.

[12]Wells, *op. cit.*, II, 300–1.

[13]*The Works of John Adams*, II, 406–7.

[14]Dr. Joseph Warren to Samuel Adams, May 17, 1775, in Richard Frothingham, *Life and Times of Joseph Warren*, 485.

[15]*The Works of John Adams*, II, 410.

[16]*Ibid.*, 415.

[17]*Journals of the Continental Congress*, 112.

[18]*The Works of John Adams*, III, 16.

[19]Frothingham, *op. cit.*, 485.

[20]Cited in E. C. Burnett, *The Continental Congress*, 74.

[21]Resolution of the Continental Congress, June 7, 1775, printed in *The Works of John Adams*, III, 17.

[22]Excerpt from the Diary of John Adams in *Works*, II, 415–16.

[23]*Ibid.*

[24]*Ibid.*

[25]*Ibid.*, 417.

[26]*Ibid.*

[27]John Adams in Autobiography in *Works*, III, 18.

[28]John Adams to Dr. J. Morse, January 1, 1816, in *Works*, X, 197.

[29]Jonas Clarke, "A Sermon Preached before His Excellency, John Hancock," 1781.

BIBLIOGRAPHY

A. DEPOSITIONS

The original depositions taken at the direction of the Second Provincial Congress, were sworn to on April 23, 24, and 25, 1775, in Lexington, in Concord, and in Charlestown. Twenty-one separate documents were gathered and are now at the Library of Harvard College and at the University of Virginia.

1. Solomon Brown, Jonathan Loring, and Elijah Sanderson, all of Lexington
2. Elijah Sanderson (supplementary to the above)
3. Thomas Price Willard, of Lexington
4. Simon Winship, of Lexington
5. John Parker, of Lexington
6. John Robbins, of Lexington
7. Benjamin Tidd and Joseph Abbott, of Lexington
8. Nathaniel Mullekin, Philip Russell, Moses Harrington, Thomas and Daniel Harrington, William Grimer, William

Tidd, Isaac Hastings, Jonas Stone, Jr., James Wyman, Thaddeus Harrington, John Chandler, Joshua Reed, Jr., Joseph Simonds, Phineas Smith, John Chandler, Jr., Reuben Lock, Joel Viles, Nathan Reed, Samuel Tidd, Benjamin Lock, Thomas Winship, Simeon Snow, John Smith, Moses Harrington, 3rd, Joshua Reed, Ebenezer Parker, John Harrington, Enoch Willington, John Hosmer, Isaac Green, Phineas Stearns, Isaac Durant, and Thomas Headly, Jr., all of Lexington

9. Nathaniel Parkhurst, Jonas Parker, John Munroe, Jr., John Winship, Solomon Pierce, John Muzzy, Abner Mead, John Bridge, Jr., Ebenezer Bowman, William Munroe, 3rd, Micah Hagar, Samuel Sanderson, Samuel Hastings, and James Brown, all of Lexington

10. Timothy Smith, of Lexington

11. Levi Mead and Levi Harrington, both of Lexington

12. William Draper, of Colrain

13. Thomas Fessenden, of Lexington

14. John Bateman, of the British Fifty-second Regiment

15. John Hoar, John Whitehead, Abraham Garfield, Benjamin Munroe, Isaac Parks, William Hosmer, John Adams, and Gregory Stone, all of Lincoln

16. Nathaniel Barrett, Jonathan Farrer, Joseph Butler, Francis Wheeler, John Barrett, John Brown, Silas Walker, Ephraim Melvin, Nathaniel Buttrick, Stephen Hosmer, Jr., Samuel Barrett, Thomas Jones, Joseph Chandler, Peter Wheeler, Nathan Peirce, and Edward Richardson, all of Concord

17. Timothy Minot, Jr., of Concord

18. James Barrett, of Concord

19. Bradbury Robinson, Samuel Spring, and Thaddeus Bancroft, all of Concord, and James Adams, of Lexington

20. James Marr, of the British Fourth Regiment

21. Edward Thornton Gould, of the King's Own Regiment

These depositions were published in Force, *American Archives*, 4th Series, II, 487–501.

A separate set of depositions was taken in 1825, fifty years after the event, from ten surviving witnesses or participants: Elijah Sanderson, William Munroe, John Munroe, Ebenezer Munroe, William Tidd, Nathan Munroe, Amos Lock, Joseph Underwood, Abijah Harrington, and James Reed. These are the garrulous recollections of old men, solicited to refute a claim advanced that the first active resistance to the British took place at Concord rather than at Lexington. It was in these depositions that the myth of Captain Parker's directing his men to "stand your ground" had its roots. They were first printed in Elias Phinney, *History of the Battle at Lexington*, in 1825.

In 1827, two years later, in answer to Lexington's claims, four new affidavits, by John Richardson, Samuel Hartwell, Robert Douglass, and Sylvanus Wood, were published in Ezra Ripley, *History of the Fight at Concord*, a contentious reply to Phinney.

In 1835, Josiah Adams, a native of Acton, published, in his address on the centennial of that town, six more depositions by four Acton citizens: Thomas Thorp and Solomon Smith, members of Captain Isaac's company that led the fighting at Concord's North Bridge; Charles Handley, a Concord spectator; and Hannah Davis Leighton, Captain Davis' widow. All these later depositions, made fifty to sixty years after the events, by aged men in an atmosphere of inter-town feuds, must be used with caution; but some of them add interesting and entirely plausible detail.

B. OTHER CONTEMPORARY ACCOUNTS

Adams, John, is the major source on the second session of the Continental Congress. His diary, autobiography, and correspondence for the period are in Charles Francis Adams, ed., *The Works of John Adams*, 10 vols. Boston, 1850–56.

Baker, Amos, The Affidavit of, is an Appendix to Robert Rantoul, Jr., *An Oration Delivered at Concord on the Celebration of the Seventy-fifth Anniversary of the Events of April 19, 1775,* Boston, 1850.

Barker, Lieut. John, *Diary,* is a highly critical account by an officer of the light infantry company of the King's Own Regiment. It was published in the *Atlantic Monthly,* XXXIX, 389–401, 544–54, and in Elizabeth E. Dana, ed., *The British in Boston,* Boston, 1924.

Barrett, Amos, "Concord and Lexington Battle," in Henry True, *Journals and Letters,* Marion, Ohio, 1906, is a sprightly, concise account by a provincial participant in the Concord battle.

Belknap, Dr. Jeremy, *Journal of My Tour to the Camp,* in First Series, Massachusetts Historical Society *Proceedings,* IV, 77–86, contains information gathered from personal interviews with participants in the battle.

Clarke, Reverend Jonas, "Opening of the War of the Revolution," an appendix to his anniversary sermon preached on April 19, 1776, *The Fate of Blood-thirsty Oppressors,* and reprinted by The Lexington Historical Society, 1901, is a brief, reliable account but carefully phrased to intensify anti-British feeling as the war moved into its second year.

De Berniere, Henry, *Narrative of Occurrences, 1775,* is a straightforward, sober chronicle by an ensign of the British Tenth Regiment, written in Boston in 1776 and originally published there in 1779; also in Second Series, Massachusetts Historical Society *Collections,* IV, 204 ff.

Emerson, Reverend William, Diary of April nineteenth, 1775, is inserted as a manuscript facsimile in the back matter of *Proceedings of the Centennial Celebration of Concord Fight,* Concord, 1876. Though he reported with the militia early in the morning, Emerson stayed on the Concord side of the North Bridge during the fight to protect his wife and children at the manse near the formation of the British. His diary account is reliable and informative.

Gage, General Thomas, "A Circumstantial Account of an Attack that Happened on the 19th April, 1775," was originally sent to the colonial governors to counteract the provincial propaganda; it is published in Force, *Archives,* 4th Series, II, 435, and in Second Series, Massachusetts Historical Society *Collections,* II, 224 ff. This is Gage's fullest account, based on the reports that he had from the field officers but full of unsubstantiated assumptions about the first firing at Lexington. Gage's reports to the ministers at London are in *The Correspondence of General Thomas Gage* (New Haven: 1933): to Lord Dartmouth, I, 396; to Lord Barrington, II, 673. The letters are sparse and, of course, defensive. Gage's manuscript papers are at Clements Library, University of Michigan.

Gordon, Reverend William, "An Account of the Commencement of Hostilities between Great Britain and America, in the Province of Massachusetts Bay," was written May 17, 1775, following the author's interviewing of participants, including the British prisoners. Gordon, pastor of the Third Church at Roxbury and also chaplain of the Provincial Congress, wrote his valuable account in the form of "a letter to a gentleman in England" and gave authority for all his statements. The letter is in Force, *Archives,* 4th Series, II, 625 ff. Gordon's *History of the Rise, Progress and Establishment of the Independence of The United States of America,* 4 vols., was begun in 1776 and published in London in 1788. It is partisan and unreliable.

Heath, General William, the first American general officer on the scene, gives his own account in his *Memoirs,* Boston, 1798. He was a field officer of indifferent ability, but his account is simple, direct, and reflects his limited military insight. Heath's papers are in Fifth Series, Massachusetts Historical Society *Collections,* IV, and Sixth Series, IV and V.

Lister, Ensign Jeremy, of the British Tenth Regiment, wrote

an account of his experiences in 1782, particularly valuable for the fight at Concord. It was published with the title, *Concord Fight,* Cambridge, 1931; and it is discussed carefully by Allen French in *General Gage's Informers,* Ann Arbor, 1932.

Mackenzie, Lieutenant Frederick, of the Royal Welch Fusiliers, *Diary,* was published in 2 vols., Cambridge, 1930. This is an excellent journal by an observant, sensible, and experienced officer.

McClure, Reverend David, "Diary," in First Series, Massachusetts Historical Society *Proceedings,* XVI, 155 ff. contains an account of his interviews with participants, including British wounded.

Percy, Hugh, Earl, *Letters,* published in Boston, 1902, and edited by C. K. Bolton, contains his account of the retreat in an official report to Gage and in two informal letters.

Pitcairn, Major John, gives a concise, direct report of the battle at Lexington Common in his letter to Gage. It is printed in *General Gage's Informers,* 55 ff.

Pope, Richard, apparently a Boston loyalist volunteer who went to Concord with Lord Percy's force, wrote an account, much of it based on what he had heard from others. It was published, together with a long and valuable letter of Lieutenant William Sutherland (*q.v.*) under the title *Late News,* Boston, 1927.

Quincy, Dorothy, gave her version of Hancock's stay at Lexington to General William H. Sumner in 1822; it was published in *New England Historical and Genealogical Register,* VIII, 188.

Revere, Paul, left two excellent accounts of his activities on the night of April eighteenth, 1775. The first was an unsworn deposition, probably written shortly after the event; the second, a letter, expanding on the events, addressed to Jeremy Belknap, Secretary of the Massachusetts Historical Society, was dated January 1, 1798. It is in the First Series, Massachusetts Historical Society *Collections,* V, 106 ff. and *Proceedings,* XVI, 371 ff. The deposition is in Goss, *Life of Colonel Paul Revere,* I, 180 ff.

Smith, Lieutenant Colonel Francis, wrote an official report to

General Gage, printed in First Series, Massachusetts Historical Society *Proceedings,* XIV, 350. Its value is limited by Smith's propensity to be late everywhere. Allen French discovered a more important letter from Smith to Major R. Donkin, dated October 8, 1775, in the Gage MSS., and discusses it in *General Gage's Informers,* 61 ff.

Sutherland, Lieutenant William, an enterprising and responsible officer, wrote a narrative letter to Sir Henry Clinton, April 26, 1775, and another to General Gage, the following day. The former was published in *Late News,* and the latter in *General Gage's Informers.*

C. LOCAL HISTORIES

Indispensable to the student of the American Revolution are the local histories, most of them written by dedicated and industrious town and city historians of the last century. Of widely varying literary quality, sometimes of uneven scholarship, occasionally rather over prideful and in some cases not too discriminating between tradition and research, they nevertheless contain a wealth of detail which would not otherwise be so conveniently available. Among those listed here, Hudson's long history of Lexington, despite its aggressive local pride, is particularly noteworthy, as are Paige's Cambridge and Shattuck's Concord. Allen French's wholly admirable and judicious work is in a category of excellence by itself. Josiah Adams, Phinney and Ripley are argumentative and defensive and must be used with care. The following local histories were all of some value:

Adams, Josiah, *Acton Centennial Address,* Boston: 1835

Brown, Francis H., *Epitaphs in the Old Burying-Grounds of Lexington, Massachusetts,* Lexington: 1905

Butler, Caleb, *History of the Town of Groton,* Boston: 1848

Drake, Samuel Adams, *Historic Fields and Mansions of Middlesex,* Boston: 1879

———, *History of Middlesex County, Mass.*, 2 vols., Boston: 1880

French, Allen, *Day of Concord and Lexington,* Boston: 1925

Green, S. A., *Groton during the Revolution,* Boston: 1890

Hudson, Charles, *History of the Town of Lexington, Massachusetts,* Boston: 1868 (revised and reprinted in two volumes by the Lexington Historical Society in 1913, with an invaluable genealogical register)

King, Daniel P., *Address Commemorative of Seven Young Men of Danvers,* Salem: 1835

Lexington Historical Society, *Proceedings,* 4 vols., 1886–1912

Mann, Herman, *Annals of Dedham,* Dedham: 1847

Massachusetts Historical Society, *Collections,* various series

———, *Proceedings,* various series (Significant items are noted by author.)

Morison, Samuel Eliot, *Three Centuries of Harvard,* Cambridge: 1936

Paige, Lucius R., *History of Cambridge,* Boston: 1877

Phillips, James Duncan, *Salem in the Eighteenth Century,* Boston: 1937

Phinney, Elias, *History of the Battle at Lexington,* Boston: 1825

Ripley, Ezra, *A History of the Fight at Concord, on the 19th of April, 1775,* Concord: 1827

Shattuck, Lemuel, *History of the Town of Concord,* Boston and Concord: 1835

Smith, Frank, *History of Dedham,* Dedham: 1936

Smith, Samuel Abbott, *West Cambridge on the Nineteenth of April, 1775,* Boston: 1864

Smith, S. F., *History of Newton,* Boston: 1880

Sumner, William H., *History of East Boston,* Boston: 1858

Wheildon, William W., *New Chapter in the History of the Concord Fight: Groton Minutemen,* Boston: 1885

Winsor, Justin, ed., *Memorial History of Boston,* 4 vols., Boston: 1881

Worthington, Erastus, *History of Dedham,* Boston: 1827

Harold Murdock's three skeptical papers on Concord and Lexington were published under the title, *The Nineteenth of April, 1775,* Boston, 1923. Informed, critical, witty, the essays are of immense value for the lines of inquiry that they suggest and for the sprightly persistence with which Mr. Murdock tracked down some of the atrocity myths—both of which historical excursions were highly important to this book.

D. BIOGRAPHY AND LETTERS

For the principal figures in this book, I have generally relied on their own works and those of their contemporaries. There are no biographies of the Lexington figures, although there are some useful sketches in the *Proceedings* of the Lexington Historical Society, already noted. For the Harvard teachers and clergy who taught the Samuel Adams generation, Sibley's *Harvard Graduates* and Josiah Quincy's *History of Harvard,* both noted below, are necessary. John Adams is best revealed in his own *Works* and *Familiar Letters,* noted below. There is no adequate general biography, though Catherine D. Bowen's *John Adams and the American Revolution* is an interesting and careful reconstruction. Samuel Adams is best treated in John C. Miller's *Sam Adams, Pioneer in Propaganda,* which, however, has some omissions. Ralph Harlow's study of Adams from the Freudian point of view is not entirely successful. William V. Wells, Adams' grandson, wrote a long biography, which omits some unfavorable episodes but contains a great deal of reliable material not elsewhere available. J. K. Hosmer's briefer biography is good but uncritical. The best Hancock biography is by Herbert S. Allan, who is careful, thorough, and unprejudiced in his research but somewhat partisan in his conclusions. The *Dictionary of American Biography* is, of course, excellent for all the major Revolutionary figures.

Adams, Charles Francis, ed., *The Works of John Adams with a Life*, 10 vols., Boston: 1856

——, *Familiar Letters of John Adams and His Wife Abigail during the Revolution*, New York: 1876

Allan, Herbert S., *John Hancock, Patriot in Purple*, New York: 1948

Armory, Thomas C., *Life of James Sullivan*, 2 vols., Boston: 1859

Arnold, Isaac, *The Life of Benedict Arnold*, Chicago: 1880

Bowen, Catherine D., *John Adams and the American Revolution*, Boston: 1950

Bradford, Alden, *Memoir of the Life and Writings of Rev. Jonathan Mayhew, D. D.*, Boston: 1838

Brown, Abram English, *John Hancock, His Book*, Boston: 1898

Carter, Clarence, ed., *The Correspondence of General Thomas Gage with the Secretaries of State and with the War Office and Treasury*, 2 vols., New Haven: 1931–33

Chamberlain, Mellen, *John Adams, The Statesman of The American Revolution*, Boston: 1884

Chinard, Gilbert, *Honest John Adams*, Boston: 1933

Cushing, Harry A., ed., *The Writings of Samuel Adams*, 4 vols., New York: 1904–8

Davol, Ralph, *Two Men of Taunton*, Taunton: 1912

Decker, Malcolm, *Benedict Arnold*, Tarrytown: 1932

Dictionary of American Biography, Allen Johnson and Dumas Malone, eds. 21 vols., New York: 1928–37

Forbes, Esther, *Paul Revere and the World He Lived In*, Boston: 1942

Freeman, Douglas S., *George Washington*, 5 vols., New York: 1948–52

Frothingham, Richard, *The Life and Times of Joseph Warren*, Boston: 1865

Goss, E. H., *The Life of Colonel Paul Revere*, 2 vols., Boston: 1891

Harlow, Ralph V., *Samuel Adams, Promoter of the American Revolution*, New York: 1923

Hilldrup, Robert L., *Life and Times of Edmund Pendleton,* Chapel Hill: 1939

Holland, H. W., *William Dawes and His Ride,* Boston: 1878

Hosmer, James K., *Samuel Adams,* Boston: 1896

Knollenberg, Bernard, *Washington and the Revolution,* New York: 1940

Lucas, Reginald, *Lord North,* 2 vols., London: 1913

Martyn, Charles, *The Life of Artemas Ward,* New York: 1921

Mays, David John, *Edmund Pendleton,* 2 vols., Cambridge: 1952

Miller, John C., *Sam Adams, Pioneer in Propaganda,* Boston: 1936

Nettels, Curtis P., *George Washington and American Independence,* Boston: 1951

Pell, John, *Ethan Allen,* Boston: 1939

Quincy, Josiah, *Memoir of the Life of Josiah Quincy, Junior,* Boston: 1825

————, *The History of Harvard University* (Vol. II for the eighteenth century presidents and the Harvard clerics), Cambridge: 1840

Sears, Lorenzo, *John Hancock, The Picturesque Patriot,* Boston: 1913

Shipton, Clifford K., *Isaiah Thomas, Printer, Patriot and Philanthropist,* Rochester: 1948

Sibley, John Langdon, *Biographical Sketches of the Graduates of Harvard University,* Cambridge: 1873–

Stillé, Charles J., *Life and Times of John Dickinson,* Philadelphia: 1891

E. THE REVOLUTION: POLITICAL, SOCIAL, AND RELIGIOUS BACKGROUND

The number of provocative and valuable monographs on the American Revolution is tremendous and growing. Only those with a special relevance to the thesis of this book are listed here. Of immeasurable value also have been various original documents, especially some of the sermons of the New England clergy.

Adams, Randolph G., *Political Ideas of the American Revolution,* Durham: 1922

Andrews, Charles McLean, "Conditions Leading to the Revolt of the Colonies," in *Selected Essays in Anglo-American Legal History,* Boston: 1907

———, *The Colonial Period of American History,* Durham: 1922

———, *The Colonial Background of the American Revolution,* New Haven: 1924

Baldwin, Alice M., *The New England Clergy and the American Revolution,* Durham: 1928

Clarke, Jonas, *The Importance of Military Skill, Measures for Defence and a Martial Spirit, in a Time of Peace,* Boston: 1768

———, *The Fate of Blood-thirsty Oppressors and God's Tender Care of His Distressed People, A Sermon Preached at Lexington, April 19, 1776,* Boston: 1776

———, *A Sermon Preached before His Excellency, John Hancock,* Boston: 1781

Greene, Evarts B., *The Revolutionary Generation, 1763–1790,* New York: 1943

Holyoke, Edward, *Integrity and Religion,* Boston: 1736

———, *Obedience and Submission,* Boston: 1737

Howard, George Elliott, *Preliminaries of the American Revolution, 1763–1775,* New York: 1905

Humphreys, Edward F., *Nationalism and Religion in America, 1774–1789,* Boston: 1924

Jameson, J. Franklin, *The American Revolution Considered as a Social Movement,* Princeton: 1926

Kraus, Michael, *Intercolonial Aspects of American Culture on the Eve of the Revolution,* New York: 1928

Lothrop, Samuel K., *History of the Church in Brattle Street, Boston,* Boston: 1851

Mayhew, Jonathan, *The Snare Broken, A Thanksgiving Discourse Preached at the Desire of the West Church in Boston,* Boston: 1766

Moore, Frank, ed., *Patriot Preachers of the American Revolution,* New York: 1862

Sprague, William B., *Annals of the American Pulpit,* New York: 1857

Thornton, J. W., ed., *The Pulpit of the American Revolution,* Boston: 1860

Van Tyne, Claude Halstead, "Influence of the Clergy, and of Religious and Sectarian Forces, on the American Revolution," in *American Historical Review,* XIX, 44–64

Weedon, William B., *Economic and Social History of New England,* 2 vols., Boston: 1891

F. THE REVOLUTION: OTHER SPECIAL STUDIES

For the uses of the battle of Lexington for propaganda purposes both in the colonies and in England and aspects of Massachusetts history accounting for the local attitudes before and after the nineteenth of April, 1775, other special studies have been stimulating and valuable. Philip Davidson's study of propaganda and the Revolution set for itself a rather ambitiously inclusive goal, which makes an otherwise interesting work perhaps too general. Such inquiries as Arthur M. Schlesinger's *Prelude to Independence* deal more manageably with individual aspects of the subject.

Adams, Brooks, *The Emancipation of Massachusetts,* Boston: 1887

Adams, Randolph G., "New Light on the Boston Massacre," American Antiquarian Society *Proceedings,* V., 47 ff.

Alden, John Richard, *General Gage in America,* Baton Rouge: 1948

Beer, George Louis, *The Commercial Policy of England toward the American Colonies,* New York: 1893

———, *British Colonial Policy, 1754–1765,* New York: 1907

Brigham, Clarence L., *History and Bibliography of American Newspapers, 1690–1820,* 2 vols., Worcester: 1947

Burnett, Edmund C., *Letters of Members of the Continental Congress,* Washington: 1921–36

———, *The Continental Congress,* New York: 1941

Clark, Dora M., *British Opinion and the American Revolution,* New Haven: 1930

Coupland, R., *American Revolution and the British Empire,* London: 1930

Cross, Arthur Lyon, *The Anglican Episcopate and the American Colonies,* Cambridge: 1902

Cushing, Harry A., *History of the Transition from Provincial to Commonwealth Government in Massachusetts,* New York: 1896

Davidson, Philip, *Propaganda and the American Revolution,* Chapel Hill: 1941

Duniway, Clyde A., *The Development of Freedom of the Press in Massachusetts,* Cambridge: 1906

Fisher, Sydney George, "The Legendary and Myth-Making Process in Histories of the American Revolution," in American Philosophical Society *Proceedings,* LI, 53–76

French, Allen, *General Gage's Informers,* Ann Arbor: 1932

Hinkhouse, Fred Junkin, *The Preliminaries of the American Revolution as Seen in the English Press,* New York: 1926

Howe, Mark Antony De Wolfe, *Boston Common, Scenes from Four Centuries,* Cambridge: 1910

Loring, James S., *The Hundred Boston Orators Appointed by the Municipal Authorities and Other Public Bodies, from 1770 to 1852,* Boston: 1853

Mott, Frank Luther, "The Newspaper Coverage of Lexington and Concord," in *New England Quarterly,* XVII, 489–505

Mowat, R. B., *England in the Eighteenth Century,* New York: 1933

Mullett, Charles F., *Fundamental Law and the American Revolution, 1760–1776,* New York: 1933

Scheide, J. H., "The Lexington Alarm," in American Antiquarian Society *Proceedings,* L, 49–79

Schlesinger, Arthur M., *Prelude to Independence, the Newspaper War on Britain, 1764–1776,* New York: 1958

Tyler, Moses Coit, *The Literary History of the American Revolution, 1763–1783,* 2 vols., New York: 1897

G. THE REVOLUTION: GENERAL WORKS

The best general history of the Revolution is still Trevelyan. The best long history of the United States is Channing, and the best short history is Morison and Commager, *The Growth of the American Republic.* John C. Miller's two studies are excellent, and so is Carl Becker's too brief *The Eve of the Revolution.* A general bibliography of the Revolution is not attempted here, of course, but the works listed provide the necessary framework in which to consider the limited area of this book.

Becker, Carl, *The Eve of the Revolution,* New Haven: 1921

Carpenter, William Seal, *The Development of American Political Thought,* Princeton: 1930

Channing, Edward, *A History of the United States,* 6 vols., New York: 1905–25

Commager, Henry Steele, *see* Morison, S. E.

Curti, Merle, *The Growth of American Thought,* New York: 1943

Force, Peter, ed., *American Archives,* 4th and 5th Series, 9 vols., Washington: 1837–53

Ford, Worthington Chauncey, et al., eds., *Journals of the Continental Congress,* 34 vols., Washington: 1904–37

Fortesque, Sir John W., *History of the British Army,* London: 1899–1929

Lancaster, Bruce, *From Lexington to Liberty,* New York: 1955

Lecky, William E. H., *The American Revolution,* 1765–1783, New York: 1898

Miller, John, *Origins of the American Revolution,* Boston: 1943
————, *The Triumph of Freedom,* Boston: 1948

Montross, Lynn, *Rag, Tag, and Bobtail: The Story of the Continental Army, 1775–1783,* New York: 1951

Morison, Samuel Eliot, and Commager, Henry Steele, *The Growth of the American Republic,* 2 vols. Third Edition, New York: 1942

Nevins, Allen, *The American States During and After the Revolution,* New York: 1924

Osgood, H. L., *The American Colonies in the Eighteenth Century,* New York: 1924

Schlesinger, Arthur M., "The American Revolution" in *New Viewpoints in American History,* New York: 1928

Trevelyan, Sir George O., *The American Revolution,* 4 vols., New York: 1899–1907

Winsor, Justin, *Narrative and Critical History of America,* 8 vols., Boston: 1884–89

Index